DISSIDENT PEACE

DISSIDENT PEACE

*Autonomous Struggles
and the State in Colombia*

ANTHONY DEST

STANFORD UNIVERSITY PRESS
Stanford, California

Stanford University Press
Stanford, California

Printed in the United States of America on acid-free, archival-quality paper

Library of Congress Cataloging-in-Publication Data
Names: Dest, Anthony, author.
Title: Dissident peace : autonomous struggles and the state in Colombia / Anthony Dest.
Description: Stanford, California : Stanford University Press, [2025] | Includes bibliographical references and index.
Identifiers: LCCN 2024047843 (print) | LCCN 2024047844 (ebook) | ISBN 9781503642409 (cloth) | ISBN 9781503642997 (paperback) | ISBN 9781503643000 (epub)
Subjects: LCSH: Peace-building–Colombia. | Political violence–Colombia. | Government, Resistance to–Colombia. | Colombia–Politics and government–1974-
Classification: LCC JZ5584.C7 D48 2025 (print) | LCC JZ5584.C7 (ebook) | DDC 327.1/7209861–dc23/eng/20250305
LC record available at https://lccn.loc.gov/2024047843
LC ebook record available at https://lccn.loc.gov/2024047844

Cover design: Jason Anscomb
Cover photographs courtesy of the author
Typeset by Newgen in 10/15 Source Serif Pro

The authorized representative in the EU for product safety and compliance is: Mare Nostrum Group B.V. | Mauritskade 21D | 1091 GC Amsterdam | The Netherlands | Email address: gpsr@mare-nostrum.co.uk | KVK chamber of commerce number: 96249943

CONTENTS

Preface: Toward an Ethnography of Struggle　　　　　　　vii

INTRODUCTION
Unsettling Peace in Colombia　　　　　　　　　　　　1

1　**Alfonso Cano's Grave: Vanguardism and the**　　　　34
　FARC-EP in Northern Cauca

2　**The Coca Enclosure: Drug Trafficking and the**　　　61
　Settler Colonization of Struggle

3　**Making Peasants Count: Creole Whiteness**　　　　91
　and the Politics of Recognition

4　***¡Tod@s Somos Primera Línea?*: Preliminary**　　　125
　Notes on the 2021 Uprising in Cali

CONCLUSION
The Doing of Dissidence　　　　　　　　　　　　152

Acknowledgments　　　　　　　　　　　　　　　163

List of Acronyms　　　　　　　　　　　　　　　167

Notes　　　　　　　　　　　　　　　　　　　171

Bibliography　　　　　　　　　　　　　　　　197

Index　　　　　　　　　　　　　　　　　　　221

PREFACE

TOWARD AN ETHNOGRAPHY OF STRUGGLE

Alexandra Nariño wrote down my information at the entrance to the disarmament camp in Buenos Aires, Cauca. Better known by her legal name, Tanja, the Dutch-national turned guerrilla of the Revolutionary Armed Forces of Colombia–People's Army (Fuerzas Armadas Revolucionarias de Colombia–Ejército del Pueblo, FARC-EP) passed me a freshly printed business card and a blue lanyard indicating my visitor status at the FARC-EP's fifty-third anniversary celebration in May 2017.[1] It was their first aboveground anniversary since the signing of the Peace Accords with the Colombian government in August 2016, and the occasion transformed the encampment into festival grounds complete with fireworks, live music, a traveling theater troupe, busloads of college students, and special guests who included former President Ernesto Samper. Despite the palpable yearning for a new era of peace at the event, the forces of war continued to undermine the ability of people to live freely.

During the eight months leading up to the FARC-EP's anniversary, I lived and worked in the northern region of the department of Cauca. Notorious for its reputation as a hotbed of violence and insurgency, the region is home to some of the most vibrant experiments in autonomous struggle in Colombia. I first got involved with struggles for black autonomy in northern Cauca in 2010 as a solidarity activist primarily associated with the Black Communities' Process (Proceso de Comunidades Negras, PCN) social movement. The human rights organization where I worked at the time was engaged in an intense fight against the U.S.-Colombia Free Trade Agreement, and on March 2, 2010, we hosted the event "Resisting Internal Displacement from Ancestral Lands: Afro-Colombians in Northern Cauca," about the refusal of the people of La Toma to leave their territory despite threats from armed groups that did the bidding of gold miners from outside the community. Our guest was Francia Márquez Mina, who at the time served as vice president of the Afro-Colombian Community Council of La Toma and was later elected vice president of Colombia in 2022.

I missed the first part of the event because I was having a hard time adjusting to the frantic pace of human rights advocacy in Washington, DC. It was my second month working at the Washington Office on Latin America (WOLA), and I was probably printing sign-in sheets or making sure that guests had enough coffee instead of introducing myself to Francia when she arrived. When I finally made it to the event, I had brought a digital camera with me to boost the organization's social media presence. Standing in the back of the fourth-floor conference room overlooking one of the many Starbucks that line Connecticut Avenue NW, I snapped a few shots. To my surprise, Francia stopped midsentence and covered her face with her jacket. She addressed me as a potential spy from the Colombian embassy, whose office was just a few blocks away. She told the audience not to take photos of her because she was already assuming risks by coming to the United States to tell her story. Feeling embarrassed, I think that I muttered something about working at WOLA, apologized, and excused myself from the room. Back in my windowless office, I reflected on how I fit into the life-and-death stakes of the work.

La Toma's inspiring struggle resonated with my desire to contribute to movements on the frontlines of making change. As an adolescent, I became deeply committed to social justice after racist classmates bullied me for being "Mexican" upon learning that I spoke

Spanish at home—never mind that I thought of myself as a white kid whose mom happened to be Colombian. Angry and determined to fight back, I joined a progressive youth organization thanks to a suggestion from a perceptive teacher. Participating in organizing efforts shaped my approach to study, which included studying in Cuba and researching the history of violence in Colombia before beginning to work at WOLA.

Francia and I ended up becoming close friends while working together to stop the eviction of her community in northern Cauca. Meeting Francia and other members of PCN offered me the opportunity to apply myself more purposefully, particularly as my own political commitments became clearer and I grew more critical of WOLA's approach to human rights advocacy. I learned about the struggles of black people in Colombia by participating, and I remember being struck by how the concept of autonomy was at the core of so many of our conversations. My early understanding of PCN led me to believe that their approach to territorial autonomy seemed to be in line with another movement that was beginning to shape my consciousness: the Zapatista Army of National Liberation (Ejército Zapatista de Liberación Nacional). Although I now understand more about the differences between the Zapatistas and PCN (particularly in relation to their analysis of the state and capital), PCN's confrontational and unapologetic attitude appealed to me and distinguished it from other, more conciliatory organizations that I had encountered in my solidarity work.

Over the course of years, my relationship with PCN transformed into more than a political affiliation. The members of PCN became my friends, confidants, mentors, and *compas*.[2] As a white guy from the United States working among black communities in Colombia, I was acutely aware that I was an outsider, and—in dialogue with PCN—we tried to leverage the power and privilege that came with it to advance the goals of the organization. These kinds of comradely conversations also took the form of risk analysis. When my friends told me it was too dangerous to visit a place, I listened. After all, the struggle is not only a beautiful space for rehearsing emancipatory praxis—it is also deadly and contradictory.[3] My *compas* from PCN continue to confront systemic violence in the form of death threats, forced displacement, attacks, and murders.

By working with PCN and joining a community of activist scholars in Austin, Texas, I also learned more about the need to engage with the contradictions of struggle.[4] I saw how apparent victories in passing a law or winning an election did not necessarily translate into significant change on the ground, how supposedly autonomous governance structures could reflect the oppressive and corrupt forms of state power, and how people I respected were capable of ignoring problematic developments within an organization because they thought it would undermine the movement's broader aims. This became especially important as PCN faced accusations of sexual assault by one of its members in 2017. These painful experiences revealed the potential and need to do better in the struggles ahead.

This book, then, serves as my best effort to meditate on the possibilities and contradictions that took shape in the aftermath of the 2016 Peace Accords between the FARC-EP and the Colombian government. This unique conjuncture represented an opportunity for people to relate to one another in previously unthinkable ways and to imagine a radically different future.

As part of my work in 2016–2017 and thanks to my history with PCN, I supported the development of an autonomous mechanism for monitoring the implementation of the accords with the Ethnic Commission for Peace and the Defense of Territorial Rights (Comisión Étnica para la Paz y la Defensa de los Derechos Territoriales), a coalition of black and indigenous organizations that developed in the context of the Colombian government's negotiations with the FARC-EP. Although the mechanism never took off in a formal way, the many workshops we organized in black and indigenous communities throughout the region served as a pretext for discussing the contents of the Peace Accords and learning about how the communities wanted to maneuver through the new institutional framework to advocate for themselves.

I still reflect on the period between August 2016 and May 2017 as a honeymoon of sorts. During that time, we could more easily travel to areas that were once strictly controlled by the FARC-EP (figure P.1).

FIGURE P.1

The FARC's fifty-third anniversary celebration at the Carlos Patiño
disarmament camp in Buenos Aires, Cauca (photo by author, May 2017)

The novelty of the moment eclipsed many people's ability (including
mine) to face up to how the underlying conditions of the war remained
mostly intact. Even with the numerous challenges that emerged, we
stubbornly believed that the Peace Accords represented a break in Colombia's bloody history. People felt inspired to experiment.

This sentiment led me to break out of my own comfort zone—if such
a thing could exist in this context. Feeling compelled to get away from
the day-to-day operations of movement organizing, I moved to the
pseudonymous Afro-Colombian Community Council of Nuevo Amanecer to learn more about how people who did not think of themselves
primarily as organizers interpreted the situation. In *This Land Is Ours
Now*, Wendy Wolford notes that the "process of subject elision (of con-
flating the individual with the collective) is common to both the practices and analyses of social movements, for reasons that are strategic,
ideological, and analytic."[5] As I spent more time in communities away
from the activist spaces that I was familiar with, I grew increasingly

cognizant of how "subject elision" framed my understanding of the situation in Colombia, particularly in terms of how at times I accepted certain narratives about the political conjuncture emanating from organizations and political leaders as truth. As a result of this shift in thinking, I started to establish relationships with people from other organizations and formations throughout the region that may have been at odds with PCN and the Ethnic Commission, including former FARC-EP combatants who signed the Peace Accords.

This effort to get a fuller understanding of the conjuncture was ultimately how I wound up at the FARC-EP's fifty-third anniversary celebration. The FARC-EP's anniversary also marked the end of the honeymoon period of the Peace Accords (figure P.2). Just a few weeks before, my hosts in the Afro-Colombian Community Council of Nuevo Amanecer suggested that I might want to leave the municipality for a little while. New armed groups were gaining power in the absence of the FARC-EP, and my involvement in organizing workshops with the Ethnic Commission, particularly in relation to the chapter in the accords on illicit crop substitution, became too risky. The leadership of the community council could not guarantee my safety, and they did not want to be held responsible if something happened to me. I appreciated their honesty and packed my things.

After I returned from the FARC-EP's anniversary, my interactions with powerful people known to exert violence haunted me. I felt exposed, as if they knew too much about me. I could no longer retreat to a state of denial that allowed me to believe that the intensely violent environment did not affect me. The sounds of motorcycles and footsteps kept me awake at night. Unlike many of my *compas* who risked their lives to defend the rights of their communities, I could leave the region without seriously disrupting the life of the community. And I did. Throughout the remainder of my time in Colombia in 2017 and upon returning to the United States, I tried to manage looming bouts of paranoia and guilt with meaningful work. That did not mean that I stopped returning to Colombia or abandoned the movement. It did, however, mean that my trips felt more guarded. Even that had its exceptions, as my experiences during the 2021 uprising in Cali suggest.[6]

FIGURE P.2

Laundry at the Carlos Patiño disarmament camp in Buenos Aires, Cauca (photo by author, May 2017)

In what follows, I take autonomy seriously as an organizing principle and emancipatory horizon. It is not something that lies out there waiting to be unlocked after being recognized by a state or some other entity—it is manifest in our everyday actions. The promise of the concept lies in its starting point: naming the dominant state of affairs as unacceptable. In this sense, it tracks closely with a quote from John Berger's *And Our Faces, My Heart, Brief as Photos* that I often returned to while writing this book: "When something is termed intolerable, actions must follow. These actions are subject to all the vicissitudes of life. But the pure hope resides first and mysteriously in the capacity to name the intolerable as such: and this capacity comes from afar—from the past and from the future. This is why politics and courage are inevitable."[7]

While I remain skeptical about the possibility of a "pure" hope, his invitation to act resonates with me in a way similar to Francia's indignation in a sterile conference room many years ago. Taking the "vicissitudes of life" seriously obligates us to engage in self-criticism in step with our actions, or *caminar preguntando* (asking as we walk) as the Zapatistas would say.[8] In Cauca, this approach to autonomous praxis is eloquently expressed in the following reflection by Nasa indigenous people on the words of Alvaro Ulcue, a Nasa priest murdered for defending the rights of indigenous peoples in Cauca in 1984:

> *La palabra sin la acción es vacía. La acción sin la palabra es ciega. La palabra y la acción por fuera del espíritu de la comunidad: son la muerte.*

> (Words without action are empty. Action without words is blind. Words and action outside of the spirit of the community are death.)

DISSIDENT PEACE

MAP 0.1

Colombia (*top*), Cauca (*bottom left*), Afro-Colombian Community Council of Alto Mira and Frontera (*bottom right*)

INTRODUCTION
UNSETTLING PEACE IN COLOMBIA

ON OCTOBER 5, 2017, STATE forces opened fire on a group of protesters in the small community of El Tandil close to the border with Ecuador. During the ten days leading up to the massacre, coca growers in El Tandil demanded that the Colombian government implement the 2016 Peace Accords with the FARC-EP. The accords supposedly guaranteed support for coca growers willing to substitute their illicit crops and transition into a legal economy. Instead of providing the coca growers with alternatives, the state killed seven people and injured more than twenty.

Although government officials later blamed the violence on so-called FARC-EP dissidents (*disidentes*), witnesses affirmed that the massacre was unprovoked.[1] More than five years later, the perpetrators of the massacre still have not faced justice, and the coca cultivations in the region around El Tandil continue to produce cocaine for the global market.

José Hernán de la Cruz, one of the survivors of the massacre, told *El Espectador*:

I think we are dealing with a ruse [*engaño*]—those of us living amid bullets, amid the armed conflict. What a damn ruse to learn that the

1

military and police arrive and that it's practically the same as dealing
with your worst enemies!

How am I supposed to trust them after what they did to me? They
destroyed my arm. All of this arm is reconstructed. [. . .]

It still does not make sense in my mind or for my way of living that I
could exercise my rights before this authority and that same authority
would start shooting at us, the peasants.

We were demanding something that was just.[2]

The El Tandil Massacre shattered the illusion of peace that the Colombian government tried to project to the world, but it was not a surprise to people familiar with the violent means used to suppress social change in the country. In the immediate aftermath of the Peace Accords, the communities that stood to benefit the most from peace continued to face oppression, and the steady elimination of former FARC-EP combatants who participated in the process had already begun. War continued.

The "ruse" that de la Cruz referred to after the El Tandil Massacre is at the core of the social contract that theoretically holds together the place called Colombia. It is the foundational and ever-present violence of the state and capitalism.[3] The state, like capitalism, is not a transhistorical feature of human history.[4] It is a historically specific form of patriarchal authority whose birth was intertwined with the racist foundations of colonial-capitalist modernity. Colombia, as one such instantiation of a state, gained its independence from Spain in 1819, and its rulers set out to establish dominion within its perennially changing borders through violence and the rule of law. With Christopher Columbus as its namesake, Colombia forged a citizenry and national identity over the course of centuries. As a state in search of subjects, the discourse of national belonging hinged on forms of racialized and gendered dominance with creole whiteness as its idealized form.[5] This established indigenous peoples and the descendants of enslaved Africans—along with their diverse and at times contradictory relationships to the territory—as an obstacle to Colombian state formation. Thus, the Colombian state took shape through the inherently violent imposition of a social contract premised on the maintenance of colonial capitalism.[6]

In 2022—260 years after Rousseau wrote *On the Social Contract; or, Principles of Political Right*—Gustavo Petro and Francia Márquez promised a "new social contract" on the first page of their program that pledged to turn Colombia into a "world power for life" and bring about "total peace."[7] Their election marked the inauguration of the first progressive government in the country's history. Petro, a former M-19 guerrilla who claimed that Rousseau inspired his interest in history as an adolescent, embarked on a mission to transform the state by expanding its realm of influence.[8] During his victory speech, he told the crowd, "We are going to develop capitalism in Colombia. Not because we worship it, but because first we must overcome premodernity in Colombia."[9] In doing so, he reiterated a popular trope about state formation that attributes violence, backwardness, and underdevelopment to the absence of capitalism and the state.[10] This trope not only concealed the multiple ways in which the state and capital are present in regions labeled as unruly frontiers; it also established the state and capital as the solution to violence, thereby ignoring their active role in producing it. Despite the claims of newness, the Petro administration's approach to the social contract and what would become known as total peace remained explicitly committed to a form of capitalist development facilitated by the state.

For centuries, the idea of social contract as the basis of political community has served as one of the primary justifications for the sovereignty of states.[11] Through the social contract—so the story goes— men submit to a higher authority in the name of a loosely defined common good.[12] However, the term "contract" suggests conscious agreement consummated by law, and the countless people slaughtered in the name of state formation did not willingly sign their lives away in its service. Writing in 1762 as the forces of European colonialism continued to expand throughout the globe, Rousseau included the following warning in his treatise on the social contract: "Under bad governments this equality is only apparent and illusory; it serves only to keep the poor in their misery and the rich in their usurpations. In fact, laws are always useful to those who possess and injurious to those that have nothing."[13] As de la Cruz attested in his denunciation of the

El Tandil Massacre, the social contract was not as democratic, just, or egalitarian as it might seem.

Since the earliest days of colonization, the law—particularly in relation to private property—has been crucial for the codification and continuation of colonial capitalism and state formation.[14] From the *resguardo* (indigenous reservation) system and *gracias al sacar* (the legal right of enslaved Africans to "purchase whiteness") established by the Spanish Empire to contemporary forms of multicultural recognition, these laws extended the promise of what Silvia Rivera Cusicanqui calls "conditional inclusion" to those willing to abide by the rules of the colonial project and punishment for those who rebel.[15] This colonial project has hinged on ensuring submission to a particular form of authority emanating from Europe that derived its strength by eliminating alternatives to the system through violence and assimilation.

Framed in this light, the prevailing discourse around peace in Colombia should be understood within a longer history of pacification (*pacificación*), which shares the Latin root word *pax*. The origins of pacification in what is now called Colombia can be traced at least as far back as 1573 with King Felipe II's mandate to abandon the language of *conquista* (conquest) for that of *pacificación* (pacification). The Spanish Empire's "Ordinances Concerning Discovery, New Settlements, and Pacification of the Indies" were made law amid self-serving critiques from other European powers about Spain's ostensibly exceptional brutality as a colonizing force. The rhetorical shift toward pacification in the official language of the Spanish Empire did not inspire a divergence from the genocidal structure of colonial capitalist development, but it did reveal an anxiety about exposing the hollowness of the religious and moral convictions that served as ideological justifications for colonization. In *The Conquest of America*, Tzvetan Todorov argues, "The text [of the Ordinances] could not be more explicit on this point: it is not conquests that are to be banished, but the word *conquest*; 'pacification' is nothing but another word to designate the same thing."[16] By the twentieth century, "pacification" became part of the lingua franca of counterinsurgency as colonial powers the world over attempted to quell native resistance and consolidate their control over land and life.

Returning, then, to the root word of both "peace" and "pacification" is instructive. According to Mark Neocleous in *War Power, Police Power,* "What is connoted by the word *pax,* and thus 'peace,' is not an absence of conflict or making of a pact but, rather, the imposition of hegemony and domination achieved through conquest and maintained by arms [. . .]. *Pax* was and is a victor's peace achieved by war and conquest."[17] By operating through the seemingly more palatable language of *pax,* pacification served as one of the primary methods of settlement in the Americas and peace its progeny.

This book explores how the dominant discourse of peace in Colombia is shaped by and shapes colonial capitalism. By establishing the consolidation of the state's sovereignty as the antidote to violence, it takes for granted how state-centric peace consists of a totalizing form of settlement dependent on genocide and the elimination of alternatives to it.[18] Peace, like war, imposes a framework for thinking and acting politically that shapes social relations. This process of subjugation, however, is always incomplete.

Another one of the survivors of the El Tandil Massacre described his efforts to achieve justice through the legal system as "swimming against the river."[19] This frustration has emerged at nearly every meeting, march, or mobilization that I have attended. From survivors of the El Tandil Massacre to Afro-Colombian community councils on the Pacific coast to resistance points in the city of Cali, people share stories about how violence, capitalism, and the state impede their ability to live freely as they struggle for a better future. In theory, the state should be there to protect them, but instead it mostly manifests in the form of a hostile police officer or a useless bureaucrat. Dissident forms of peace emerge from their rejection of the status quo and the potential of their struggles for autonomy from it.

"DO NOT TOUCH"

Despite the widespread media coverage of the El Tandil Massacre, reports about the massacre rarely specified that it occurred in the Afro-Colombian Community Council of Alto Mira and Frontera.[20]

Founded by the descendants of enslaved Africans, the community council adopted its name from its location on the upper part of the Mira River and the border (*frontera*) it shares with Ecuador. During the 1990s, the black communities that lived in the Mira River basin organized themselves as community councils to assert the newly recognized multicultural rights for black and indigenous peoples in the 1991 constitution.[21]

Among a myriad of reforms that included decentralizing governance structures and overhauling the judicial system, the new constitution recognized "the ethnic and cultural diversity of the Colombian Nation" for the first time and established the conditions for the second-largest black population in Latin America to acquire collective land titles, access to affirmative action policies, and congressional seats designated for Afro-descendants. It also included stipulations for expanding a similar set of rights for indigenous peoples. As a result, many of the black and indigenous organizations that pushed for these constitutional reforms accompanied communities around the country in an unprecedented struggle to make these new possibilities a reality.[22] According to Tianna Paschel, "The recognition of collective territory for indigenous peoples and black communities meant the biggest agrarian reform in that country's history."[23] As of January 2025, black communities held collective titles to 5.7 million hectares of land, and another 34.8 million hectares were legally recognized as indigenous territories. This form of state recognition was supposed to guarantee a degree of community control over the management of land and resources.

In the Afro-Colombian Community Council of Alto Mira and Frontera—as in many other black and indigenous communities throughout Colombia—these legal rights did not safeguard the communities from people willing to use force to steal land and acquire wealth. Alto Mira's fertile land and location made the community vulnerable to predatory prospectors encouraged by the state's neoliberal reforms. During the 1990s, oil palm companies intensified a land grab just as black communities throughout the region started to demand collective rights through Law 70 of 1993, which laid out the parameters for how blackness would be recognized by the state. The multicultural rights associated with the 1991 constitution operated through what Michael Taussig calls a "logic of camouflage" that feebly disguised "a terrible mess, a hazy morass of words that work through lies and subterfuge to the benefit of the large landowners throughout Colombia, which, so it is claimed has the most extreme maldistribution of land in all of Latin America."[24] Through the discourse of rights and recognition, neoliberal multiculturalism took much more than it seemed to offer by metabolizing resistance through inclusion and deepening the expansion of colonial-capitalist relations.[25]

Arriving under the pretext of eliminating communist guerrillas, paramilitary death squads worked with local elites, oil palm companies, and representatives of the state to dispossess the impoverished rural masses. In the process, the land grab expanded the infrastructure for extracting resources for capital and exacting tribute for the state. They used an assortment of tools—from guns and chainsaws to government contracts and payouts—to gain footing and inspire fear throughout the country. In 1998, Francisco Hurtado Cabezas—the first legal representative of the Afro-Colombian Community Council of Alto Mira and Frontera—was murdered by paramilitaries for standing up to the oil palm companies. They left a note on his dead body that read "Por molestarnos con tu ley 70" (For bothering us with your Law 70).[26]

Between 1996 and 2017, five members of the leadership of the Community Council of Alto Mira and Frontera were murdered as were another twelve community activists from the community council.[27] According to one independent report, the war in Colombia resulted in the theft of more than 6.6 million hectares of land between 1980 and 2010 (without including the territories of ethnic communities), and the United Nations identified approximately 7.4 million internally displaced people in Colombia in 2017.[28] Reports by local organizations and other experts demonstrate that black and indigenous communities were particularly affected by the conflict in the aftermath of the paramilitary onslaught. Despite the risks associated with resisting violence and dispossession, black and indigenous communities and organizations continued to struggle for territorial rights, autonomy, and self-determination.[29]

Following the murder of Hurtado Cabezas in 1998, the situation in the community deteriorated further as the U.S. and Colombian governments expanded the so-called war on drugs and aerial fumigations of coca crops increased throughout southern Colombia. The fumigations were not as precise as policy makers suggested, and the planes dumped herbicide on the jungle and anything else in their flight path (villages, schools, subsistence crops, rivers, etc.). This strategy resulted in a massive exodus of coca farmers to other parts of the country in search of new places to grow their crop. Some of these coca-farming émigrés arrived in Alto Mira and Frontera along with the FARC-EP.[30] Together, they acquired land and expanded coca cultivations inside the territory of the Afro-Colombian Community Council of Alto Mira and Frontera, eventually making it one of the most important coca-growing regions on earth. Many of the newly arrived coca farmers also became more involved with the modest Peasant Association of the Mira, Nulpe, and Mataje Rivers (Asociación de Juntas de Acción Comunal de los Ríos Mira, Nulpe y Mataje, ASOMINUMA) as a space for organizing outside the purview of the Afro-Colombian community council.

Even after the community council of Alto Mira and Frontera received official notice of its collective land title to 24,790 hectares in 2006, it continued to face enormous challenges that undermined its ability to become an effective authority in the region. As ASOMINUMA grew in size and influence throughout the middle of the first decade of the 2000s, the community council felt pressure from various sides: the oil palm companies, the paramilitaries, the guerrillas, drug traffickers, and ASOMINUMA itself. By the later years of that decade, the FARC-EP took a more overtly aggressive position against the Afro-Colombian community council. In a move that awkwardly reflected the state's neoliberal policies and the strategies deployed by extractive industries during land grabs, the FARC-EP tried to force the community council to respect individual—*not* collective—land titles in the territory and banned any utterance of the words "community council."

The community council rejected this encroachment on their autonomy at great cost. In 2008, the FARC-EP murdered two leaders from the community council of Alto Mira and Frontera: Pablo Gutiérrez and Armenio Cortés.[31] Between 2008 and 2013, the leadership of the region's community councils could not risk staying in the territory. They left for larger cities where they tried to slip into anonymity or fled the country altogether. In early 2013, shortly after the onset of the peace negotiations with the FARC-EP and the Colombian government, I spent several weeks in Tumaco working with the Black Communities' Process (PCN) and other black social movements to document the forms of racist dispossession confronting black communities in the region. Dreading retaliation, people spoke to me on the condition of absolute confidentiality. Their fears were encapsulated in a story one person shared with me about a ramshackle raft sent down a sparsely populated river. The four black cadavers on the raft were tied together with no explanation except for a handmade sign: "No Tocar" (Do Not Touch). The dead people bore the signs of torture, and the spectacle's private audience—the black peasants living alongside the riverbanks—were intended to absorb it in silence. This violence expressed another form of torture, or what Christen Smith calls "sequelae," naming the "the gendered, reverberating, deadly effects of state terror that infect the affective communities of the dead."[32] The raft was swept anonymously down the Mira River and into the Pacific Ocean. Their names—unlike the victims of the El Tandil Massacre—remain unspoken.

With little expectation for the ongoing peace negotiations between the FARC-EP and the Colombian government in Cuba, leaders from the community council of Alto Mira and Frontera decided to return to the territory in 2014 without permission from any of the armed groups. By that time, people antagonistic to the community council established themselves as the de facto bosses of the territory. They openly mocked the traditions of the black community, even prohibiting the singing of traditional funeral rites (*velorios*) for murdered constituents of the community council. Gunshots, *rancheras*,[33] and brothels replaced the sounds of the marimba and forms of communal exchange such as the local *trueque*. The people committed to the community council's struggle for autonomy and self-determination felt compelled to re-claim their land with or without support from the government that was supposed to guarantee their rights.

"YOU CAN'T ACHIEVE CHANGE BY FOLLOWING THE RULES"

Pablo Catatumbo folded his fingers into the shape of a gun and pointed it at me. It was June 2018, and he was weeks away from his inauguration into the Colombian Senate thanks to one of the stipulations of the Peace Accords. Before becoming a member of the secretariat, the highest level of the FARC-EP's hierarchy, Catatumbo commanded troops throughout southwestern Colombia. His menacing gesture punctuated the climax of his story about why he joined the guerrillas nearly fifty years ago. In his upscale Bogotá apartment adorned with colorful paintings by ex-combatants, our conversation created an illusory distance between the promise of peace and the continuation of war.

After years of avoiding them, I hustled to secure interviews with Catatumbo and other members of the FARC-EP. Their reputation for kidnapping and killing had always deterred me from initiating contact. That changed in June 2016 when the Ethnic Commission for Peace and the Defense of Territorial Rights—a coalition of black and indigenous organizations that formed in the context of the peace process—invited me to accompany their meetings with representatives of the FARC-EP in Havana, Cuba, and the Colombian government in Bogotá, Colombia.[34]

I was somewhat expecting the out-of-touch thugs portrayed by the media, but the FARC-EP leadership in Havana surprised me. As a revolutionary cadre that survived more than half a century of war, the FARC-EP's spokespeople exhibited confidence and clarity about their decision to negotiate with the Juan Manuel Santos administration. According to them, if the Ethnic Commission felt excluded by the course of the negotiations, then it was the government's fault. Throughout the week of meetings at the Martin Luther King Center in Havana, the guerrillas' delegates—Pablo Catatumbo, Jesús Santrich, Victoria Sandino, and Benkos Biohó—spoke of the need to struggle side by side with the Ethnic Commission against their common enemy: the elites in control of the state.

Unconvinced by the FARC-EP's rhetoric of unity, members of the Ethnic Commission criticized the guerrillas for systematically using violence to shut down black and indigenous calls for autonomy and self-determination, even charging them of genocide at one particularly tense moment of the proceedings. The FARC-EP, unfazed by the condemnations, attributed past errors to the inherent excesses of war and not their vanguardist approach to liberating the people.[35] They refused to acknowledge military defeat; for them, the imminent accord with the Colombian government represented a moral victory and marked the beginning of a new era.

Back in his Bogotá apartment, Catatumbo told me, "You can't achieve change by following the rules." He was in the middle of a story about how the police beat him with their helmets for tagging revolutionary slogans on walls as a youth. He recalled the moment that cemented his decision to join the FARC. It occurred the night that the 1970 presidential election was stolen by the political establishment, an event that also triggered the formation of the M-19 guerrilla group that Gustavo Petro belonged to.

According to Catatumbo:

> That day we went out to protest and throw rocks at the police. That was a really an intense confrontation. President Lleras Restrepo imposed a curfew. You had to get inside before 8 p.m. because they enforced the curfew with bullets. So we left. We said, "Let's get out of here because this is fucked, brother." I was walking with two girl friends [*muchachas amigas*] from the university. We were embracing as we walked and talked about the protest. I was so careless and excited about having my two friends with me and about the protest that I didn't realize where I was going.
>
> We had to travel on foot because there weren't any buses in the area. They suspended the public transit, and I remembered what I was telling them when all of a sudden a truck of *aguacates* [avocados] arrived. We called the police *aguacates* because they wore green. I yelled, "You *aguacate* sons of bitches!" and we started to pick up rocks

to throw at them. Just as I said that, I felt a strong hand slap me across the face like I had never been hit before. I felt a strong hand hit me and throw me to the ground. Then he hit me with his rifle and said, "Which *aguacates*? You son of a bitch!" I turned around to look, and it was a big powerful black police officer beating me with the butt of his rifle. He grabbed me and said, "Get over there!" We were in front of the main police station in Cali, and I was talking bad about the cops. He took me and told the girls to "leave, leave." He took me alone.

When I arrived at the station, he said, "Look, this is the one who calls the cops *aguacates*. He's a son-of-a-bitch subversive." They started beating me with their war helmets. They hit my head and punched me until they left me in the yard, which was full of people. I arrived over there and said to myself, "All right. I messed up, man . . . Talked too much."

I was there and people kept arriving. More people came and suddenly a shoe-shiner arrived in the yard [. . .], and they treated him badly. They kicked him and threw him over there. So the kid gets up and says, "You know what, lieutenant? You're nothing more than a coward. Why are you hitting me? You're armed, and I'm unarmed. It's obviously easy with a rifle." The lieutenant paused and said, "Well, I'll lose the rifle." He put the rifle aside, and they came to blows. The shoe-shiner was winning the fight. Really, the kid got the better hand and was beating him down until the other cops arrived. About ten police showed up with batons. They massacred him, leaving him practically unconscious.

That's when I thought to myself, "What cowardice! I could be that kid! The lieutenant was fighting with him man to man. Why is it the kid's fault for winning the fight? That's not worth it! That's not worth it!"

I remembered that I once read something about Che Guevara when he was younger. They invited him to throw rocks at a student protest, and—I'm not sure if this is true or not, but I read it—Che said, "No. Not with rocks. That must be done with weapons." He said, "I don't participate in those stone-throwing protests. For what?" Che never participated in those stone-throwing student protests in Argentina. I remembered that episode and said, "Che was right. This can't be done with heroism. What we need are weapons."

I was in prison for two days before they released us. They said, "Get out of here!" I left thinking about everything and said, "Ah! I'm joining the guerrillas, brother."

The struggle between the shoe-shiner and the police officer transformed Catatumbo's perspective on politics: the impossibility of a square fight required the adoption of more aggressive measures. In the crude dialectic that emerged for the burgeoning guerrilla movements of the era, only the revolutionary vanguard could amass the strength necessary to overthrow the elites that controlled the government and take over the state. Their formula flattened the diversity of struggles and often placed the guerrillas at odds with their supposed class allies. Over the years, the FARC increasingly reflected the authoritarian power relations of their enemies that controlled the state. Nearly fifty years after the fight in the prison yard, the political establishment still had the upper hand, and the FARC-EP found itself negotiating the terms of its inclusion in the state that it once sought to conquer.

Colombian President Juan Manuel Santos concisely laid out the limits of the peace process from the outset of the negotiations. In November 2012, he said, "The economic and political model is not up for debate with the FARC."[36] His speech served as a response to a polemic statement by Iván Márquez, a member of the FARC-EP's negotiating team in Norway, one month earlier. Márquez had criticized the government's policy of "accumulation by dispossession" and affirmed that "[the negotiations] were not a space to resolve the particular problems of the guerrillas, but the problems of society as a whole."[37] In light of the FARC-EP's ambitious agenda, Santos needed to reassure the decidedly anti-FARC political establishment that he was not willing to yield to pressure from the guerrilla group to extend the reach of the peace negotiations beyond the FARC-EP's disarmament.

Ultimately, the 2016 Peace Accords included a series of reforms laid out in six main chapters: (1) Toward a New Colombian Countryside: Comprehensive Rural Reform, (2) Political Participation: A Democratic Opportunity for Peace Building, (3) End of the Conflict and Disarmament, (4) Solution to the Problem of Illicit Drugs, (5) Agreement on the Victims

of the Conflict, and (6) Implementation, Verification, and Public Endorse-
ment of the Accords. The 310-page document written in drab technical
language over the course of four years fulfilled Santos's promise: the political and economic model survived. Capitalist development remained at
the heart of the deal, and the state sought to ensure the expansion of the
rule of law through it. The Peace Accords' two flagship policies for rural
Colombia—the Comprehensive Rural Reform (RRI) and the National
Comprehensive Program for the Substitution of Illicit Crops (PNIS)—
gestured toward the allocation of government funds for infrastructure
projects, community participation, and a moderate land reform. Thus,
they reflected the anti-communist reforms associated with the Alliance
for Progress more than the FARC-EP's road map to revolution.

Nevertheless, Colombia's notoriously conservative political establishment rejected anything that could be perceived as a concession to
the FARC-EP. On October 2, 2016, the Peace Accords failed to garner
enough public support to clear the national plebiscite that was supposed
to rubber-stamp the accords. This was due in large part to a reactionary
campaign against the Peace Accords that coalesced around combating
their supposed gender ideology and an allegedly lenient approach to
prosecuting the FARC-EP guerrillas for crimes committed during the
war. According to Diana Gómez Correal, critics of the "gender ideology"
were concerned about how the contributions of the Subcommission on
Gender for the Peace Accords might challenge the "patriarchal ontol-
ogy" of the Colombian nation-state by giving voice to women and LGBTI
communities during implementation.[38] As a consequence of the failed
attempt to gain popular support for the peace process through the plebiscite, the Santos administration invited spokespeople from the opposition—namely, the right-wing Democratic Center Party and evangelical
Christian religious denominations—to renegotiate the sections of the
accords that they found problematic. The new version of the Peace Accords excised much of the language around specific programs designed
to encourage the participation of women and LGBTI communities.

After the plebiscite fiasco, Rodrigo Londoño (alias Timochenko)
and Juan Manuel Santos unironically signed the second version of the
Peace Accords on November 24, 2016, at the Christopher Columbus

Theater in Bogotá. The accords thus represented an updated—yet remarkably stubborn—version of the social contract. With its reverence for private property, the relegation of the ethnic chapter to a three-page appendix, and the contributions of the Gender Subcommission all but eliminated, the Peace Accords conveyed the colonial-capitalist roots of Colombian society.

"WHAT PEACE ARE THEY TALKING ABOUT? THEY ARE KILLING US"

In December 2014, some of the founders of the Ethnic Commission invited a delegation of indigenous activists from Guatemala to northern Cauca to share their experiences with the so-called postconflict moment in anticipation of the possibility of a peace agreement. The Guatemalan indigenous activists were emphatic: "Things will get worse. Many of your friends will die. Only now, nobody will believe you."[39] By March 2017, banners made by mourners at the funeral for Javier Oteca, an indigenous activist murdered on the grounds of the Incauca sugarcane refinery in northern Cauca, declared their collective frustration with the empty promises of the peace process: "What peace are they talking about? They're KILLING us" (figure 0.1).

Genaro García was one of the community leaders present at the meeting with the Guatemalan indigenous activists in December 2014. Largely unknown in the world of professionalized human rights activism in Bogotá, García served as the legal representative of the Afro-Colombian Community Council of Alto Mira and Frontera. In October 2014—two months before meeting with the Ethnic Commission and the Guatemalan indigenous activists visiting northern Cauca—the FARC-EP summoned García and other community council leaders. They reportedly told him, "We are not going to talk about Law 70 or the community councils here. We are going to talk about unity and ASOMINUMA."[40]

Less than one year later, on August 3, 2015, the Daniel Aldana Mobile Column of the FARC-EP called García in to another meeting. About ten kilometers from the location, four armed men stopped his convoy on the way to the meeting. They made everyone get out of the

FIGURE 0.1

Javier Oteca's funeral (photo by author, March 2017)

car and asked the driver for the keys. After reviewing the passengers' IDs, they said, "Ah, Genaro García, move over there. Get on the floor facedown and put your hands behind your head." García replied, "But, why? I haven't done anything to you." Two men on a motorcycle approached the scene. They dismounted, and one of them shot him in the head and legs. The shooter turned to the witnesses: "Don't say anything. Grab him and throw him in the car." The two people traveling in the car with García protested and said that they wanted to stay with the body. Before departing, the murderer told them, "Say that he was killed for being a snitch [sapo] or a thief."[41]

García's assassination temporarily rattled the ongoing peace process, particularly because the murder constituted a violation of a unilateral ceasefire declared by the FARC-EP two weeks before. On August 24, 2015, Pablo Catatumbo read out a communiqué from the guerrilla group in Havana acknowledging that the Daniel Aldana Mobile Column of the FARC-EP was responsible for the "condemnable act" that "contradicts the FARC-EP's politics regarding its relationship with the civilian population and its respect for ethnic communities."[42] I followed up with Pablo Catatumbo about García's murder during my interview with him in 2018. He continued to believe that the FARC-EP acted appropriately following the murder of García: "What happened with Genaro was handled well. We recognized that it was something very badly done." The 2015 communiqué was intended to salvage the FARC-EP's reputation and ensure the continuity of the negotiations. To a certain degree it worked. After the FARC-EP's admission of guilt, press outlets and politicians responded somewhat favorably to the guerrillas' willingness to accept responsibility for the murder. Exactly one year later, on August 24, 2016, the FARC-EP and the Colombian government announced that they had reached an agreement.

Sara Quiñonez replaced Genaro García as the leader of the community council. She and other people from her community knew that García's murder was not an exception: it was the predictable outcome of the FARC-EP's strategy to vanquish the Afro-Colombian community council in their quest for territorial control. Quiñonez and I became friends in 2013 during a two-week political advocacy workshop that PCN invited me to facilitate in Bogotá. I spoke with Quiñonez about the situation in the community council in 2016, while government-provided bodyguards from the National Protection Unit (Unidad Nacional de Protección) leaned on the hood of her bulletproof SUV that was also provided by the unit. Quiñonez asked her mother, Tulia Maris Valencia, to join our conversation as her daughter played in the living room. Unbeknownst to us at the time, we would not have another chance to talk in person until years later, after Quiñonez and her mother were released from prison.

The threats against the community council did not end with García's assassination. In October 2017, an offshoot of the FARC-EP murdered Jose Jair Cortes—yet another leader from the community council of Alto Mira and Frontera—for encouraging peasants to participate in a government-sponsored coca substitution program. On April 20, 2018, Quiñonez and her mother were arrested on charges of rebellion (*rebelión*) and falsely accused of supporting the National Liberation Army

(Ejército de Liberación Nacional) guerrilla group. The day after their arrests, a collective from northern Cauca named the Afro-descendant Women's Mobilization for the Care of Life and Ancestral Territories published a statement with a clear message for the government: "Stop fucking with us and using us for your interests!" They went on to say, "We want Sara and Tulia Maris to be free, like all other people that are caretakers of life. We want all of us to get together and simply say that our efforts are collective and that progress must cease to mean pain and death for species and peoples."[43]

Their arrests were representative of the state's strategy to use the judicial system as a weapon to neutralize social movement organizing. For example, former President Álvaro Uribe Vélez often conflated human rights activists with guerrillas by openly referring to activists as "spokespeople for terrorism" and the like.[44] In 2012, another PCN activist, Felix Banguero, was arrested in northern Cauca after being falsely accused of belonging to the FARC-EP. Banguero spent more than two years in an overcrowded prison and was released because of insufficient evidence. Quiñonez and Tulia Maris were released in July 2019 after spending more than a year in pretrial detention. All three PCN activists maintained their innocence throughout the proceedings and remained committed to the struggle for Afro-Colombian rights. According to PCN, "If our leaders stay in the territory, they are murdered—if they leave the territory, they are criminalized."[45] These leaders were targeted by the state—both inside and outside prisons—because they represented a threat to the status quo: they refused to acquiesce.

STATE-CENTRIC PEACE

The Afro-Colombian Community Council of Alto Mira and Frontera's struggle for autonomy offers a partial insight into violence surrounding the 2016 Peace Accords. Since then, the situation confronting the black communities in Alto Mira and Frontera has only deteriorated, and the members of ASOMINUMA have not fared much better. Far from ameliorating the conditions of genocide and immiseration, the abortive disarmament of the FARC-EP gave rise to ever more splintered war machines that continued to enclose the community council within colonial-capitalist relations.

As a consequence of the failures of the 2016 accords, peace remained on the agenda during the 2022 presidential elections. The Petro campaign made "Total Peace" a cornerstone of its agenda, while the right-wing opposition demanded "Peace with Guarantees." It is pertinent, then, to return to the question asked by the attendees of Javier Oteca's funeral: "What peace are they talking about?"[46]

The Colombian government has engaged in some sort of "peace negotiations" with either guerrilla groups or paramilitary groups on a more or less continual basis since the early 1980s. Proceeding by fits and starts punctuated by dramatic breakdowns, these talks tended to emphasize the need to stop the bloodshed. This approach, deemed "negative peace" by activists and scholars, has focused primarily on bringing an end to outright hostilities.[47] Yet even when negotiations culminated in an agreement, peace—in any meaningful sense of the term—remained elusive, as in the cases of the Popular Liberation Army, Quintín Lame Armed Movement, and M-19. Rather than calling these agreements "negative peace," they should be understood as armistices or negotiated surrenders.

The Uribe administration's negotiations with the United Self-Defense Forces of Colombia (Autodefensas Unidas de Colombia, AUC) between 2002 and 2006, however, were qualitatively different from the talks with the guerrillas. As a paramilitary group, the AUC sought to expand state power and capital through vigilante violence. For example, Carlos Castaño, one of the cofounders of the AUC, reflected on the meeting that gave rise to the most influential iteration of paramilitarism of the last forty years:

> The first meeting of cattle ranchers, farmers, and businessmen was at the end of 1982. About 250 businessmen organized to defend themselves from guerrilla attacks on the basis of the legal framework of 1965 and 1968 that permitted citizens to bear arms. The spirit of the law invited citizens to organize themselves and take care of their property in collaboration with the armed forces. Since it was legal, the first collective self-defense association was formed: the Peasant Association of

Cattle Ranchers and Farmers of Magdalena Medio [Asociación Campesina de Ganaderos y Agricultores de Magdalena Medio].[48]

The association went on to build forty-two schools where teachers were
instructed to teach students the Colombian national anthem and how
to participate in patriotic marches in order to "recover the values that
had been lost over the course of ten years of guerrilla infiltration."[49]
Some of the participants in the meeting later launched the AUC on the
basis of these principles. The AUC's official disarmament under Uribe
thus functioned as a tautological integration into a state they were already a part of. With more than one-third of the Colombian Congress
investigated for having ties to the AUC and many more officials sympathetic to their cause, the AUC was not bargaining with adversaries in
the state.[50] To retain a semblance of legitimacy, the terms of the AUC's
negotiations needed to be strict enough to admonish violations of the
rule of law but loose enough to ensure the AUC's submission. More
than fifteen years after the dissolution of the AUC, paramilitary groups
continue to collude with state officials to threaten, kill, and displace
people they consider to be subversives or dissidents, and the vast majority of the AUC's abuses remain in complete impunity.

The negotiations that resulted in the 2016 Peace Accords with the
FARC-EP took a different course. After more than fifty years of fighting,
the FARC-EP claimed the mantle of the oldest guerrilla movement in
the Western Hemisphere, and as such, they rejected the possibility of
disarming without reforms that reflected their political project. The
Santos administration understood this and adopted a more flexible approach to the negotiations in order to successfully disarm the FARC-EP.

As the negotiations gained momentum, demands for participation
took on new force. The FARC-EP believed that broader civil society
participation would expand the reach of the accords, and civil society organizations understood the conjuncture as an opportunity to
intervene on their own behalf. Counter to the Santos administration's
efforts to delimit participation and keep the negotiations from becoming unwieldy, civil society organizations demanded "nothing about us
without us." In an effort to appear more democratic, the negotiations

ultimately included mechanisms to expand participation beyond what international humanitarian law calls the parties to the conflict (i.e., the FARC-EP and the state forces). The accords proclaimed that "more than 3,000 victims participated in four forums in Colombia organized by the United Nations and the National University, and seventy victims traveled to Havana to give their direct testimony to the Negotiating Table and offer their recommendations with support from the Episcopal Conference, United Nations, and National University. That does not include the more than 17,000 proposals that were sent by victims and other citizens through various means to the Negotiating Table."[51] The Gender Subcommission was internationally celebrated and widely reported as the first of its kind in peace negotiations, despite being significantly undercut after the plebiscite. Black, indigenous, and Rom communities, in contrast, never received a formal invitation to participate in the negotiations. Risking the threat of legal action against them, representatives of black and indigenous organizations traveled to Cuba on their own behalf in 2016 to meet with the negotiating teams. Ultimately, their efforts resulted in the adoption of the ethnic chapter of the Peace Accords at the last moment in another first with tepid results. This civil society participation created the illusion of an inclusive process that expressed the possibility of a positive peace and spoke to the conditions that created the conflict (figure 0.2).

While these forms of civil society participation revealed the reformist bent of the process, they occluded how bourgeois interests influenced the negotiations. Business conglomerates, economic elites, multinational corporations, and imperialist forces undoubtedly swayed the outcome of the accords. From the productivist logic of the Comprehensive Rural Reform to the squeamishness regarding the redistribution of private property, the accords reinscribed the colonial-capitalist character of the state.

The plebiscite debacle in 2016 also provided reactionary forces inside and outside the government with an opportunity to spoil the implementation process. As FARC-phobia spread throughout the institutions responsible for implementing the agreement during the twilight of the Santos administration and right-wing opposition to the Peace

FIGURE 0.2

Charo Mina Rojas, member of PCN and the Ethnic Commission, conducting a workshop on the contents of the 2016 Peace Accords in Puerto Tejada, Cauca (photo by author, October 2016)

Accords consolidated under Iván Duque's neoliberal authoritarian administration (2018–2022), the Colombian government's flirtations with promoting the Peace Accords were systematically undermined until the inauguration of Gustavo Petro and his support for "Total Peace."[52]

The idea of total peace connected with many people's frustrations regarding the unfulfilled promises of the 2016 Peace Accords. Signed into law on November 4, 2022, Law 2272 formally recognized that "peace policy is state policy." The Total Peace Law opened the door for the state to begin dialogues with any illegal group willing to abide by the law, and—in a pivot away from limiting negotiations to "political actors"—this included groups primarily involved in drug trafficking and other illicit activities. In addition to its emphasis on negotiations with armed groups, the new law also created the Social Service for Peace, which provided Colombian citizens with an alternative to obligatory military service.

Despite the rhetorical flourish around total peace, the concept appeared to be unmoored from a legible political philosophy. In one of the few articles to critically assess the terms of total peace during the debates leading up to the passage of the law, Sergio de Zubiría Samper argued that the absence of a foundational document defining the administration's approach to total peace constituted a "structural limitation" to the concept.[53] However, even in the absence of a foundational document or perhaps in part thanks to that absence, "total peace" became an empty signifier that reinforced state-centric understandings of peace that position the state as its guarantor.[54] This was evident in the Ministry of Interior's statement celebrating the passage of the Total Peace Law as "the new social contract that guarantees the fundamental rights of the people in President Gustavo Petro's Government of Change."[55]

It remains to be seen if the Petro administration's approach to "total peace" can overcome "the economic and political model" that Juan Manuel Santos said was "not up for debate." This "economic and political model" of colonial-capitalist state formation constitutes the basis of state-centric peace. In both its negative and its positive variants, state-centric peace hinges on the state for enforcement and reinforces the logic of elimination at the core of settler colonialism.[56]

It is likely for this reason that the Mother Earth Liberation Process (Proceso de Liberación de la Madre Tierra, PLMT) says, "For us, peace—a word we do not use—is land: freedom, equilibrium, harmony."[57] As one of the most radical expressions of indigenous politics in Colombia, the PLMT has reclaimed more than 12,500 hectares of land in the Cauca River Valley through direct action. By insisting that peace is "a word we do not use," the PLMT refuses state-centric peace as its horizon. Instead, it centers land and freedom as the basis of a peace worthy of struggle. They organize *mingas*—a form of collective labor indigenous to the Andes—to cut down sugarcane monocultures and create "liberation points" on the freed land. This has come at great cost: fourteen liberators have been murdered since the PLMT's foundation in 2014 and more than six hundred have been injured during confrontations with the police and military. There are also more than a hundred arrest warrants out for people associated with the PLMT.[58] These hostilities between the PLMT and the state have continued under the Petro administration and its policy of Total Peace because that land is considered to be under the state's dominion. At best, state-centric peace might offer reprieve from more brutal forms of dispossession, but it is not analogous with liberation because the state is the instrument par excellence of settler colonialism. And settler colonialism is war.

DISSIDENT PEACE

> *Y aunque mi amo me mate*
> *A la mina no voy*
> (Even if my master kills me
> I won't go to the mine)

I first heard "La Mina" in a music video produced in collaboration with the Afro-Colombian Community Council of the Iscuandé River.[59] The video juxtaposes beautiful images of life along the Iscuandé River with clips of large mechanical excavators tearing at the earth's surface while black workers get their hands dirty mining gold. Despite the song's contested origins, it emerged from the struggles of black communities on the Pacific coast of Colombia.[60] Similar to W. E. B. DuBois's description of the general strike of formerly enslaved black people after the Civil War in the United States—"This was not merely the desire to stop work. It was a strike on a wide basis against the conditions of work"[61]—the lyrics to "La Mina" express a shared desire for radical transformation. KiKe's acoustic performance of the song cuts across time and space enunciating a passionate refusal of the colonial-capitalist order.

As the Colombian government and the FARC-EP negotiated in Havana, I frequently found myself listening to the song and watching this music video. It gave voice to a sense of defiance emerging from my friends struggling for peace in northern Cauca. In 2014, a large illicit gold mine in San Antonio (Santander de Quilichao, Cauca) collapsed killing at least twelve miners, many of whom resided in the neighboring black communities. With over 150 excavators operating just minutes from the Pan-American Highway, the mine employed thousands of workers trying to make a living. Bus companies in Santander de Quilichao offered routes to San Antonio, and a bustling boom economy took shape around the mine. Despite its location in a highly militarized part of the country, mafias associated with guerrilla and paramilitary groups controlled the gold mines in San Antonio and throughout northern Cauca. Like the Afro-Colombian Community Council of Alto Mira and Frontera, these communities also confronted a dire situation that placed them at odds with predatory armed groups, a hostile state, and the need to provide their constituents with a means of subsistence.

Later that same year, the Afro-descendant Women's Mobilization for the Care of Life and the Ancestral Territories formed after a group of black women from northern Cauca declared that they had had enough.[62] Again, like the leadership of the Afro-Colombian Community Council of Alto Mira and Frontera, they decided that death threats and the forces of dispossession could no longer constrain their lives. In the opening lines of their first statement, the Mobilization defined its struggle by connecting the legacy of enslavement with the ongoing need to ensure the livelihoods of their posterity, or *renacientes*:

> We are black women from northern Cauca: the descendants of enslaved Africans and experts on the ancestral value of our territories. We know that many of them paid for our freedom with their lives. We know about the blood that our ancestors shed to get these lands. We know that they worked for years and years under enslavement in order to leave it for us. They taught us not to sell the land. They understood that we should guarantee the permanence of our *renacientes* in the territory.[63]

To make themselves heard by national authorities, they organized a march from the Afro-Colombian Community Council of La Toma in Suárez, Cauca, to Bogotá because legal recourse at the local level did not work.

Upon arriving in Bogotá, the Mobilization met with government officials at the Ministry of Interior's offices next to the Presidential

Palace. Hours of roundabout negotiations went nowhere, and the women refused to leave until they reached a solution. While the Mobilization occupied the offices of the Ministry of Interior overnight, dozens of supporters outside held a vigil singing songs and holding candles in the hope that increased outside attention would keep the anti-riot police from pulling them out by force.[64]

As the meetings continued, the members of the Mobilization felt increasingly frustrated by the government's inability to take meaningful action. Francia Márquez Mina, one of the founding members of the Mobilization, passionately confronted the government officials:

> What was this Colombian state created for? Wasn't it supposed to serve the people? Wasn't it [supposed] to protect every Colombian man and woman? If not, what was this Colombian State created for? What was the object of creating this state? If it wasn't for that, then tell us. If the objective is to pillage our territories, if the objective is to hand it over to other countries, if the objective is to produce war by way of all these phenomena. [. . .]
>
> Mining and the so-called engines of development are not generating peace. The only things that they are generating are misery, poverty, hunger, and displacement! And if it's not, go ask every one of the four million displaced people why they were displaced from their territories. We are not willing to be one more! We are not willing to have our children in the streets at the traffic lights so that people in suits and ties can look at them as if they were garbage! We are not willing to allow that to happen. We will remain in our territory because the territory has been our father and our mother, and it will continue to be for our children.[65]

A recording of Márquez's speech went viral, launching her into the spotlight of international struggles for environmental and racial justice and thereby drawing more attention to the Mobilization's demands on the state.

Her intervention also signaled a turning point for the other participants in the Mobilization by exposing the state's hollow promises of peace. Sofía Garzón Valencia, another one of the protagonists in the Mobilization, reflected on the moment with me in 2018:

It's just that we were not even asking them to give us something. So when Francia said, "What are you here for?" I thought, "Wow . . . they're here to guarantee that we're not free, and they're here to guarantee that we can never be equal." Right? So she said that, and we all started to cry. I wasn't the only one to tear up. I turned around and all of us were crying because I felt that all of us realized at that moment that we arrived with the hope of getting a response from the state. But the faces of the people listening and the welcoming that they gave us could not compare with the gestures of love from people that accompanied us throughout our walk there. It was like, "No. No. Nothing is going to happen here." [. . .] It was like when you're at a movie and you realize who the bad guy is, "Ohhh! That person who always said they were my friend is the same person that put me in this truly bad situation." It was like that. *We finally became disenchanted with the state.* (my emphasis)

Even so, the participants in the Mobilization eventually signed an agreement with the government that included several promises to address illegal mining and recognize the collective rights of black people in northern Cauca. They decided to sign the agreement out of a shared sense of obligation not to return home empty-handed, many of them knowing that the document itself would amount to little more than a piece of evidence in a future court case. Within weeks of returning to northern Cauca, the Mobilization denounced the presence of seventeen more excavators in the community, and they subsequently received death threats from paramilitary groups. Within a couple of years, Márquez Mina was forcibly displaced from La Toma because of death threats. By 2022, drug traffickers and gold miners had sparked enough divisions in the community to provoke part of the community council of La Toma to break off and form their own community council (figure 0.3).

In spite of the disappointing results, Garzón Valencia reflected on her experience of the Mobilization with reverence years later:

I feel like it helped me position myself. Right? To know not to expect anything. It's different when I relate to the "other" knowing that I can't expect anything from them. I feel like a lot of people keep expecting

FIGURE 0.3

An International Committee of the Red Cross (ICRC) helicopter flies above an Afro-Colombian community council in northern Cauca (photo by author, August 2016)

things from the state. When we expect something from the state, we don't take control over our lives because we have ceded control over our lives to someone or something else.

Garzón Valencia considered the Mobilization's 2014 march to Bogotá as integral to the process through which she ceased to consider herself as a subject of the state, as someone subjected by the state. Her disidentification flipped the logic of colonization by labeling the state as the Other. Garzón Valencia eschewed the hollowness of the social contract and demanded a framework that centered her freedom both as an individual and as part of a collective.

This "generative refusal," as Leanne Betasamosake Simpson might call it, serves as the basis for dissident peace.[66] Garzón Valencia conveyed a deeply felt knowledge that the mobilization deserved more and that the state could not and would not provide it. In doing so, she opened up the terrain of struggle in search of something else beyond colonial-capitalist relations. In *Wayward Lives, Beautiful Experiments*, Saidiya Hartman explores the potential and promise of this drive for "something else" in the fugitive pursuit of freedom by black women in early twentieth-century United States.[67] In Colombia, fugitivity, particularly in the form of marronage, figures prominently in black freedom struggles. PCN—the organization through which Garzón Valencia and I met in 2012—calls its regional collectives *palenques* (maroon societies) in the spirit of sustaining the connection between the struggle of their African ancestors and their struggle now. Yet interpreting fugitivity or marronage as merely escape obscures how these praxes necessarily imply confrontation. The conditions for flight are dependent upon challenging the ideological and material forms of domination that attempt to lock subjects into a position of subjection.[68]

In this spirit, Emmanuel Rozental and Vilma Almendra, two people based in northern Cauca committed to autonomous struggle and associated with Pueblos en Camino, manifested the need for a "peace of the peoples without owners" in a 2013 article:

> Neither the state nor the insurgency has the legitimacy to negotiate peace in the name of or in representation of the Colombian people. Colombia, its transformation, its peoples, and peace do not fit in that negotiation between the state and the insurgency. The country cannot and should not be negotiated at those tables. Even if participation is expanded to other sectors, those sectors and the future would be subject to the armed actors and their interests, as well as the structural conditions imposed by the economic model under which they are being negotiated.[69]

The publication of this article led to a flurry of death threats against them from dogmatic leftists and reactionary right-wingers alike. By challenging conventional wisdom about conflict resolution, they bristled at the state-centric orientation of the dominant peace paradigm and expanded the potential for dignity and autonomy.

The desperation provoked by colonial capitalism, however, heightens the demand for deliverables—that technocratic neologism used to obscure the commonsense understanding that the current system does not deliver. Particularly in the context of war, people grasp at instruments that might provide them with some wiggle room to sustain the conditions for survival. Violence pushes people into desperate circumstances, thereby exacerbating the pressure to address their immediate needs.[70] For example, Márquez made a conscious shift in her approach to politics after the 2014 mobilization. During an interview following her unsuccessful run for Congress in 2019, she told me:

> I wanted to see what possibilities there were with more black people occupying those spaces [in government]. Others arrive in Congress to persuade the people to support the politics of death [la política de muerte]. The majority of them . . . But what do they want power for? To keep fucking [jodiendo] with the lives of people? They're building power, but for the traditional elites. What kind of power could that be? It's very difficult to break with that.
>
> We have tried to build autonomy, but the people side with the politicians. The movements are on the outside trying to build the consciousness of the people. The others use power to legitimize themselves before the people, to implement policies, to kill. We're simply in the rearguard resisting and resisting while they kill us and kill us. [. . .]
>
> That's the risk that I assumed. I was fearful about going into electoral politics, but I saw it as an alternative that could slow down the politics of death. I saw it as an opportunity to use the campaign as a space to reflect on ways to end the politics of death. I knew that I would not change the minds of all of the politicians, but I could use my voice as a platform to send another message to the people. I wanted to generate a political platform to organize the people from another political perspective.

Márquez Mina's decision to embark on electoral politics represents an attempt to challenge state power on its own terms. Encapsulated in her 2022 campaign's slogan "From Resistance to Power," the state became the locus of transformation, not a patriarchal relation that reproduced the conditions of subjugation.[71] Hardly "disenchanted with the state," Márquez Mina deliberately became part of the state with her 2022 election to the vice presidency, and the new administration recruited heavily from the activist milieu that she and I belonged to. As a result, many of the activists whom I have worked with for years assumed posts within the government, thus opening the door to confronting the contradictions implicit in representing the state that they sought to transform or abolish.

In a searching reflection on the limitations of "progressive" governments in Venezuela, Bolivia, and Ecuador, Raquel Gutiérrez Aguilar reflected on an "apparent paradox" expressed by comrades in Ecuador that referred to their experience under Rafael Correa: "We were never weaker as social and indigenous organizations as when we participated in the government." According to Gutiérrez Aguilar:

> The paradox is simple to understand: whoever occupies the government in a rush to push political transformation has to govern and they have to do it according to the inherited rules and institutions, which establish immediate and rigid limits on political action that go beyond the constituent processes that have occurred in various countries. The tragedy—which is no longer a paradox—is that the mobilized societies and the multiple and polyphonic associations of men and women in struggle lose their force and capacity to intervene in political questions when their most developed cadre or the people close to them "occupy the government."[72]

During the first years of the Petro-Marquéz administration, the trend toward co-optation threatened the potential of the autonomous struggles that many of the activists turned officials seemed to represent. That is the tension that Almendra evokes in her book *Between Capture and Emancipation* on the Nasa indigenous people's struggle in northern Cauca. It is also the existential question driving the lyrics to "La Mina." The struggle for autonomy is, as Ana Cecilia Dinerstein suggests, "above all a creative contradictory process."[73] Under the conditions of state-centric peace, it is exceedingly so (figure 0.4).

FIGURE 0.4

Non–Nasa Yuwe speakers tend to refer to Çxhab Wala Kiwe as the region of northern Cauca in southwestern Colombia. A direct translation of the term from Nasa Yuwe would be "Territory of the Great People" in English or "Territorio del Gran Pueblo" in Spanish. (*Source:* Çxhab Wala Kiwe ACIN, Tejido de Defensa de la Vida y los Derechos Humanos 2025)

Homicides in Çxhab Wala Kiwe (2009-2024)

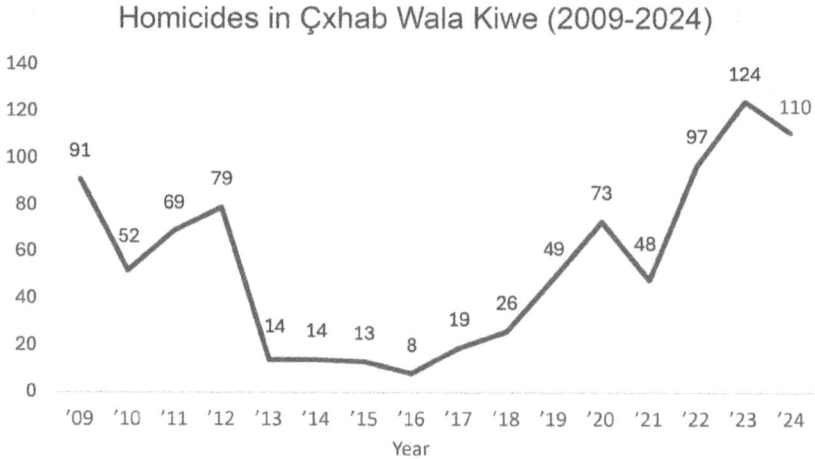

Carlos Rosero, cofounder of PCN, casually shared the following quote with me as he cooked lunch one afternoon in 2016: "Cuando entramos en la lógica del otro, estamos perdidos" (When we enter into the logic of the other, we're lost). We were preparing for one of the many workshops with the Ethnic Commission in northern Cauca. He didn't recall exactly where he picked it up, but the quote struck me as a useful insight into how to resist the colonization of struggle. It remains key to my thinking about dissident peace because it reveals how and why critical consciousness is essential to struggling for autonomy and liberation.[74] After all, the state not only consists of the individuals and institutions that claim it; it is also an alienating logic that permeates our consciousness. Recognizing it as such allows us to face the contradictions of political practice and sustain principled forms of struggling through them. Without critical consciousness developed through praxis, the centripetal force of the state can transform our struggles into normative activities that sustain the structures of domination. This is the challenge facing many activists who now occupy positions within state institutions. Unsettling peace therefore involves a double move: the first is to question the conditions and contradictions of so-called peace, which are unsettling in their own right; the second goes further to challenge the settler colonial premises of the state-centric peace by creating space for more liberatory forms of peace through the struggle for autonomy.

The following chapters explore how struggles for dissident forms of peace confront entanglements with the state and capital.[75] Each chapter is based on unresolved political questions facing the social movements, organizations, and communities that I have accompanied for years. My intent is to reflect on the potential of peace as a horizon rather than an attainable state.

1 ALFONSO CANO'S GRAVE

Vanguardism and the FARC-EP in Northern Cauca

Let us first consider the question: who are the combatants in a guerrilla war? On one side we have a group composed of the oppressor and his agents, the professional army, well-armed and disciplined, in many cases receiving foreign aid as well as the help of the bureaucracy that is beholden to the oppressor. On the other side are the people of the nation or region. It is important to emphasize that guerrilla warfare is a war of the masses, a war of the people. The guerrilla band, as an armed nucleus, is the combative vanguard of the people. Its great force is drawn from the mass of the people themselves.

—Ernesto "Che" Guevara, *Guerrilla Warfare* (1961)

We continued marching, sometimes at night. Comrade Pablo [Catatumbo] had the hardest time because the cast on his arm caused him to lose his balance. I always marched with him during those dark nights. I held his hand, and I watched his steps. There were moments when I got angry with myself for not having more strength to sustain him. When he slipped, he would hit his arm. *The most difficult days during those times were when we had to walk through the trenches where we had laid the landmines ourselves.*

—Camila Cienfuegos, "The Last Embrace with
Comrade Alfonso" (2017; my emphasis)

Why was Guillermo León Sáenz Vargas, an anthropologist from Bogotá, hiding out in the mountains of northern Cauca in 2011? His contemporaries built their careers writing about violence and social change in Colombia, not absconding from the Colombian military. Accompanied by a small security detachment, Sáenz had shaved off the thick beard that distinguished him as "Alfonso Cano," the top commander of the FARC-EP.

At his hiding place, overlooking where the Marilopito and Inguitó Rivers merge into Salvajina reservoir, his two dogs—Conan and Pirulo—had plenty of room to roam the grassy slopes. Their safe house had not drawn much attention from the neighboring communities, an area without paved roads or reliable cell phone service, until low-flying helicopters swept past the mountain ridge opposite Cano's safe house interrupting breakfast on November 4, 2011. Thanks in large part to the United States, the Colombian military boasted one of the largest helicopter fleets in the world, including the AH-60L Arpías, similar to the Black Hawks used in the military raid on Osama Bin Laden's compound in Pakistan earlier that year.[1] Jorge, who heard the helicopters that morning, guessed that the police were planning to eradicate coca crops or attack a guerrilla or drug-trafficking outfit nearby. Sitting at his kitchen table with me six years later, Jorge reflected on the attack:

> Fortunately, the raid occurred during the day because that was the most spectacular thing that I've ever seen in war. Seriously. It was around eight in the morning, and we had been working at my neighbor's house. I was sitting down for breakfast when I saw two lights in that area over there. Moments later, the explosions . . . Just like a few days before—a few months before—when I heard an explosion over in that other village where a few of their guys, the guerrilla's guys, died. I said, "Who's getting themselves killed over there again?" because it hadn't been that long. When all of a sudden, within three or four minutes, more than forty helicopters flew over us. [. . .] At that moment, I said, "All right, they killed or captured someone important," but I never knew that the comandante was over there.
>
> You could look over here and see how the helicopters passed by closely, and I said, "Something serious is going on." And we had to wait because the communication is bad here. So we had to wait for

the midday or evening news. That was how we found out on the seven o'clock news that the operation was against Alfonso Cano. We finally found out because, honestly, we were uncertain all day because we didn't know what happened. Seeing all of that, many people had nervous breakdowns and were evacuated or taken to hospitals. Some people are still affected by it. They hear a helicopter fly overhead, and they get lost. They were left with that psychosis.

Carmen waited to fill in the gaps of her husband's retelling until after I turned off the recorder. She described how the schoolchildren rushed home in a panic during the bombing and framed the raid on Alfonso Cano within the context of the violence that drove her out of her home in southern Cauca years before. Her solemn account of the attack did not exhibit any of the bravado espoused by many of the men from the community who rehearsed the *zip* of the bullets and the *boom* of the bomb explosions. Those polished stories were meant to be heard and relished. Carmen and Jorge's testimonies, in contrast, revealed a more intimate appraisal of the residual and accumulating effects of violence on their experiences living in a battleground. Even so, Carmen said, "with the exception of that"—pointing toward the mountainside where Cano died—"we have lived nicely here" (figure 1.1).

News reports later paraded the image of Cano's corpse stretched out on top of a body bag with a cleanly shaved face, as if he was kin to Samson in the biblical Book of Judges. In the FARC-EP-produced documentary *Moral de Combate* commemorating the life of Alfonso Cano, secretariat member Ricardo Tellez recalled that Cano once told him, "Mr. Santos wants to take my cadaver to the negotiating table." Less than a year after his death, delegations from the Colombian government and the FARC-EP arrived in Havana, Cuba, to formally commence the negotiations that promised to bring an end to more than fifty years of conflict. In 2017, five years and one peace accord later, the site of Operation Odysseus—the Colombian government's name for the raid on Cano's hideout—was practically indistinguishable from the surrounding mountains. Nevertheless, Alfonso Cano continued to serve as a model of self-sacrifice and commitment for former FARC-EP combatants confronting the challenges of adapting to reintegration.[2]

FIGURE 1.1

The site of the raid on Alfonso Cano's hideout (photo by author, October 2017)

This chapter analyzes the FARC-EP's distinctive approach to vanguardism, particularly in relation to the so-called indigenous question in northern Cauca. Although largely absent from academic explorations of social movement theory, vanguardism remains central to centuries-long debates about revolutionary strategy. At its core, vanguardism emphasizes the pivotal role of leadership in determining the outcome of revolutionary situations. The qualities, contents, and aims of that leadership vary across tendencies, but vanguardism usually implies the necessity of a cadre of professional revolutionaries with sophisticated political analysis and military expertise that represent the revolutionary aspirations of the people (*pueblo*).[3]

Throughout its history, the FARC-EP espoused its desire to foment what Che Guevara called "a war of the masses" by expanding its reach beyond a committed core of revolutionaries.[4] Yet their reputation for kidnapping and drug trafficking tends to overshadow the guerrilla group's avid ability to build organic connections within some sectors of impoverished rural populations throughout Colombia. However, the FARC-EP's particular class-based conception of the people along with their reliance on violence to settle disputes pushed away potential allies, particularly among some of the black and indigenous organizations and communities that I worked with in northern Cauca. The divisions between the FARC-EP and black and indigenous communities of northern Cauca exposed concrete political differences based principally on the question of autonomy.

BECOMING THE "TRUE REPRESENTATIVES"

During insurrections, earning the trust and support of the people preoccupies guerrilla leaders and state officials alike. Former U.S. President Lyndon Johnson famously said, "We must be ready to fight in Viet-Nam, but the ultimate victory will depend upon the hearts and the minds of the people who actually live out there."[5] According to Mao Zedong, Johnson's counterpart in China, "The guerrilla must move amongst the people as a fish swims in the sea."[6] Both heads of state understood their relationship with the people based on the conditions of war, and their insights remain central to understanding the fraught relationships forged in armed conflicts today.

Living through war forces people to take positions that are not necessarily tethered to explicit political convictions. Their position in relation to an armed actor can change depending on the balance of power, the likelihood of being exposed as a traitor, or the ephemeral conditions of a conversation. For guerrilla movements, building durable connections with the people is—at least in theory—vital to their survival and the creation of a broad-based movement in support of the revolution. The liberal nation-state, on the other hand, ostensibly regards the people as rights-bearing citizens, and the state should thus protect their individual rights as legal subjects to offset the potential for revolution.

The evolution of the FARC from a small self-defense militia of peasants organizing semiautonomous communities in the 1950s to an army with the capacity to overtake cities at its peak in the 1990s reveals how the confluence of compelling ideas, experiences with state violence, precarious socioeconomic conditions, a hefty war chest thanks to various forms of illicit revenue, and military force made it possible for the guerrilla group to grow.[7] Throughout its history, the *pueblo* (people)—and in particular the *campesinado* (peasantry) and *colonos* (settlers) displaced by violence and dispossession—remained central to the FARC-EP's political agenda.

The Agrarian Program, originally written in 1964 and amended during the FARC-EP's Eighth Conference in 1993, laid out the core of the FARC-EP's grievances, and it was the first thing that Camila Cienfuegos recommended that I read during one of our conversations at the FARC-EP's reintegration camp in Buenos Aires, Cauca, in May 2017.[8] She joined the FARC-EP as a teenager and rose through the ranks, eventually becoming part of the Central General Staff of the FARC-EP and one of the most vocal proponents of the FARC-EP's own brand of feminism: *feminismo insurgente* (insurgent feminism). Having spent much of her life in the FARC-EP, she strongly identified with the *cultura fariana* (FARC culture) based on camaraderie, discipline, and a strong sense of purpose (figure 1.2).

In *Chronicles of Hard Times*, a compilation of Alfonso Cano's diaries posthumously released by the FARC, Cano echoes Camila's passion: "This is what is truly transcendental: fidelity to the cause, faith in our own efforts, unity, and confidence in the capacity of the people [*pueblo*] to interpret the message of their true representatives."[9] Yet as the war dragged on over the course of decades, the FARC-EP's claims to becoming the true representatives of the people rang hollow.[10]

There are several potential explanations for the FARC-EP's lagging support: mass kidnapping, multimillion-dollar revenues from drug trafficking, arbitrary murders of civilians, and the collapse of Soviet-style communism as an alternative to capitalism, for example. Taken together, these factors are referenced by critics as evidence of the FARC-EP's conversion into a narco-terrorist group devoid of a political agenda and motivated solely by profit. They were stigmatized as bandits, and these critiques became more resonant during the 1990s when the FARC-EP deepened its relationship with drug-trafficking networks and expanded its use of kidnapping as the costs of war continued to rise. The consolidation of right-wing paramilitary groups and the shift of coca production from Peru and Bolivia to Colombia

FARC guerrilla participating in a workshop at the Carlos Patiño
disarmament camp in Buenos Aires, Cauca, with a large cutout photo
of Alfonso Cano in the upper-left corner of the photo (photo by author,
March 2017)

represented another facet of Colombia's escalating war. Instead of
peace and democracy following the Constitutional Assembly of 1991,
many of Colombia's *violentólogos* (scholars of violence) suggested the
onset of an era of degradation (*degradación*) in the war.[11] These circumstances led many analysts to believe that Colombia was on the verge of
becoming a "failed state" by the end of the 1990s, due in large part to
the FARC-EP's insurgency.[12]

Yet these explanations tended to leave out the multidecade, mul-
tibillion-dollar counterinsurgency strategy financed in large part by
the United States. During an interview with me in June 2018, Pablo
Catatumbo rejected the dominant narrative that made the FARC-EP
appear anachronistic and predatory. Pablo offered a different explanation for why the FARC-EP did not achieve its revolutionary objectives
through armed struggle:

Well, the oligarchy has illegitimate power in Colombia, and we thought it would be possible to start a popular insurrection. [Manuel] Marulanda [cofounder and former top commander of the FARC-EP] knew that guerrillas don't win wars. Guerrillas need more than strength to win wars—they must be able to connect. There must be a link with the popular urban struggles because Colombia is a country of cities and those guerrilla struggles. If you study the experiences of Russia and Cuba, that is what happened. In Cuba, Castro did not win alone. He only had three thousand guerrillas, but he was able to link the armed struggle with the struggle of the masses. And he was successful in overthrowing the system. In Russia, too. Lenin had a broad mass movement that rebelled. They rose up, and then they formed guerrilla groups. The same thing happened in Vietnam and everywhere else. But the oligarchy here caught on. The Colombians, and especially the gringos, knew how to study these dynamics.

The entire strategy of the state has been to block the link between the revolutionary struggle and the struggle of the masses. They resorted to the stigmatization, repression, and murder of leaders that could guarantee that kind of change. They carried out an anticipated counterrevolution. That's why it didn't bother them to murder the Patriotic Union.[13] That's why it doesn't bother them to kill leaders. They've always had the pretext of, first, the armed struggle and, second, narcotics trafficking.

That is really the problem here in Colombia. Wars shouldn't last this long because they generate a lot of hate. When we [the FARC-EP] conceived our plan entitled the "Strategic Plan," Colombia had 110,000 soldiers. Now there are 500,000. As the war continued, the Army successfully strengthened its military equipment, which is possibly the strongest in Latin America. I would say that not even Brazil has an army as big as Colombia's. But the Colombian Army is also very well equipped. They have a lot of helicopters and assistance: sophisticated state-of-the-art systems for gathering intelligence, as well as support from the United States, Israel, and England. Ultimately, it was very difficult without a strategic leap in the correlation of forces. Now it's very difficult to win a war because you cannot win it without tanks, artillery, or planes. You can't confront 500,000 men equipped with the best helicopters in the world. Colombia has the best helicopter fleet in the world with more than five hundred Black Hawk helicopters. Only Israel has a helicopter fleet of the same caliber.

In addition to the dirty war, there was a propaganda campaign for twenty years calling us narcotics traffickers, terrorists, and bandits. Well, that discouraged the people in the cities that didn't know us. The people in the countryside know us, and they know that we aren't bandits. But the majority of people live in cities, and they believed us to be narcos and bandits. They conducted psychological warfare that was very, very, very well done. But the dirty war eliminated a lot of leaders, as well. Right?

Catatumbo played a pivotal role in strengthening the FARC-EP's political and military capacity for more than forty years, eventually becoming a member of the secretariat and a senator following the Peace Accords. His insistence that "the entire strategy of the state has been to block the link between the revolutionary struggle and the struggle of the masses" reflected a frustration regarding the FARC-EP's inability to bridge the urban-rural divide. Yet in rural northern Cauca—where Alfonso Cano was killed and Pablo Catatumbo previously exercised influence as the commander of the FARC-EP's Joint Western Command (Comando Conjunto de Occidente, CCO)—the guerrillas met staunch resistance from indigenous organizations, such as the Çxhab Wala Kiwe Association of Indigenous Cabildos of Northern Cauca (Asociación de Cabildos Indígenas del Norte del Cauca, ACIN) and the Regional Indigenous Council of Cauca (Consejo Regional Indígena del Cauca, CRIC).[14]

These indigenous struggles challenged the FARC-EP's claims to being the true representatives of the people. They reflected a form of political consciousness and organization that clashed with the FARC-EP's approach to revolutionary politics.[15] The tense relationship between the FARC-EP and some rural communities of northern Cauca exposed the shortcomings of the FARC-EP's analysis of the political conjuncture that assumed a knowledge of the motivations of people based, ipso facto, on their narrow understanding of class.[16] Although the FARC-EP and the Colombian state seemingly foreclosed the emergence of alternative political visions within the context of war, expressions

of self-determination—especially by black and indigenous peoples—
challenged claims to either representing a totality of the people. The
landmines that Camila Cienfuegos referred to in the second epigraph
to this chapter therefore serve as more than a troubling reference to
the dangers of an indiscriminate weapon of war—they should also be
understood as a metaphor for the (self)destructive nature of the FARC-
EP's vanguardist approach to politics. Vanguardism not only justified
violence against perceived enemies but, in its flawed pretense of representation, ensured a form of authoritarian politics that ultimately
alienated the guerrillas from their supposed base.

MEETING WITH THE *PROFES*

His clicking pen broke the silence. Tomás was facilitating a workshop
on the contents of the Peace Accords with the Afro-Colombian Community Council of Nuevo Amanecer, and it was the community's first
formal meeting with a representative of the FARC-EP since the signing
of the Peace Accords. Nearly four hours into the meeting held in a pool
hall turned town hall, a coca grower in his sixties asked Tomás why the
Bojayá Massacre was a "political act."

The question caught the ex-guerrilla off guard. "Bojayá was not
a 'political act'—it was an act of war," retorted Tomás. The mestizo
FARC-EP leader's demeanor changed as he recalled his involvement
in the massacre:

> We accept that it was an act of war, and we apologized to the victims
> because we cannot say that it wasn't us. It was us. And we accept it. And
> we asked for forgiveness from the victims. But it wasn't our policy, and
> it wasn't planned. It was not something where we said, "We're going to
> do this." Because those things . . . Just, no. It was an act of war.

One hundred nineteen people were killed during the 2002 massacre in
Bojayá. Images of a mutilated Christ statue recovered from the rubble
of a bombed-out church feebly stood in for one of the most notorious
episodes of the conflict. In the days leading up to the massacre, both
the paramilitaries and the FARC-EP murdered suspected informants

in the black community of Bojayá in the department of Chocó. More than three hundred people sought refuge from the violence in a Catholic church, and the paramilitaries used the hallowed grounds as a shield to take cover from the FARC-EP's assault. According to accounts from inside the church, the FARC-EP launched a weaponized gas cylinder (*cilindro-bomba*) that exploded on the altar, killing seventy-nine people and injuring dozens more.[17]

The eighteen people in Nuevo Amanecer listened closely to Tomás's story. Nobody expected that one of the guerrillas who participated in the Bojayá Massacre would conduct a workshop on behalf of the FARC-EP regarding the contents of the Peace Accords in their community. That massacre occurred hundreds of miles away more than fifteen years before the meeting, but it irrevocably changed the way that many black people related to the FARC-EP. According to one leader from the Black Communities' Process (PCN), the 2002 Bojayá Massacre and the National Liberation Army (ELN) bombing in Machuca in 1998 represented a turning point in the way he related to the insurgencies: "The guerrillas turned us into their enemies. It became painfully clear that their ideas about liberation did not include us. It was possible that at certain moments before we could have understood them to be on our side, but not after that. If you look at the victims of those massacres, they were all black people—our people."

Not everyone shared the PCN leader's conviction, however. Throughout the meeting, Tomás insisted that the implementation of the Peace Accords depended on the peasants' ability to organize and not the FARC-EP. One man in the audience wearing a large straw hat retorted:

> You all know this better than anyone. We're really good at criticizing, but in terms of organizing ourselves . . . not so much. So what do I say? I think that the FARC shouldn't forget about the campesinos because the FARC really has been the army of the people. So I think the accords may have been signed, but I think that the FARC should continue organizing, helping, and participating in the organizations. Right? Because as a political movement it will be much easier. As a guerrilla group, it was a little tough because they couldn't travel freely whenever they

wanted or leave at any hour of the day. But as a political movement I think the FARC should provide accompaniment because I think the FARC has a lot more knowledge about how to negotiate and organize than any of us.

His desire for more leadership by the FARC-EP—not less—surprised me. Was he just trying to ingratiate himself to the powerful outsider, or was I missing something important?

Tomás responded to the man's comment:

I'm going to tell you a story, so forgive me for a minute. I tried to join the guerrillas when I was eleven years old. Eleven years old! I quit school to help my mother because my father tossed us aside and we stayed with her. She was a campesina who had to watch over six children including the two boys. I left school when I was seven years old and started to pick coffee in order to work. Ultimately, the paramilitaries arrived. In two years there were four massacres in the village where I lived. They killed twenty-three people in one of the massacres. The only option was to join the guerrillas. I tried to join them when I was eleven years old, but they didn't let me. They excluded me until I was fifteen because those are the rules for recruitment.

I joined the guerrillas without knowing how to read or write, and I was very lazy about studying. Lazy! It's obligatory to study in the FARC. Obligatory! It's not about whether or not you want to. No. You have to study. I would even volunteer to stand guard in order not to study! Just so I wouldn't have to study! But then a comrade told me, "If you think you left home so that you wouldn't have to study then you're screwed. If you're here, you've got to get to it." She made me do homework in her bunk from seven in the morning until four in the afternoon. She taught me how to read and write a little bit. From there, her husband got a hold of me, and he gave me books: "Look, you've got four days to read this book and give me a report on it." Today, I'm proud because I'm addicted to reading. For me, talking about my studies is like a sport. I am obsessed with reading about economics, history, and philosophy!

So if I was capable of doing this, that means that we have to stop being lazy. It's mental laziness [*pereza mental*]. Leaders like you all need to take an hour in the afternoon to read, even if it's just a few pages before bed. That's what I do. I read two pages, four pages, or ten pages before going to sleep, then two more when I wake up, and the rest of my day is free. I write poetry. That's what I do. If I have free time, I write a poem. I have a book of poems that I'm thinking about publishing. If I was able to do this, why aren't you? Aren't we all campesinos?

The group of fifteen men and three women laughed about his passion for poetry. Tomás's charisma contrasted greatly with the stale technocratic workshops typically offered by nongovernmental organizations and universities. He was one of them, or at least he made himself appear as such.

His ability to connect the struggles of the guerrilla movement with the difficulties of living in a peasant community corresponded with the FARC-EP's political and military strategy to bring the people onto their side. Drawing on his personal experiences as an example, Tomás embodied the possibility of transitioning from an illiterate campesino into an empowered, intelligent leader. His combat boots, muscular physique, and commanding persona gave the impression of masculine authority exemplified in action movies and television shows. The six-hour meeting evoked the teachings of Paulo Freire's *Pedagogy of the Oppressed* and Antonio Gramsci's reflections on the revolutionary potential of organic intellectuals.[18] Tomás appeared to enter into communion with the people through jokes based on shared hardship and insider knowledge of the peasant experience.[19] He encouraged them to take control over their lives and contribute to society. Even his discussion of the Bojayá Massacre seemed to entertain some of the men present as he shared war stories about shooting up the paramilitaries. One of the Afro-Colombian community council's leaders later told me somewhat embarrassedly that the folks in attendance were not as sympathetic to the FARC-EP as it may have seemed, but—on the basis of my experience in many political organizing meetings throughout the region—the connection felt real.

These questions about how to raise political consciousness and establish connections with the people are primary concerns for aspiring revolutionaries. As indicated by the pleas from the man in the straw hat, the FARC-EP positioned itself as the vanguard of the revolution by offering a political analysis that provided a framework for understanding and struggling against the structures of inequality and violence that people confronted in their everyday lives.

This approach to becoming the true representatives of the people reflected the impulse of an often-cited quote from Lenin's "What Is to Be Done? Burning Questions of Our Movement": "Class political consciousness can be brought to the workers only from without."[20] Marxist-Leninist vanguardism informed the FARC-EP's approach to political organizing and caused sectarian tensions that often resulted in bloodshed. According to that framework, the success of the revolution depended on their capacity to impose their particular—and supposedly correct—analysis of the objective conditions of struggle to take state power. Drawing from aspects of democratic centralism, Bolivarian thinking associated with Hugo Chávez in Venezuela, and—most importantly—their own history of confrontation with the Colombian government, the FARC-EP advocated for people to join their revolutionary struggle to topple the Colombian oligarchy described by Pablo Catatumbo. Refusing to join, however, placed a person, community, or organization at odds with the FARC-EP and potentially in the camp of the enemy. This reality corresponded more with what Antonio Gramsci called "bureaucratic centralism," whereby the leadership "[turns] into a narrow clique which tends to perpetuate its selfish privileges by controlling or even by stifling the birth of oppositional forces."[21] This tendency opened the FARC-EP up to criticism that its strategy mirrored the power relations of the oligarchy it sought to overthrow.

In response to what they considered a pedantic and misguided approach to politics, some black and indigenous activists unaffiliated with the FARC-EP ironically called guerrilla leaders *profes* (short for *profesores,* or "professors"). The FARC-EP's attitude toward organizing the masses conflicted with alternative approaches to struggle causing strife with rural communities, social movements, and political parties. Jorge, who witnessed the raid on Alfonso Cano's encampment, remembered when the FARC-EP first arrived in his hometown:

> They came in saying that they were going to organize the peasants in order to help them. At first, it seems true. They make you see things as if they were true. But as time passed and as the coca crop cultivations grew, that view gets distorted. They didn't organize the peasants; they disorganized themselves [*ellos mismos se desorganizaban*]. They committed the errors of displacing, killing, and threatening people. That's when things practically changed.

These "errors" constitute a breaking point, where revolutionary rhetoric collides with the practicalities of conducting war, and war means violent confrontation. Tomás never said that the Bojayá Massacre was a political act during the meeting in the community council, but the people in attendance interpreted his presentation that way. By trying to distinguish between a political act and an act of war, Tomás attempted to distance the FARC-EP's discourse of liberation from their use of violence, the logical outcome of the FARC-EP's raison d'être: revolutionary armed struggle. This distance, however, is impossible.

ON OPPOSITE SHORES OF THE SAME RIVER?

Ten months after replacing Manuel Marulanda as the top commander of the FARC-EP, Alfonso Cano penned a letter in March 2009 to "the indigenous communities of Cauca." In it, he responded to an open letter signed by the Çxhab Wala Kiwe ACIN and CRIC indigenous movements that accused the FARC-EP and the Colombian government of attempting to "force them into the logic of war." These two letters marked the beginning of an epistolary exchange that included at least ten correspondences between 2009 and 2013 covering issues ranging from the use of gas cylinder bombs to indigenous jurisdiction over captured FARC-EP guerrillas.[22] In addition to addressing the impacts of the war, the letters also revealed two contrasting perspectives on the role and reach of indigenous autonomy in the struggle.

The relationship between the FARC-EP and the indigenous communities of Cauca predated the intensification of the armed conflict
during the 1990s and into the next decade. The sixth point of the FARC-
EP's foundational Agrarian Program declared:

> Indigenous communities will be protected and given sufficient land
> for their development by returning the lands usurped by the *latifundis-
> tas* [large-scale landowners] and modernizing their systems of culti-
> vation. The indigenous communities will enjoy all of the benefits of
> the Revolutionary Agrarian Policy. [The Agrarian Program] will also
> establish an autonomous organization for the communities respecting
> their *cabildos* [councils], way of life, culture, languages, and internal
> organization.[23]

The founding members of the FARC expected that the impoverished
indigenous populations would ally with them in their efforts to over-
turn the quasi-feudal relations in the countryside.[24] Many members of
the FARC-EP were of indigenous descent themselves. Yet their treat-
ment of the indigenous question provided little space for dialogue or
reimagining the contents of the revolutionary program beyond the
FARC-EP's mandates.[25] In relation to the so-called indigenous question,
José Carlos Mariátegui—a Peruvian socialist praised by the FARC-EP
in a 2012 letter and strongly associated with forging a distinctly Latin
American style of leftism in the early twentieth century—repeated the
following phrase verbatim throughout his writings: "The solution to
the problem of the Indian must be a social solution. It must be worked
out by the Indians themselves."[26] However, the FARC-EP's contradictory approach to the indigenous question in Cauca hardly allowed
space for the Nasa indigenous peoples to work it out for themselves
despite their rhetorical support for doing so.

Cano's 2009 letter repeated the FARC-EP's "full and unconditional
support" for indigenous struggles as "evidence of [their] permanent
commitment and positive disposition toward the indigenous cause, to
the point that today, various fronts and innumerable guerrilla units are
made up primarily of combatants from different ethnic groups: heirs
of the epic struggle for freedom by important indigenous heroes in

national history." Equating the individual participation of indigenous people in the ranks of the FARC-EP with the support for the FARC-EP by indigenous political platforms functioned as a way for the FARC-EP to sidestep criticism. For example, during the June 2016 meetings in Cuba between the FARC-EP and the Ethnic Commission for Peace and the Defense of Territorial Rights, one FARC-EP leader scoffed at the idea that the FARC-EP needed to consult with black and indigenous organizations about the contents of the Peace Accords: "Why do you talk so much about prior consultation if we have an indigenous and black base?" His words minimized the space for a debate about potentially divergent expressions of black and indigenous demands.

The Çxhab Wala Kiwe ACIN's 2012 letter to Timochenko—Rodrigo Londoño, successor of Alfonso Cano as commander of the FARC-EP and cosigner of the 2016 Peace Accords—challenged the FARC-EP's politics of representation: "We can't deny that indigenous *milicianos* [militants] are indigenous; we're not blind. But the moment that they decided to become permanent members of a military organization they renounced their status as civilians and placed themselves outside of our political community."[27] For the Çxhab Wala Kiwe ACIN, becoming part of a guerrilla group or the Colombian military separated an indigenous individual from the indigenous political community.

This concept of an indigenous political community developed out of centuries of autochthonous struggles to resist colonization, international frameworks supporting indigenous rights in the latter half of the twentieth century, and historical memory linking the past with the present.[28] For example, the formation of the CRIC served as a key moment in defining indigenous political community during the latter half of the twentieth century. In 1971, indigenous commoners (*comuneros*) from Cauca split off from Colombia's largest peasant organization, the National Association of Peasant Users (Asociación Nacional de Usuarios Campesinos, ANUC), and formed the CRIC. These indigenous members of the ANUC did not feel represented by the ANUC's class-based demands that sidelined indigenous difference.[29] According to Gregorio Palechor, one of the CRIC's leaders at the time, "ANUC accused us of being racist, pro-indigenous, trade-unionist. They slandered our leaders. They were out to swallow up our organization and manipulate it for their own ends."[30]

The CRIC's approach to indigenous political community centered the principles of unity, land, culture, and autonomy.[31] Over the course of the following decades, the efforts to build indigenous political community frequently clashed with the state and the FARC-EP, as well as other armed groups. These confrontations became more violent and led to the creation of new indigenous political formations to defend the territory. For example, the Quintín Lame Armed Movement (MAQL) drew inspiration from its namesake, an indigenous leader from Cauca who led a series of land occupations to reclaim territory in the early twentieth century.[32] The MAQL emerged as an armed self-defense group for the indigenous communities of northern Cauca in the early 1980s and quickly entered into direct conflict with the FARC-EP, as well as other guerrilla factions, the army, police, and local landowners. The escalating conflict in Cauca resulted in the drafting of the Vitoncó Resolution of 1985, in which the CRIC asserted its "right to autonomy, that is to say, the right of the *cabildos* and the communities to control, monitor, and organize their social and political life in the *Resguardos* and to reject the policies imposed from outside, regardless of where they come from."[33] As a result of pressure by the communities, the FARC-EP signed an agreement in 1987 with the CRIC reaffirming the need to respect the sixth point of the Agrarian Program.[34] Nevertheless, the presence of the FARC-EP continued to cause friction with the region's indigenous communities.[35]

These conflicts bled into the twenty-first century. On July 9, 2011, the FARC-EP detonated a bus full of explosives next to a police station on market day in Toribío, a town in northern Cauca with the reputation for being the most attacked by guerrillas in the country. The explosion killed five people, injured more than a hundred, and destroyed several homes. In addition to the *chiva-bomba* (bus bomb) in Toribío, the FARC-EP conducted coordinated attacks in the municipalities of Corinto, Caldono, Jambaló, and Páez at around the same time. The attacks appeared to serve as a diversionary tactic by the guerrillas to ensure safe passage for Alfonso Cano, who was en route to the Pacific coast after escaping his besieged camp in Cañon de las Hermosas in the neighboring department of Tolima.

In response to the bombings and the systematic attacks on its leadership, the Çxhab Wala Kiwe ACIN published a strongly worded statement on July 20, 2011, "Ending the War, Defending Our Autonomy, Reconstructing the Public Good, and Building Peace," demanding the "demilitarization of indigenous territories."[36] They also amplified the activities of the Indigenous Guard (Guardia Indígena)—a volunteer community watch group for indigenous people armed only with wooden batons and walkie-talkies—to monitor the conflict in the area and provide a semblance of protection for communities associated with the Çxhab Wala Kiwe ACIN (figure 1.3).[37]

Equating the role of the FARC-EP in the communities with that of the state and therefore distancing their autonomous political project from either, the Çxhab Wala Kiwe ACIN argued, "Both the invasion of our territories by the official Army and the occupation of our com-

FIGURE 1.3

Indigenous Guard (photo by author, March 2017)

munities by the insurgency promote an extractive territorial and economic model that is dependent on the profitability of natural resources therefore reproducing a system of dispossession and annihilation that indigenous peoples have known for centuries."[38]

Following Operation Odysseus in November 2011, which targeted Alfonso Cano's hideout, the FARC-EP retaliated with another series of attacks on police and military outposts throughout Cauca. In March 2012, they published a video, "Report on the War: 'Comandante Alfonso Cano Present and in Combat,'" documenting their exploits with clips of the attacks in January and February along with body counts for each battle.[39] That same month, the FARC-EP's CCO issued a statement addressed to the indigenous communities of northern Cauca: "Once again we appeal to the word that—like a bridge—can communicate between opposite shores of the same river: the civil struggle of the indigenous communities and the armed resistance of the people. Both are fundamental for the struggle of Colombians to build dignified future for everyone."[40] The tone of the FARC-EP's March 2012 statement turned sharply after seven paragraphs criticizing the government's neoliberal policies, taking credit for successful efforts to reclaim indigenous land, and lamenting the involvement of indigenous commoners (*comuneros*) in the war:

> In that context, the erroneous and deceitful interpretation of Autonomy spread by certain "leaders" cultivates hatred among the *comuneros* and promotes a confrontational spirit in the assemblies—not only against the presence of guerrillas but also against their own indigenous brothers who distance themselves from policies that are amenable to the State. In that regard, they promote hostile actions that end up turning the Indigenous Guard into a mere extension of the policing arm of the Establishment and converting their hostility into the best weapon in support of the governing elites and the Empire's transnationals. [. . .]
>
> Just like the immortal José Carlos Mariátegui, we believe that "the land has always been the joy of the Indian" (regarding its material and spiritual value). That is why we think that as long as the indigenous territories are not effectively secured for their peoples, as long as "self-governments" [*gobiernos propios*] are not a guarantee for social

justice and order in their communities, as long as the military maintains a threatening presence, and as long as there is a risk of exploiting the natural resources in the territories, the presence of the FARC-EP will continue to be legitimate in those territories.[41]

The FARC-EP's full-throated critique of the Çxhab Wala Kiwe ACIN and CRIC's efforts to build forms of autonomy conformed to their wider practice of stigmatizing and attacking black and indigenous communities that advocated for self-determination, as evidenced by their relationship with the Afro-Colombian Community Council of Alto Mira and Frontera. Letters by the Çxhab Wala Kiwe ACIN and CRIC, as well as statements by other black and indigenous organizations throughout Colombia, consistently condemned violence against their leadership and denounced the formation of parallel organizations by the FARC-EP as strategies to undermine the authority of the *cabildos*, community councils, and other ethnoterritorial authorities.

Yet according to the FARC-EP's analysis of neoliberal multiculturalism in the context of a protracted counterinsurgency campaign, their opposition to this form of autonomy was consistent with their revolutionary program. According to one mestizo ex-FARC-EP guerrilla whom I interviewed, state recognition of black and indigenous autonomy created a "minority trap" that benefited the capitalist state:

> It's a minority trap where every minority gets their own space: "I recognize you as a minority. I'll give you your autonomy. Now leave me the hell alone. The rest of the world keeps moving to the beat of my drum." And the minority from its local autonomous zone says, "OK. You leave me the hell alone, and I'll be fine here in my reduced space." We think that it shouldn't be reduced to local autonomies. Instead, we must struggle to find themes that cut across all of the spaces and sectors of society in Colombia, regionally and globally. That is to say, we must find universalisms because the world will never be transformed if we don't.

According to him, these forms of territorial autonomy were another example of the doomed efforts to "change the world without taking power," an unprovoked reference to John Holloway's homonymous book, which he identified as "another cool poem, but it means very little in real terms." Instead of advocating for what he would probably consider vulgar identity politics, oppressed people needed to develop an all-encompassing "universalist" framework for transforming society that included taking state power. However, as indicated by the alienating aspects of the FARC-EP's class-based approach to politics for organizations like the Çxhab Wala Kiwe ACIN and CRIC, the FARC-EP's ability to make the people "interpret the message of their true representatives" appeared unlikely to succeed without resorting to world-shattering levels of violence.

In their first of two letters to Timochenko, the Çxhab Wala Kiwe ACIN responded to the FARC-EP's condemnation of indigenous autonomy:

> In order to oppose our project of territorial autonomy, the CCO talks about supposedly "real autonomy," which consists of something that apparently appeals to the guerrilla commanders. That's the same autonomy that the government talks about, one that takes orders from their ministers and generals. But when we say "self-determination," we mean "self-determination," not authorized autonomy [*autonomía tutelada*]. Autonomy does not consist of an armed actor or an intellectual or a politician or a religious person or a legal or illegal entity giving us a blessing with respect to how we should exercise it. Autonomy refers precisely to the contrary: that indigenous authorities and leaders are not accountable to anyone other than the organized community.
>
> In that regard, we are very distant from one another. If that's the FARC's position, then it is even more backward than that of the capitalist States that at least approve of the United Nations Declaration on the Rights of Indigenous Peoples in word. The leaders of the CCO say that indigenous peoples can't have autonomy as long as there are certain threats that they will "combat" (their exact words). The first of which are the "self-governments" [*gobiernos propios*]—that is to say, our indigenous governments that "are not a guarantee for social justice and order in their communities." We ask, From here on out is the FARC going to "combat" the *cabildos* of the ACIN and CRIC? What an enemy to pick: the popular organizations! If that's not what you meant to say, then why did you write it? To intimidate us? Is it a typo? Whatever

the reason, the indigenous peoples of Cauca are not going to give up politics for fear.[42]

The Çxhab Wala Kiwe ACIN's position delineated a clear opposition to the FARC-EP's hypocritical stance on autonomy and their violent approach to getting the support of the people. According to the Çxhab Wala Kiwe ACIN, "We are not on opposite shores of the same river, as the CCO statement says. In reality, we're on two different rivers. It might be possible that both rivers flow into the same sea, but we think that yours will be hard-pressed to reach the sea of a more just country."[43]

ACTING LIKE A STATE

"The FARC's politics and indigenous politics aren't different. They're almost the same. The only difference is the use of arms. It's not anything else. That's why, if you review the FARC's politics and the indigenous movement's politics, it's the same. They just thought about it differently. That's why we can't fight each other after the peace process. We need to unite our forces to confront our common enemy." I would dismiss this assertion as naive by almost anyone other than Jhon. We had our first conversation on the *malecón* in Havana during a round of negotiations between the FARC-EP and the Ethnic Commission for Peace and the Defense of Territorial Rights in June 2016, where he participated as a representative of one of the indigenous organizations associated with the Ethnic Commission. Throughout the tense proceedings that reflected the tone of the aforementioned letters, he observed quietly as the other spokespeople for the black and indigenous social movements confronted the FARC-EP about being excluded from the negotiations with the government. That night, as we stared into the Caribbean Sea and took in the lively atmosphere near La Rampa, he said, "You know . . . I was in the FARC for six years."

He went on to tell me about his life manufacturing artisanal explosives for the FARC-EP before becoming the governor of an indigenous *cabildo* in northern Cauca. Jhon joined the FARC-EP in the middle of the first decade of the 2000s as a *miliciano* at around the age of sixteen mostly out of curiosity. He decided against becoming an active guerrilla because that meant that he would have to give his entire life over to the guerrillas. As a *miliciano*, he got to live at home and served as an informant for the local guerrilla units, occasionally participating in specific combat operations when the FARC-EP called on him. He eventually received training on how to make explosives like the cylinder bombs and grenades used in the 2012 attacks in northern Cauca and during the Bojayá Massacre. Over the course of those six years, he and his classmates in the training "simply became a shopping center. The guerrilla units would show up, pack their bags, and leave." Only two out of the ten *milicianos* from his course were still alive when we spoke.

Although he still thanked the FARC-EP for instilling him with discipline, Jhon ultimately chose to get out after his sister was killed. According to his mother, Jhon's sister joined the FARC-EP to search for him and as an excuse to escape the strict rules at home. Within two months of her departure, the family received news that the military captured her during a raid on a FARC-EP camp and tortured her before dismembering her body. Feeling responsible for her death and acquiescing to the pleas of his mother, Jhon assumed the risks of abandoning the FARC-EP. A couple of weeks after Jhon left, he received a veiled threat from one of his former comrades for abandoning the guerrillas. Despite the potential for retaliation, he joined the state-sponsored demobilization program Regreso a Casa (Return Home), resolved his legal status, and moved to a rural indigenous community in northern Cauca, where he grew coca and participated in the community organizing efforts. However, once some of the community leaders learned about his past, they kicked him out of the *cabildo*. He eventually arrived in his current *cabildo* after the owner of a coca farm a few hours away in a different municipality invited him to work on his land as a *raspachín* (coca picker) until he could purchase his own piece of land. Eventually, Jhon's reputation as a good soccer player earned him friends, and someone from the *cabildo* recruited him to get more involved in community organizing.

Jhon did not cite Marx or rave about the motorcycles, women, and money associated with joining the FARC-EP. He did not talk about the

FARC-EP's Agrarian Program or the Çxhab Wala Kiwe ACIN's autonomous Life Plans (Planes de Vida). He presented himself as someone
whose decisions hinged on growing up poor and disenfranchised. He
wanted to better the life of his community. As governor of the *cabildo*,
he built the foundations of a gymnasium and attempted to facilitate
the reincorporation of FARC-EP guerrillas into the area surrounding his community after the Peace Accords. Yet the scant implementation of the Peace Accords frustrated his efforts at the *cabildo*, and
many ex-guerrillas joined armed groups that filled the void left by the
FARC-EP. New drug-trafficking organizations and guerrilla groups
recruited ex-FARC-EP members and constituents of the *cabildo* by
providing them with a shortcut to power and authority in the form of
weapons and income.

Reflecting on the changing makeup of the ranks of the FARC-EP,
Pablo Catatumbo acknowledged the conditions that led many youths
to join the guerrillas:

> For many young men and women, the guerrillas meant, first, sexual
> liberty and, second, social liberty. With the guerrillas, they could
> easily get a motorcycle, a gun, a man . . . So, many people that joined
> the guerrillas didn't join because they were conscious revolutionaries.
> That's not why they joined. They joined because their parents' homes
> were strict. Because they didn't have money. In the guerrillas it's easy.
> Within two days you've got a motorcycle and a pistol, and the guys have
> a girlfriend—not a girlfriend, but a lover or a wife—with everything
> paid for because they didn't have to work. The guerrillas would give
> them clothes. Everything. Everything. And that was an incentive [to
> join].
>
> For many of the guerrillas, the disarmament was complicated be-
> cause many lost out, and that's why they joined the dissidents. Not all
> of them were in the FARC because of ideals. In a certain regard, the
> guerrilla is like the paramilitaries. Not everyone in the paramilitaries
> was an anti-communist. They were there because it was a way to sur-
> vive. They paid. They gave you a weapon. You got nice clothes. You got
> a motorcycle. You had authority.
>
> That's the problem.

For many onlookers, the participation of these seemingly apolitical youth in the war reflected its so-called degradation.[44] These recruits contrasted with the conscious revolutionaries who joined the guerrilla groups during what Pablo Catatumbo calls the "boom following the death of Che Guevara [. . .] when youthful students would say, 'If you're a revolutionary do what Che did: Go to the jungle! If you're not a revolutionary guerrilla, then you're trash [*pacotilla*] or better yet a coffee-shop revolutionary [*revolucionario de cafetín*]!'"

Alfonso Cano and Pablo Catatumbo joined the FARC during the era of revolutionary fervor in Latin America. They became close friends when they traveled to Moscow in the early 1970s. In the USSR, they participated in a course hosted by the Communist Party's All-Union Leninist Young Communist League (KOMSOMOL), where they received instruction on the tenets of Marxism from political exiles like Rodney Arismendi from Uruguay, Luís Carlos Prestes from Brazil, and refugees from the Spanish Civil War, as well as important Communist Party officials from the Soviet Union such as Mikhail Suslov. Upon returning to Colombia, they upheld their commitments as revolutionary cadre and joined the FARC. As with Jhon's cohort from the explosive training, violence decimated Cano and Catatumbo's Colombian cohort from the Young Communist League of more than a dozen people. But unlike Jhon's cohort, these professional revolutionaries dictated the political and military strategy of the guerrilla movement that sought to take control of the state in the name of—and often at the expense of—systematically oppressed peoples in Colombia.

The death of Alfonso Cano and the subsequent signing of the Peace Accords further unraveled the FARC-EP's aspirations to become the revolutionary vanguard. Over the course of the 2010s, vigorous debates emerged within the FARC-EP about the possibility of forming strategic alliances with other political formations outside the guerrilla group and how to democratize its internal hierarchy. The "April Theses" published by the FARC in 2017 as guidelines for their new political party state, "We are based on the notion of an expansive political party, understanding that our party represents one of the nodes in the revolutionary camp. We understand ourselves not as the revolutionary party in Colombia, but as one of the organizations struggling for that purpose."[45] On paper, the shift in language represented an important departure from the bulk of the FARC-EP's nearly fifty-three years of armed struggle. However, their ability to transform the vanguardist aspects of the *cultura fariana* has proved more difficult. Five years after the Peace Accords, Comunes, the FARC's political party, was in shambles. Many former guerrillas and party members wrote their own letters announcing their resignation from the party and denouncing enduring forms of vanguardism and hierarchy within the party.[46]

In its violent and racist reaction to indigenous calls for self-determination and autonomy, the FARC-EP harmed the people it claimed to represent. It attempted to extinguish the potential of alternatives to their state-centric approach to revolution. The authoritarian politics at the core of the FARC-EP's effort to become the true representatives of the people revealed the tribulations inherent to acting like a state.[47]

This tendency, however, was not limited to the FARC-EP. The centripetal force of colonial-capitalist state formation and its promise of power also affects social organizations and communities that embrace increasingly state-centric routes for redressing forms of oppression.[48] That is why movements like the Liberation of Mother Earth Process in northern Cauca reject the FARC-EP's approach to politics in asserting, "We don't have external spokespeople, we [*nosotras y nosotros*] speak for ourselves."[49]

2 THE COCA ENCLOSURE

Drug Trafficking and the Settler Colonization of Struggle

NEARLY TWO HUNDRED PEOPLE PILED into the white plastic chairs and wooden benches that filled the dusty pool hall. Others watched from outside. The crowd of mostly men arrived at the Afro-Colombian Community Council of Nuevo Amanecer by foot or on horseback. In a couple of months, some of them would be able to use their motorcycles on the freshly inaugurated road built by a private energy company with economic interests in the region. That morning in late September 2016, some of the attendees hiked under the sun for up to three hours in order to learn about a topic that drew more attention than any other local issue in the immediate aftermath of the Peace Accords—the accords' chapter 4, "The Solution to the Illicit Drugs Problem."

For the first time since the signing of the Peace Accords in August 2016, people had the opportunity to learn more about chapter 4. They listened intently to the various perspectives shared by the people sitting at the front of the room, which included the governor of a neighboring indigenous *resguardo* (reservation), the legal representative of the Afro-Colombian Community Council of Nuevo Amanecer, a member of the municipal council, and me. The attendees responded to the presentations by voicing their aspirations and concerns regarding the government's National Comprehensive Program for the Substitution of Illicit Crops (PNIS), which was created by the accords. Given the tenuous standing of the accords before the October 2 plebiscite, many people wondered out loud whether the implementation of the Peace Accords would actually occur. Nevertheless, the possibility of acquiring resources from the state and minimizing the risks associated with cultivating coca served as an impetus to participate in the planning process.

Instead of focusing on the minutiae of the accords, the facilitators of the meeting emphasized the power of the communities to influence the terms of the coca substitution programs. In the past, coca catalyzed community resistance to outside intervention. During the region's first major coca boom late in the first decade of the 2000s, the military attempted to forcibly eradicate the crops by sending in regiments of soldiers armed with guns, shovels, and pesticides. The military intervention caused an uprising among the region's coca growers, or *cocaleros*. In a rare convergence of their political energies, people from the surrounding black, indigenous, and mestizo peasant communities confronted the troops and threatened to escalate the protests if the military did not retreat. Although small compared with other parts of the country with longer histories of growing coca, the coca cultivations in this part of northern Cauca played an important role in the local economy, which depended primarily on the production of coffee.

Formally founded in the early 2000s, the Afro-Colombian Community Council of Nuevo Amanecer's original membership included just a few families. They learned about the potential benefits of organizing themselves as a community council from black organizations with a historical presence in the area. Interest and membership did not swell in the community council of Nuevo Amanecer, however, until the military threatened to forcibly eradicate the coca cultivations in the area. According to one member of the community council, "People started to join the community council when the military came in because they said that the only way to protect the territory was by being indigenous or Afro . . . or by being recognized as either one of those two . . . because they have a special recognition or something like that where the military can't show up as if it were just a peasant zone without any . . . How can I say it? Well, without being tied to an important organization." As a result of this widely held impression about the reach of multicultural rights enshrined in Colombia's 1991 constitution, many black and mestizo people from the region signed up to join the community council, but they were not the only ones. By 2009, several families of *colonos cocaleros,* or "coca-growing settlers," from other parts of the country signed up to become part of the Afro-Colombian community council as well.

Unlike the founding members of the community council, the *colonos cocaleros* arrived in the region in the middle of the first decade of the 2000s searching for a recondite place to grow coca after state-led eradication efforts forced them out of their homes in other parts of the country. Although very few, if any, of the *colonos cocaleros* self-identified as black, they believed that the Afro-Colombian community council could provide an extra layer of protection against the government's counter-narcotics policies because black communities have the internationally recognized legal right to free, prior, and informed consultation. In their estimation, this meant they could use the courts, on the basis of their recognition from the state as a black community, to halt any public policy or development project that might negatively affect their livelihoods through an extensive consultation process. The legal representative of the Afro-Colombian Community Council of Nuevo Amanecer at the time welcomed the newcomers because he believed that the community council could harness the explosion of interest in the entity to defend the community's rights.

The protests against the military-led forced eradication continued, and the government eventually reached an agreement with the communities after two weeks of negotiating. The troops retreated, and the bureaucrats promised to implement a series of state-supported programs that would provide the communities with incentives such as credits and roads to encourage the *cocaleros* to voluntarily substitute the illicit crop. The government never made good on its promises, and the *cocaleros,* in turn, did not uproot their coca, leaving the community council with a dilemma. It could no longer convene enough of its members to hold an official assembly because the coca-growing settlers now found little use in engaging with the community council. During the protest, the official membership of the community council grew from around 25 families to 250. According to the internal regulations (*reglamento interno*) of the community council, they needed at least half of the registered members to participate in a meeting to hold quorum. The inability to make decisions effectively stalled the community council's efforts to function as an administrator or to defend the territorial rights of the community.

In the late 2010s and early 2020s, the community confronted a similar situation. People in the region would say "*la coca convoca*" (coca convenes), because meetings related to the substitution or eradication of coca crops summoned many more people than meetings related to unreliable teachers at the school or repairing washed-out roads. Even topics like the possibility of acquiring collective land titles tended to elicit ambivalence—and even outright resistance—from community members.

This chapter analyzes coca's power to transform social and economic relations, and it reveals how the settler colonial project and the attendant structural inequalities of Colombian society are reproduced in regions where coca is cultivated. Rather than stigmatizing the crop and the people who grow it, this chapter examines the contradictions that arise as communities become increasingly dependent on drug trafficking and subsequently tied to state bureaucracies, neoliberal markets, U.S.-sponsored militarization campaigns, illegal armed actors, and the racial hierarchies associated with the illicit economy.

The first section of this chapter, "Colonizing the Margins," critically examines processes of *colonización* (colonization). In Colombia, contemporary uses of the word *colonización* are not usually associated with the legacy of the Spanish *conquista* (conquest). Instead, *colonización* names an ongoing process whereby *colonos* settle Colombia's hinterlands, which are often imagined as uninhabited or primed for the civilizing force of *colonización*.[1] The separation implied by the different usage of the terms *conquista/colonización* and *conquistador/colono* thus masks the continuities between Spanish colonialism and Colombian state formation. Like many other countries in the region, Colombia had its own government agencies officially tasked with shepherding processes of colonization throughout the twentieth century such as the Institute for Colonization and Immigration. These agencies were created to modernize the countryside and implement a modest version of land reform, and their successors in the 2016 Peace Accords were supposed to do the same thing.[2] Although these processes of state-led colonization often failed to deliver on their promises, they were accompanied by other waves of informal settlement that also transformed the Colombian frontier, often in tandem with the expansion of illicit crops and other boom economies.[3] Consequently, most academic studies of *colonización* focus on the subject of the *colonos*.[4] As people whose lives have been shaped by what Francisco Gutiérrez-Sanín calls "institutionalised calamity," *colonos* offer an important perspective into the contradictory terrain of state formation because they are both its grist and its protagonists. In places like northern Cauca, however, locals do not call the settlers *colonos*. Instead, they call them *foráneos* (outsiders) to indicate their imposing status. This key insight has been largely sidelined in much of the literature on *colonización* in Colombia; that is, *colonización* is part of an ongoing process of settlement (i.e., settler colonialism). Thus, it is important to attend to not only the subjects of *colonización* but also those subjected by it in the regions being colonized.

In the middle of the first decade of the 2000s, many people in southern Colombia became *colonos cocaleros* as they fled their homes as a consequence of Plan Colombia, a U.S.-backed antidrug and counterinsurgency strategy. The second section of the chapter, "Imperialism and Colonization," explores the ways in which the drug war transformed the social, cultural, political, economic, and physical landscape. The United States had provided the Colombian government with more than $10 billion in primarily military aid since 2000 and contributed to the forced displacement of over seven million people. By analyzing the demographic changes and shifts in coca cultivation patterns, the section reveals how Plan Colombia disrupted the concentration of coca cultivations in eastern and southern departments of Colombia and contributed to the spread of coca cultivations to other parts of the country. The Pacific coast, a predominantly black and indigenous region, became Colombia's most strategic drug-trafficking route as planes fumigated the dense coca cultivations in southern Colombia with glyphosate, drug interdictions expanded in the Caribbean Sea, and *colonos cocaleros* trekked out in search of safer places to grow coca.

In addition to the crops, the settlers also brought what some community leaders call the *anticultura de la coca*, or "anti-culture of coca," the title of the third section, which is associated with new forms of consumerism, violence, and an extractive relationship to the land. This section provides an ethnographic analysis of the friction between these ways of life—one based primarily on subsistence and the other on the accumulation of wealth. Despite the community council's role in protecting the people from state-led coca eradications, the survival of the crops proved to be double-edged. As the coca cultivations became more entrenched in everyday life and outsiders gained more influence in the communities through *colonización*, the anti-culture of coca increasingly determined the region's political economy and transformed its racial formation.

Encounters with *colonización* along northern Cauca's "narcofrontiers" are important sites for understanding enclosure.[5] Enclosure, according to James Scott, is "an effort to integrate and monetize the people, lands, and resources of the periphery so that they become, to use the French term, *rentable*—auditable contributors to the gross national product and to foreign exchange."[6] Yet by confining enclosure to a narrow definition of political economy, we risk obscuring its social, cultural, and territorial aspects in a settler colonial context. In Nuevo Amanecer, the coca enclosure signals the destruction of alternative ways of life in order to consolidate social relations amenable to the expansion of capitalism and settler colonial state formation by undermining struggles for autonomy and self-determination.[7]

COLONIZING THE MARGINS

> Birds, monkeys, ocelots, turtles, tapirs, big white and yellow fish below the surface of the water . . . The skies full of rain . . . The virgin jungle of the Amazon . . . The large impassible rivers and the still intact

lands . . . Between the expansive plains and the green immensity of the Amazon, at first glance the Macarena is a paradise far away from men. It was named a biological reserve in the 1940s by governmental decree, but the government is far away. With or without decrees, thousands of *colonos* have moved into these lands that are put aside and protected by the Law for the infinite variety of species of Amazonian flora and fauna. *Campesinos* lured in by the illusion of land without owners, guerrillas arriving to occupy the space left behind by the centralist state, and the coca thrill-seekers . . . The cocaine that sells at the price of gold in the streets of the United States and Europe brings the poor out of poverty in this remote region in exchange for the devastation of Colombia's last virgin jungles.

This prologue to the 1989 documentary *La ley del monte* (The law of the jungle) provides a firsthand look at the bustling coca boom in Caquetá and the Macarena region of central Colombia. It was filmed in 1987 at the tail end of a failed peace process with the FARC-EP and the National Liberation Army (ELN). Adelaida Trujillo—who produced and directed the film with Patricia Castaño—describes the lush jungle that appears on the grainy footage. Suddenly, the view changes when she speaks about the campesinos: a boat approaches a group of wooden homes with zinc roofs on the banks of a river; a man speaks into a bullhorn in a crowded marketplace; a Communist Party of Colombia (Partido Comunista de Colombia) sign displaying a hammer and sickle encrusted in a red star hangs from a building; a store named Almacén El Combate advertises itself as *"el revolucionario de la economía"* (the revolutionary store of the economy); a *cocalero* stuffs a waist-high burlap bag with coca leaves; and a frothy white substance that will be transformed into coca paste pours out of a red bucket. The film cuts to Manuel Cano, a mustached mestizo man with a deep voice smoking a cigarette: "I left my woman on the corner selling blood sausages [*morcilla*] to raise my son, and I came here to work because I couldn't even cover my expenses growing corn at 300 pesos. When the coca arrived, things got better. I could educate my sons and take them to school. Now my wife is in the little house that I bought for her and so on. That's why I'll say it again, God and coca!"

La ley del monte places civilization in tension with nature, the state's sovereignty in tension with the guerrilla's control of the countryside, and the legal economy in tension with drug trafficking. Cano manifests the contradictions of the colonization of the Amazon. His arrival in the jungle and subsequent embrace of coca sprouts from material need and the hollow promises of state guarantees for impoverished people throughout the country.

Drug trafficking—and the cultivation of coca in rural areas specifically—produces social and cultural transformations that distinguish it from other extractive boom economies that stimulated previous waves of colonization. For example, coca is not bound to geographic spaces in the same way as nonrenewable resources like gold or oil are. On the contrary, some peasants say that it grows in places that most legal crops do not. A friend once asked me as we rode on his motorcycle past some recently planted coca fields, "Do you think cassava or coffee would grow on that barren mountainside? No way! That weed [coca] is the only thing that will grow there."

Almost all coca cultivation in Colombia is illegal. One exception in Colombia's legal code (Law 30 of 1986) recognizes the right of indigenous communities to cultivate and use a limited amount of the plant as part of cultural or traditional practices. However, the illicit status of coca and the violence associated with drug trafficking make the cultivations a subject of intense scrutiny by the state and sustains the profitability of the crop. Veena Das and Deborah Poole's analysis of the "margins" of the state is particularly useful for understanding the expansion of coca crops:

> Located always on the margins of what is accepted as the territory of unquestioned state control (and legitimacy), the margins [. . .] are simultaneously sites where nature can be imagined as wild and uncontrolled and where the state is constantly refounding its modes of order and lawmaking. These sites are not merely territorial: they are also, and perhaps more importantly, sites of practice on which law and other state practices are colonized by other forms of regulation that emanate from the pressing needs of populations to secure political and economic survival.[8]

According to a 2017 report by the United Nations Office on Drug Control, 30 percent of Colombia's coca cultivations were within twenty kilometers of an international border.[9] However, even in the era of satellite imagery that presumably tracks nearly every hectare of coca grown throughout the country, the margins that emerge from coca cultivations and other illicit crops such as marijuana and poppy expose the myth of totalizing state power and rule of law well within Colombia's borders. For example, the mountains of Corinto, another municipality in northern Cauca, glimmer after sunset thanks to the light bulbs used to expedite the growth of marijuana. On a clear night in Cali, the illuminated marijuana cultivations resemble villages that dot the mountainside south of the city. Many Caleños, however, are unaware that these lights that adorn their landscape are pockets of illegality. These margins in plain view serve as the site of one of the most recent waves of colonization.

Studies of colonization in Colombia expanded significantly in the 1980s as the FARC-EP gained more power and built on its historic base of peasants.[10] In these studies—many of which appeared in the pages of the discontinued journal *Estudios Rurales Latinoamericanos* (Latin American rural studies, 1978–1993)—sociologists, economists, and historians debated the divergent forms of colonization and analyzed the peasant question. Catherine LeGrand's archival research demonstrated, for example, that "frontier regions were not more democratic than the older areas of the country: in most places one finds the projection of preexistent inequalities into new regions."[11] She argued that the Colombian experience contrasts with the impression that "rural revolts originate in peasant opposition to the penetration of the market economy and the extension of state power into the countryside."[12] Instead, *colonos* sought the support of state institutions in the form of formal land titles, credit, and technical training.

Various processes of colonization facilitated the enclosure of rural territories, as violence continued to dispossess peasants of their land and subsistence. In a 1983 article for *Estudios Rurales Latinoamericanos*, Myriam Jimeno argued, "The colonizing movement is part of the constant expansion of capital and its sphere of dominance. As part of the process of developing an internal market, there is simultaneously an increase in capitalist agriculture and its diffusion in new territories."[13] Colonization thus served as an illusory promise for campesinos seeking to escape the oppressive conditions that drove them out of their homes, and the *colono* became an often-unwitting vanguard in the violent processes of rural enclosure.

According to Alfredo Molano, an acclaimed *cronista* (chronicler) of violence and dispossession in Colombia, "Colonization is always a passionate episode that feeds on the future. The *colono* is a man that desperately leaves behind his past, and he maintains a silent awareness that all of his sacrifices will be compensated. He lives off of that hope. He takes on the quotidian adversities with the composure of someone who understands that he is a pioneer."[14] Like Manuel Cano from *La ley del monte*, these "pioneers" are often portrayed as masculine and mestizo, resilient and resourceful—they are supposed to embody the nation-state, even as conservative sectors of society are quick to stigmatize them as criminal or uncouth if they transgress certain boundaries of acceptability.

In much of northern Cauca, however, the local inhabitants do not romanticize the settlers or call them *colonos*. Instead, they call them *foráneos* or *llegaderos*. Sometimes the locals refer to the *foráneos* as *pastusos* in reference to Pasto, the capital of the department of Nariño, where many of the settlers are believed to have migrated from starting around 2005.

During the crowded meetings about the implementation of chapter 4 of the Peace Accords in 2016 and 2017, the *foráneos* showed up en masse and sat quietly as they listened to the content of the meetings without participating in the discussions. The black and indigenous authorities who coordinated the meetings could not simply kick them out of the space, nor was such an option even discussed. The presence of *foráneos* at the meetings represented the threat of force. The *foráneos*' benefactors (i.e., the drug traffickers), though rarely visible or identifiable, possessed the capacity to exert violence with impunity in the event that they perceived an individual or community challenging their control over the territory.

The experiences of the inhabitants of northern Cauca undercut the teleological narratives of Colombian nation-state formation that identify colonialism as the historical epoch that preceded independence from the Spanish Empire. Instead, they demonstrate the need to link contemporary forms of *colonización* with an analysis of colonialism at large as an aspirational, always incomplete, function of capitalist modernity.[15] This does not only manifest in the ongoing coca enclosure. It also expresses itself in the struggle for multicultural recognition from the nation-state whereby many black and indigenous communities—such as the Afro-Colombian Community Council of Nuevo Amanecer—embark on a contradictory strategy of demanding autonomy through legal recourse from a nation-state built on their oppression. Ultimately, such a strategy can result in co-optation, or the colonization of struggle, even as it offers potentially unexpected openings for making demands.

By calling the coca-growing settlers *foráneos*, the inhabitants of northern Cauca draw attention to the imposition of an outside force on their ways of life. Although coca-growing settlers may seem at odds with the project of the state, the effects of drug trafficking accelerate processes of settler colonialism in northern Cauca by (1) deepening capitalist relations and cutting off subsistence-oriented economies in appealing to the fast life of drug trafficking or what local leaders call the anti-culture of coca, (2) drawing in the military apparatus of the state and subjecting the communities to the violence associated with drug trafficking, and (3) channeling the demands of black and indigenous communities into the state's legal framework. The so-called margins are produced as territories in dispute, where the state creates and differentiates its Others (the terrorist, the drug trafficker, the criminal, the indian [*indio/a*], the black [*negro/a*], the dissident peasant, etc.), where the military attempts to assert its dominance, where capitalists prey on emerging markets, and where settler dominion is established.[16] These processes are, of course, incomplete, and they continue to be met with resistance.

IMPERIALISM AND COLONIZATION

Drug trafficking and the expansion of coca cultivations exacerbated the enclosure of the Pacific region of Colombia thanks in part to another wave of colonization by *colonos cocaleros*. Before Plan Colombia, coca

cultivations were concentrated in the eastern and southern departments of the country (e.g., Caquetá, Guaviare, Meta, and Putumayo).
After Plan Colombia, the crops spread to other parts of the country
as a result of the militarized counter-narcotics policies sponsored by
the United States. Although coca can grow throughout much of the
country, the crop's adaptability alone does not explain its proliferation.
Analysts of drug trafficking call this the balloon effect, whereby coca
cultivations decrease in one place because of pressure only to bubble
up in another.[17]

The so-called war on drugs may have failed to achieve its stated
aim, but it provided the United States with a strategic foothold in the
region by pumping billions of dollars of mostly military aid into Colombia. According to Winifred Tate, "The expansion of militarized
counter-narcotics programs to primarily support the Colombian army
required ideological and institutional work including the creation of
new enemies justifying a military response [. . .]. U.S. policymakers
merged the lingering Cold War fears of communism with the escalating concern of hyperviolent traffickers."[18] In 1984, U.S. Ambassador
Lewis Tambs's designation of the FARC-EP as a "narcoguerrilla" coincided with Nancy Reagan's Just Say No campaign and the peak of Cold
War tensions in Central America. The label thus served as a premise
for the United States to take a more aggressive position against the
FARC-EP in conducting the war on drugs in Colombia, and the moniker
later took on new life when the war on drugs fused with the war on
terror in the early 2000s. The U.S. government converted drug policy
into a key component of U.S. foreign policy during the twilight of the
Cold War.[19]

As a result, the United States provided significant financial, technical, and military support for the Colombian government's offensive
against the cartels in the 1980s and 1990s. Meanwhile, the FARC-EP
expanded its base of operations throughout the country thanks in
large part to the revenues from its involvement in drug trafficking.
Before the mid-1980s, Colombia served primarily as a transshipment
point for cocaine. Colombian drug traffickers smuggled coca paste
into the country from Peru and Bolivia, converted the paste into

cocaine, and exported much of the finished product to the United States, the world's largest consumer of cocaine. However, as evidenced by the protagonists in *La ley del monte*, Colombians quickly learned that they could cut down on costs by growing coca in-country. By 1997, Colombia had become the world's largest producer of coca and cocaine, as Bolivia and Peru's share in the supply chain diminished considerably.[20]

Originally pitched as a sort of Marshall Plan for Colombia, Plan Colombia provided an opportunity for the United States to expand its position in the region, and Colombian policy makers actively sought the assistance of the United States despite protests that the policy violated Colombia's national sovereignty. Arlene Tickner called the Colombian political establishment's openness to the United States "intervention by invitation"; Kwame Nkrumah would have called it "neo-colonialism."[21] Plan Colombia was ultimately signed into law in 2000 and resulted in a military strategy that privileged the use of aerial fumigations. The ostensible targets of Plan Colombia included drug traffickers, the FARC-EP, and the peasants that grew coca in territories on the margins of Colombian society. The *cocaleros*, in addition to being identified as the base of the cocaine supply chain, were also stigmatized as FARC-EP sympathizers because a significant amount of the coca produced in Colombia was grown in FARC-EP-controlled territories.

Álvaro Uribe took office in 2002 with the mandate of "strong hand, big heart" after the failure of the peace negotiations with the FARC-EP under the Andrés Pastrana administration. The Colombian government moved decisively with the blessing of billions of dollars in primarily military aid from the United States. Right-wing paramilitary groups organized under the United Self-Defense Forces of Colombia (AUC) worked alongside the military in many parts of the country and benefited from intimate relationships with powerful politicians and private sector interests.[22] The government pursued aerial fumigations and wiped out tens of thousands of hectares of coca in the short term, despite humanitarian concerns expressed by locals and international organizations. According to victims of the fumigations, the glyphosate caused health problems and left them hungry after it destroyed the crops that they depended on to survive. The Brookings Institution reported that "the most conservative evaluation shows that for each hectare sprayed with glyphosate, coca crops are reduced by about 0.02 and 0.065 ha."[23] Clearly, official drug policy was ecologically destructive and wildly inefficient—even by its own standards of supply-side eradication.

The deepening of neoliberal reforms in tandem with counter-narcotic and counterinsurgency military operations resulted in what critics call the *descampesinazación* (depeasantization) of the countryside and exemplifies what Dawn Paley calls "drug war capitalism."[24] The regions vacated by coca growers and noncoca growers alike were subject to land grabs by multinational corporations and private sector interests in cattle ranching, extractive industries, and agribusiness (e.g., oil palm and sugarcane).[25] In 2012, the U.S.-Colombia Free Trade Agreement went into effect after it was held up in the U.S. Congress following years of concerns regarding labor rights and human rights violations in Colombia. Between 2000 and 2016, U.S. foreign direct investment in Colombia increased nearly tenfold, from $202.5 million to over $2 billion, as these forms of dispossession spread throughout Colombia.[26]

The coca boom that struck various parts of the country as a consequence of the displacement caused by Plan Colombia did not make it to northern Cauca until the first years of the 2000s. At first, people from coca-growing municipalities in Cauca like Argelia, El Tambo, and Balboa, as well as others from the departments of Putumayo and Caquetá, trickled into Nuevo Amanecer, buying up land at low prices. The locals initially feared that the swelling coca cultivations would attract the military or other armed actors, but within months the majority of the people from the community were working on the newcomers' bountiful coca farms. Their experience was not unique. As glyphosate decimated coca cultivations during the first years of Plan Colombia, the *colonos cocaleros* spread out to settle along the frontiers of the drug war (table 2.1).

TABLE 2.1

Hectares of coca by department/region

	2000	2004	2008	2012	2016	2020
Colombia (Total)	163,289	80,350	80,953	47,790	146,139	143,000
Southern/Eastern Colombia*	**121,367**	**39,395**	**26,115**	**16,393**	**46,807**	**26,503**
Caquetá	26,603	6,500	4,303	3,695	9,343	2,055
Guaviare	17,619	9,769	6,629	3,851	6,838	3,227
Meta	11,123	18,740	5,525	2,699	5,464	1,235
Putumayo	66,022	4,386	9,658	6,148	25,162	19,986
Pacific Region	**14,245**	**15,788**	**29,917**	**18,969**	**57,777**	**50,701**
Cauca	4,576	1,266	5,422	4,325	12,595	16,544
Chocó	250	323	2,794	3,429	1,803	1,468
Nariño	9,343	14,154	19,612	10,733	42,627	30,751
Valle del Cauca	76	45	2089	482	752	1,938

Source: Data from various UNODC reports.

*Caquetá, Guaviare, Meta, and Putumayo are not the only departments in southern and eastern Colombia. The annual numbers included here are for only these four departments.

The new wave of forced displacement and colonization caused by Plan Colombia brought many *colonos cocaleros* to the Pacific coast's departments of Nariño, Cauca, Valle del Cauca, and Chocó. During the late 1990s and early 2000s, the Colombian government also recognized collective land titles for the region's primarily black and indigenous populations. However, the uptick in violence—compounded with the influx of *foráneos* offering a lucrative cash crop—threatened the authority of the Afro-Colombian community councils and indigenous *resguardos*, as well as other community-based organizations.

Table 2.1 tracks the extent to which coca cultivations expanded into the Pacific coast and thereby transformed the demographic makeup of the region. For example, in Tumaco—Colombia's second-largest

municipality and home to thirteen Afro-Colombian community councils, including Alto Mira and Frontera—coca cultivations grew from
1,421 hectares in 2001 to 7,045 hectares in 2006.[27] By 2012, death threats
forced many of the elected leaders of Tumaco's Afro-Colombian community councils to flee. According to a 2017 report by the United Nations Office on Drug Control, coca cultivations increased by 32 percent
in indigenous communities and 45 percent in black communities between 2015 and 2016 alone.[28] While the growth in coca cultivations
in black and indigenous communities is intensely tracked by various
international institutions and governments, analysis of the transformations caused by the arrival of coca-growing settlers within these
communities remains scarce. In one particularly illustrative story, a
friend in northern Cauca told me that coca-growing settlers deliberately built their laboratories for processing coca paste right next to his
Afro-Colombian community council's water source. By doing so, the
settlers poisoned the water that the black community depended on for
drinking, bathing, and nourishing their crops. This colonizing tactic
designed to push people out of his community formed part of a broader
strategy to enclose and dispossess black and indigenous communities
susceptible to drug trafficking thanks in large part to a combination
of organized violence and organized abandonment by the state.[29] For
the Black Communities' Process (PCN), "Plan Colombia—a warring
and imperialist policy imposed by the United States and implemented
by Colombia's political and economic elite—led to the forced displacement of millions of people [. . .]. As black communities we understand
that the wrongly named 'War on Drugs' is really a war on us."[30]

THE "ANTI-CULTURE OF COCA"

In January 2017, stories about a gang of thieves and a series of high-
stakes robberies spread throughout Nuevo Amanecer. Juan stepped
into his parent's bedroom where my host family was watching Colombia's Next Top Model on TV. "A buyer got held up on the other side of the
river. They stole 200 million pesos. Shots were fired, and two people
got injured."[31] Just back from the farm where he worked and eager to

share the latest gossip, he had not even taken off his boots or changed out of his work clothes. The family's attention shifted from the runway models to Juan. He joked that it was time for me to start training for a potential confrontation with the gang: "Anthony can probably fire a rocket launcher like those gringos in the movies." His twenty-year-old nephew laughed, "If it was a small group of three to five guys, the community would be able to defend itself, but sixteen is a different story. It's not even worth putting up a fight because they'll kill you."

The next morning, Juan's uncle, Roberto, picked me up from the house before seven en route to his coca farm. Most of the people who reside in the cluster of homes near the soccer field are related by blood. They are mestizos and third-generation squatters without legal titles to the land, and—despite not being black—they are active participants in the Afro-Colombian community council. In the tight-knit community of Nuevo Amanecer, Juan's family was never mistaken for belonging to the new wave of *foráneos*. Juan's grandfather was an indigenous mail courier—"indio, indio" as his descendants described him with a smirk. Both his grandfather and his father worked in Nuevo Amanecer for the wealthy family from Antioquia that founded the community in the early 1900s. Now, Juan's parents, two sisters, nephew, and niece lived in what had been a kitchen but was now a four-bedroom home made of *bahareque* (a mixture of sticks and mud). The wealthy founders of Nuevo Amanecer, who were also the owners of the former kitchen, fled the region in the 1990s as a result of the FARC-EP's growing influence.

Shortly after we left the house, a neighbor stopped us along the main road that passes through the most densely populated part of the community. The neighbor covered his face with a green shirt while his dog sniffed at our feet. He told Roberto, "No hay plata ahora. No estan comprando." (There's no money now. Nobody is buying.) Beginning in November 2016, the laboratories (*chongos*) that transform coca leaves into coca paste started running low on cash after a few key arrests of money smugglers. Without cash, the buyers at the laboratories did not buy leaves from the coca growers. As the lowest rungs in the drug trade, the coca growers and *raspachines* (coca harvesters) immediately felt the effects of the sudden lack of liquidity. Many growers refrained from harvesting ripe leaves because they would drop in weight—and therefore value—if they were left to dry in storage bags. Other growers, like Roberto, made arrangements with the buyers to get paid on credit. The thieves also targeted laboratories, leading some people to think that plainclothes military officers were responsible for the thefts. The man with the dog told us, "Ahora no hay quién proteja la zona" (Now there isn't anyone protecting the zone) in reference to the FARC-EP's absence.

On our way down the steep muddy path carved into the mountain by mule trains, Roberto asked me questions about the United States, like "People are really obese there, right?" We were walking slowly, and I figured that was so that I could keep up, but I later learned that he suffered from a spinal injury attributed to years of manual labor. Back when he worked as a migrant coffee picker in the departments of Quindo, Risaralda, Huila, and Antioquia during the 1980s, he said he could lift twelve arrobas (approximately 135 kilograms) of coffee at once. His hair was long, and he wore a gold earring in his left ear. Before he left Nuevo Amanecer, his mother believed that he would not amount to anything more than a pothead, an alcoholic, or a crack-head (*bazuquero*), because he didn't like to work. He vowed to prove her wrong. Conservative landowners initially refused to hire him because he looked like a cross between a hippie and Rambo. But he told them that if he didn't pick at least ten arrobas of coffee then he would pay for his own lunch. Out in the coffee fields, he was one of the most productive workers. Other guys made deals with the devil and used drugs to boost their productivity.[32] Some covered their hands in a chemical used for gold mining that supposedly enabled them to pick coffee even faster, but it also made their hands twitch. After years of chasing the coffee harvests in various parts of the country, Roberto returned to Nuevo Amanecer to work the land and raise a family with some of the money that he had saved. Recently separated from his wife and now living alone across the street from his brother, his decision to cultivate coca was not a moral or existential conundrum.[33] A few years before, one of his neighbors accidentally allowed a brushfire to get out of control, and the fire swept through his coffee cultivation. He faced the flames alongside his neighbors to keep the fire from affecting the rest of the farms on the mountainside. After the fire, Roberto had to decide on what to do next with his farm: coca reaches maturity in a few months; coffee takes more than a year.

Two people were already working by the time we made it to Roberto's small plot of land an hour after starting our hike. They left their day bags packed with lunch and water hanging from a pine tree next to the field (figure 2.1). Before getting to work, the pickers wrapped a cloth bandage around their palms and pointer fingers. It helped offset the rashes caused by the friction between their skin and the coca. At home, they would scrub their hands with limes to remove the gummy black film that stuck on them after a day of work. In the field, lifting one leg over the bush, they bent down to grab the base,

FIGURE 2.1

Coca fields in the Afro-Colombian Community Council of Nuevo Amanecer (photo by author, January 2017)

yank off the leaves, and stuff them into the bags tied to their waists. Within a month, the bushes would bear new leaves and within another ten weeks they would be ready for harvest. That morning, the reddish-brown color of the recently stripped branches contrasted with the lush phosphorescent green of the untouched bushes. At four feet high, the bushes were about a year and a half old. Across the way, the bushes were much taller, and the cultivation was at least six times bigger than Roberto's modest plot. They belonged to a *foráneo*—Roberto didn't know his name. Close to the creek next to his coca field, a few wooden posts closed off a rustic *semillero* (seedbed), where he grew the next generation of coca bushes. Throughout the morning, the voice of one of the workers rose above the sound of coca leaves being ripped from branches and the whir of the river below the farm. She spoke in long uninterrupted monologues about the risqué activities of the girls in town and good-for-nothing husbands as she filled her nylon sack with coca leaves.

Seven hours later, a man and three mules arrived at the gate next to the entrance of the coca field. The two workers emptied the bags on their hips into the large receptacles designated to each of them for the last time that day, and Roberto made small talk with the mule driver. The young man working for Roberto propped up a scale with a broken limb hoisted between his shoulder and a tree. Roberto wrote down the weight of the coca leaves in the worn notebook that he used to account for all of his expenses. It was an average day for the young man: six arrobas of coca leaves (nearly seventy kilograms) at 7,000 pesos each meant that he took home close to US$15 after a day of working in the coca field. They loaded the coca onto the mules with heavy ropes to ensure that the bags would not fall off during the climb up the mountain to the laboratory that turned the leaves into coca paste.

A few months earlier, I heard someone refer to the "anti-culture of coca" for the first time during a two-day assembly organized by the Ethnic Commission for Peace and the Defense of Territorial Rights in October 2016.[34] Our meeting was just fifteen minutes down the road from one of the FARC-EP's temporary encampments, as the guerrilla group was still in the process of formally moving to their disarmament camp. The one hundred or so black and indigenous people in attendance broke into six small groups to discuss aspects of the Peace Accords and one group that would focus exclusively on the ethnic chapter. Many of the participants wanted to hear about chapter 4 of the Peace Accords because they grew coca themselves or worked as *raspachines* picking coca leaves for cash on someone else's farm. Other participants included community leaders who were concerned about the growing influence of coca in their communities.

Julio, a young leader from the Afro-Colombian Community Council of Nuevo Amanecer, spoke about what he called the anti-culture of coca by comparing the coca-growing *foráneos* and drug traffickers to multinational corporations: "They arrive without invitation, they don't conduct a prior consultation, they exploit the land, and they just leave when they're done. Who foots the bill? We do!"[35] For Julio, the anti-culture of coca was insidious because it transformed the moral fiber of the community.[36] He talked about how the communities used to be peaceful places, where people worked together during *mingas*, celebrated local customs, and produced the food that they needed to survive. Coca changed everything. The anti-culture of coca brought in by the *foráneos* led to the expansion of prostitution, alcoholism, violence, gambling, drug consumption, and individualism in the communities. Although Julio did not discuss the spiritual and cultural uses of coca by indigenous peoples and others at this particular meeting, he later told me that the coca plant itself was not antithetical to community life. For him, the anti-culture of coca related specifically to the cultivation of coca for the production of cocaine.

Yet for people like Roberto, cultivating coca represented—if not a shot at buying a washing machine or building a brick-and-mortar home—at least a means of enduring the precarity associated with decades of neoliberal reforms and violence in the countryside (table 2.2). For them, the critique of the anti-culture of coca espoused by social movement leaders was laudable as an aspirational ethic, but not as a realistic possibility. Of course, they publicly lamented the gradual loss of customs like *cambio de mano*.[37] But from the roadside vendor who sells empanadas and mazamorra to the baggage handler on the

TABLE 2.2

Comparison of One Hectare of Coffee with Coca in 2017

	Coffee	Coca
Number of harvests per year	1.5	4
Number of plants	5,000	10,000
Price (Col$) per arroba (~11.3 kg)	75,000	33,000
Typical harvest (arrobas)	180–200	200
Costs (Col$) per harvest (labor, fertilizer, herbicide, transport, etc.)	6,660,000	1,800,000
Colombian pesos earned per year	8,240,000	16,800,000

chiva (bus) who loads precursor chemicals on top of the bus, people had more cash in their pockets as a result of the coca boom economy.

Coca in Nuevo Amanecer extended the promise of a better life, or at least a life where material wants and needs appeared more attainable, by feeding on what Lauren Berlant might call "cruel optimism."[38] That is not to say, however, that the people of Nuevo Amanecer never worked with the crop before the middle of the first decade of the 2000s. Alfredo, the current head of the Coca Growers' Association (Asociación de Cocaleros) and a native of Nuevo Amanecer, remembered making the strenuous four-day journey over the mountains to Naya with his father to harvest coca as early as 1980 when they used straw baskets (not nylon bags) to collect the leaves. Reflecting on his trips to Naya, Alfredo said, "We would go for a month and then come back, and then we would do it again. We would fix whatever little thing back home because we had a lot of land, but the thing is that we didn't work on it [the land]. We had very little coffee, and well, during the harvest we would pick the beans, but it wasn't like the money from coffee stretched all that far. And that's how coca started showing up here. Now wherever you go in this area there is coca. It spilled over into everywhere." When the price of coffee dropped significantly in the late 1990s, many young men from Nuevo Amanecer left home and joined the thousands of other migrant *raspachines* in a rite of passage similar to Roberto's experience chasing the coffee harvests a decade before. They, too, traveled to Naya where the coca crops were well established, as well as other places renowned for coca like Caquetá, Putumayo, Meta, and Guaviare. They reflected on their time in Naya as a blur of cash, gambling, brothels, and alcohol. Although they earned much more money in Naya than in Nuevo Amanecer, the prices were inflated thanks to the booming coca economy and the costly transportation expenses. Instead of returning with savings, they brought back stories about jealous bosses (*patrones*) and card games that ended with pistols drawn.

During Holy Week in April 2001, the AUC paramilitary group asserted control of the region by murdering at least two dozen people and forcibly displacing nearly four thousand during what became known as the onset of the Naya Massacre.[39] On the premises of pursuing left-wing guerrilla groups, the paramilitaries terrorized northern Cauca and the Naya region with support from the military and business owners from the region. The troops under the command of Herbert Veloza, alias H.H.—one of the AUC leaders extradited to the United States on drug-trafficking charges—subjected the people to a new regime of social control. Anything that resembled support for the FARC-EP elicited suspicion: rubber boots, groceries that could be used to feed more than a household, and traveling either too late at night or too early in the morning. The paramilitaries murdered and disappeared people without explanation. They disposed of so many bodies in the Cauca River that H.H. referred to the river as a cemetery.[40] Violence, fear, and isolation contributed to the displacement and confinement of rural populations. In addition to clearing the land for multinational corporations and state-led infrastructure projects, the paramilitaries also facilitated the expansion of illicit gold mining and drug trafficking. During the heaviest days of the paramilitary onslaught that lasted late into the first decade of the 2000s, the *foráneos* purchased land at cheap prices brought down by violence and forced displacement.

While many black and indigenous people fled from northern Cauca into the peripheries of major cities like Cali and other regions of the country, mestizo *cocaleros* moved into the semiabandoned territories. Initially, a single settler would arrive in a remote community and employ nearby residents during the coca harvests. The workforce of *foráneos* grew steadily through word of mouth as outsiders invited families, friends, and other contacts to take advantage of the isolated terrain that—at least for the moment—appeared out of the reach of the drug war. Many of the *foráneos* who informally purchased property in Nuevo Amanecer did not reside permanently in the region and treated the land like a disposable commodity. They deserted the houses next to their coca cultivations and traveled to plots of land that required maintenance in other parts of the country. Canned food, plastic herbicide containers, and other artifacts from prior visits littered the surroundings of the houses abandoned between harvests.

Some *foráneos*, however, did choose to permanently reside in Nuevo Amanecer. One couple—Carmen and Jorge, the same couple who witnessed the raid on Alfonso Cano's hideout in chapter 1—fled their home a few hours south of Nuevo Amanecer in 2007 after a surge in violence that coincided with their coca crops getting fumigated. According to them:

> It was incredible how people arrived in Nuevo Amanecer from other parts of the country. People came to this territory from Guaviare, Meta, Pereira, Antioquia, as well as other municipalities in Cauca. But the majority came from Putumayo and Caquetá [. . .]. Some came because they were displaced, but others came because of their interest in coca. They sold their [coca] crops back where they came from, and they knew that things were just getting started around here. It was easy then because it was unoccupied terrain. Sometimes the owners of the farms would arrive and get offered a good price for the lands, and they sold them. Some of them didn't know the purpose, but others sold their farms knowing what they would be used for.

Carmen and Jorge, unlike many of the other *foráneos* that moved to Nuevo Amanecer during what they called the "coca apogee," decided to stay in the community council after a plague called the *secadera* dried out the *tinga* strain of coca in 2011. Within months, however, people started growing *guayabal*, a new strain of coca that was resistant to the *secadera* plague.

Most of the mestizo *foráneos* eventually settled in two villages that became practically off limits for the original members of the Afro-Colombian Community Council of Nuevo Amanecer. After the disarmament of the FARC-EP, new armed groups took over the exposed drug-trafficking routes around the time that the thieves targeted the coca processing laboratories. According to many people in the part of Nuevo Amanecer where I lived, the drug traffickers sought refuge in the villages occupied by *foráneos*. They circulated death threats targeting the people that organized meetings related to the coca substitution program associated with the Peace Accords, and the threats revealed their intent to "protect, strengthen, and reactivate the coca cultivations." They recruited young men from the community by offering them between 1.2 and 1.5 million pesos (US$400–US$500) per month to join their outfits. They also paid 2 million pesos per kilo of coca paste compared with the 1.2 million pesos that people received before their arrival (figure 2.2).

Not all of the death threats related specifically to coca. Armed groups in the region also protected illegal gold mining operations, settled scores for bidders, and killed social movement activists opposed to so-called development projects. For example, someone claiming to represent the Gaitanista Self-Defense Forces of Colombia (Autodefensas Gaitanistas de Colombia) paramilitary group sent the following text message directly to one of the leaders of another Afro-Colombian community council in the region in April 2017:

> All right. The time has come for the opponents from the communities in [location redacted] to pay, especially those sons of bitches from the community council who stick their noses in everything—especially [names redacted]. If you don't want what happened in [location redacted] to happen to you, we are giving you 24 h to get out of the region. We won't be held responsible for you. You already know that we are here.
>
> Autodefensas Gaitanistas.
> We know of your movements.
> Time is running out.

Between the threat of violence and the promise of wealth, natives of Nuevo Amanecer increasingly participated in coca production.

FIGURE 2.2

Coca leaves on their way to a laboratory for processing into coca paste
(photo by author, January 2017)

As of 2024, the ominous government-led eradication efforts never arrived. Back when I lived there in 2017, people like Alfredo, head of the Coca Growers' Association from Nuevo Amanecer, said that coca was the only reason they could still grow a little bit of coffee on their farms. Alfredo used the revenues from his coca cultivation to subsidize the meager revenues from coffee. In his village of sixty families, only three of the families did not cultivate coca. Jorge and Carmen stopped working with coca for the most part by 2017. Jorge, who worshipped at one of the three evangelical churches in the small community, told me about his experience:

> I used to have coca, and—as you can see—I substituted it for coffee. Sometimes I still work with coca if the situation requires it. You've got to because providing three kids with an education and wanting them to get ahead . . . well, sometimes you can't take care of everything with what you've got and you have to go [work with coca]. The truth is that coca is good economically, but if you look at the results and its final product [cocaine], then it's not. So that's why I don't grow coca.
>
> If it were up to me, I would never grow coca again. It's been three or four years since I had my own coca plants. Now I don't have any, and I've survived. I see my neighbors and they have a lot of coca, but they don't really have anything. Sometimes they even ask to borrow money. So I start to think, *What are we doing?*

"THE REVENGE OF THE SYSTEM"

Coca is not new to northern Cauca, or even the Afro-Colombian Community Council of Nuevo Amanecer. Alfredo remembers an old man who used to keep five bushes of coca, "nothing like the ones you see now." They were much bigger than the efficiently organized shrubs that people currently harvest. The old man sold the leaves to the indigenous folks who would occasionally come down from the mountains and buy it to *mambear*, or chew. Coca staved off hunger.[41] The drug war changed that. It made people hungrier.

In *Critical Thought in the Face of the Capitalist Hydra*, the Zapatistas argue, "The wasteland resulting from a war is also a commodity, as is its reconstruction. It's as if they were colonizing a totally new territory, such that they could organize it however they wanted as if from scratch."[42] The Zapatistas' reflections on ongoing forms of primitive accumulation offer a keen reminder of the centrality of violence in producing capital and transforming social relations.[43] The so-called Peace Accords hardly conceal the ongoing conflict over commodities and futures in Colombia, as colonization by *cocaleros* deepens capitalist relations and settler colonialism in Nuevo Amanecer.

The resulting tension between the prospect of earning more money by working with coca, on one hand, and confronting the transformations associated with what Julio calls the anti-culture of coca, on the other, represented a challenge for the Afro-Colombian Community Council of Nuevo Amanecer, especially considering that coca serves as a major mobilizing force in the community and *foráneos* control much of the coca production. It underscored the uncomfortable contradictions facing the community council of Nuevo Amanecer. Many of the community council's own constituents now doubted one of its ostensible premises: acquiring a collective land title. For example, two concerned men took me aside after a meeting about the Peace Accords and asked, "What exactly do you mean by 'collective land title'? Does that mean that they can sell my farm?" Their worries about losing control over their farms, along with the ongoing threats from armed groups in the region, effectively silenced the community council's organizing efforts. They also signaled how participating in the drug trade contributed to the adoption of a settler mentality within communities that have participated in historic struggles for self-determination. By May 2017, the community council's efforts to publicly engage the community about the possibility of substituting coca went underground as a consequence of the violence targeting social movement leaders.

Widespread coca cultivations and the influence of a new class of mestizo *foráneos* are evidence of the ongoing enclosure of Nuevo Amanecer and much of northern Cauca. Although their precise influence cannot be quantified, due in part to the lack of formal land titles and the impossibility of conducting an accurate census, the "structure of feeling" in northern Cauca reveals the anxieties around the most recent wave of colonization and its impact on the potential for building autonomy and self-determination.[44] For example, an old Afro-Colombian man in the Sunday marketplace turned to me to joke about a sleeping pig: "It gets tired quickly in the sun since it doesn't have hair—just like a *pastuso*." The feeling also emerges when a bumpy bus ride through the dirt roads in the mountains suddenly smooths out around coca boom towns because the coca-growing *foráneos* paid to pave the roads around their enclave.

One activist from PCN called the transformations associated with the expansion of coca cultivations "the revenge of the system." For him, the structural inequalities of Colombian society push people into cultivating coca and becoming increasingly dependent on drug trafficking as their primary source of income. Instead of providing them with a way out of poverty, the revenge of the system takes them deeper into capitalist relations that are antithetical to the autonomous forms of black community life that they struggle to build. It subjects them to violence by state forces and drug traffickers alike. These conditions are exacerbated by the false promises and paltry results of state substitution programs like the PNIS, which at best have provided participants with temporary material support and at worst exposed them to further violence and retaliation.[45] As a result, the coca chimera exploits the needs of marginalized people, and it drives another wave of colonization by outsiders in search of fortune.

The expansion of coca crops has not, however, depleted the potential for creating alternatives. During a workshop hosted by the Ethnic Commission in an Afro-Colombian community council in January 2017, the organizers asked the participants to create a short play about their own histories of resistance, both past and present. Most of the people in attendance came from black and indigenous communities in the surrounding areas. Word about the workshop filtered through to other communities, and two *foráneos* from Naya arrived. One of the *foráneos*—a middle-aged mestizo man—tried to take over the space and push for the attendees to organize through the National Coordinating Committee of Cultivators of Coca, Poppy, and Marijuana (Coordinadora Nacional de Cultivadores y Cultivadoras de Coca, Amapola y Marihuana), a new organization that formed in the context of the Peace Accords. During one of the plays, the participants acted out a storyline about the arrival of a large-scale infrastructure project in the community. The actors debated how to handle the imposition of the "megaproject" on their fictitious community. Ultimately, they rallied together and threw out the *foráneo*, who was played by the mestizo visitor, literally pushing him out of the meeting hall. The audience laughed and cheered. Stuck somewhere between autonomy and enclosure, they rejected the commodification of their lives and land.

3 MAKING PEASANTS COUNT

Creole Whiteness and the Politics of Recognition

MORE THAN FIVE THOUSAND PEASANTS from around the country converged on Popayán for the public launch of the National Coordinating Committee of Cultivators of Coca, Poppy, and Marijuana (COCCAM) in January 2017 (figure 3.1). The organizers of COCCAM wanted to create a space where peasants growing illicit crops could unite in the spirit of the 2016 Peace Accords, which included the ambitious chapter "Solution to the Problem of Illicit Drugs." For the government, COCCAM resembled a front for the FARC's political aspirations or a base for savvy drug traffickers. Leading up to the march in Popayán, concern about the accelerating growth of coca cultivations dominated the news cycle, and the government announced its goal to eliminate one hundred thousand hectares of the crop by the end of 2017.[1] According to Eduardo Díaz—the director of Colombia's newly founded Agency for the Substitution of Illicit Crops who previously served as a government negotiator assigned to the massive coca growers' protests of the 1990s— "The association should disappear," referring to the pending COCCAM march.[2] His comments provoked one participant in a plenary session of the COCCAM meeting to exclaim, "Society sees the campesino as an accomplice to drug trafficking, not a victim." The constituents of

COCCAM thus demanded special protections for campesinos who found themselves obligated to participate in the cultivation of illicit crops. They portrayed themselves as victims of the internal armed conflict, the exploitative economy, and the aggressive anti-peasant policies associated with Plan Colombia and the proliferation of free trade agreements.[3]

The number of police increased significantly as the march propelled itself into the colonial center of town. Their guns, helmets, and body armor contrasted with the peasants' colorful signs. Many of the marchers' banners proudly displayed the names of their communities and organizations. About fifty meters before reaching the end point of the mobilization under the Humilladero Bridge in downtown Popayán, the front line of the march stopped in front of a group of the Anti-disturbance Mobile Squad (ESMAD) anti-riot police. Behind them, thousands of demonstrators chanted slogans and waved flags in spite of the obvious potential for violence. Then something peculiar happened: the cars at the front of the march blasted the Colombian

FIGURE 3.1

COCCAM members singing the Colombian national anthem during a march in Popayán (photo by author, January 2017)

national anthem out of speakers facing the crowd, and the marchers placed their hands over their hearts and sang along.

The planners of the march did not stumble into this symbolically loaded act. Their display of nationalism expressed a desire for recognition from the state and society at large. The slogan at the bottom of the COCCAM banner was "We are Colombian@s, workers like you." The "@" in "Colombians" signaled that COCCAM included people of all genders. During the workshops before the march, however, the majority of the participants were male. Their identification as workers was supposed to distinguish them from efforts to stigmatize them as drug traffickers; it also reflected their class-conscious approach to organizing. For the participants in the COCCAM march, the evocation of sameness held political power.

This chapter explores how a particular form of peasant nationalism rooted in *mestizaje* mobilizes people who identify as campesino at this conjuncture of neoliberal multiculturalism in Colombia.[4] As the primary subject of the 2016 Peace Accords, the *campesinado* (peasantry) consolidated its position as one of the principal protagonists in contemporary Colombian politics. The term "campesino," however, has eluded definition for more than a century. Debates regarding its precise meaning as a social class or culture have received extensive attention elsewhere, but for the purposes of this book, "campesino" broadly refers to the subaltern class of people who live and labor primarily in rural areas, regardless of the legal status of their work.[5] However, in the era of multiculturalism, the term "campesino" increasingly refers to the mestizo peasantry that does not explicitly identify with black or indigenous organizations and ethnoterritorial authorities. Some campesino organizations point to their exclusion from the multicultural turn as yet another form of discrimination and invisibilization within the broader processes of depeasantization (*descampesinización*) that contribute to their dispossession and displacement. They argue that campesinos deserve differential legal recognition based on their historic plight and the challenges that they face in regard to land tenure. As a result, some scholars in Colombia affirm, "The central demand of the campesinos before society and the State, above all, is that they recognize them based on their condition as citizens; as citizens with full access to all of their rights."[6]

During the early twenty-first century, campesino organizations made strides in gaining recognition in Colombia and internationally, including the 2019 passage of the United Nations Declaration on the Rights of Peasants. In Colombia, campesinos gained formal recognition in 2023 as a "rights-bearing subject with special protection."[7] However, their strategy of seeking justice by appealing to recognition from the nation-state on the basis of their identity as campesinos is tenuous. In *Between the Guerrillas and the State*, María Clemencia Ramírez identifies the orientation of the demands of coca growers in southern Colombia during the 1990s the following way: "In the context of exclusion, the state also became a nucleus of affection. The population desired and demanded its presence because they felt abandoned by it."[8] In other words, the contradictory relationship between the state and the campesinos took shape as a consequence of the absence of supportive social policies and the exploitation inherent to capitalist development. Confronted with an apparent lack of alternatives, these movements resort to recognition-based strategies. This chapter, thus, explores the current predicament of campesino organizing by analyzing the efforts of elites to control and repress radical expressions of campesino organizing, as well as how race-based resentment served as an incentive for some people to join peasant organizations.

CREOLE WHITENESS

When asked about a series of protests organized by indigenous peoples in northern Cauca in 2015, Senator Paloma Valencia responded, "I think that we should propose a referendum to the department to decide if we should split it in two: one for the indigenous, so that they can have their strikes, protests, and invasions; and a department dedicated to development where we can have roads, where we can promote investment, and where we can have dignified employment for all the people of Cauca."[9] The interviewer proceeded to ask her—the granddaughter of former President Guillermo León Valencia and protégé of former President Álvaro Uribe Vélez—about the black communities that make up about 48 percent of the population of northern Cauca.[10] As an offspring of the Popayán elite and outspoken leader of the arch-conservative movement in Colombia, Senator Valencia responded that mestizos and black people get along well and said that the black communities would have to decide if they wanted a department for *"negri-tudes."* She later clarified via Twitter that she proposed "a referendum or consultation so that the department of Cauca can be divided in two. One indigenous department and another for the mestizos."[11]

Victor Hugo Moreno Mina—then legal representative of the Association of Afro-Colombian Community Councils of Northern Cauca (Asociación de Consejos Comunitarios del Norte del Cauca, ACONC) and founding member of the Ethnic Commission for Peace and in Defense of Territorial Rights—responded to Senator Valencia's proposal in an interview.[12] He argued that separating from the department of Cauca would provide the people of northern Cauca with greater independence from the elites in the departmental capital of Popayán. Although the referendum never made it beyond a brief flurry of headlines, the deep divisions exposed by the debate drive many of the conflicts in the region. Senator Valencia's racist pandering is as remarkable for its opportunistic deployment of vulgar identity politics as its baseness. Her brief mention of "mestizos," however, provides an insight into how *mestizaje* does the work of nation-state formation, even though the word "mestizo" rarely surfaces as an ethno-racial descriptor in Colombian parlance, unlike other parts of Latin America.[13]

In the 2005 National Census, for example, 84.2 percent of respondents responded "none" when asked if they recognized themselves as part of one of Colombia's ethnic groups.[14] But if they were not ethnic, then what were they? People who do not consider themselves ethnic in Colombia occasionally refer to themselves as *colombianos normales* (normal Colombians) or *ciudadanos rasos* (rank-and-file citizens).[15] They also refer to their regional identity as *caleños, paisas, costeños, rolos,* for example—all categories infused with racial connotations.[16] These terms—as with contemporary uses of "campesino"—do not explicitly reference more explicit racial markers such as *blanco* (white), *negro* (black), *indio* (Indian), *indígena* (indigenous), or mestizo. Instead, they draw on a repertoire of assumptions related to customs, stereotypes, and phenotypes that associate ethno-racial categories with regional identities. Costa Vargas's analysis of the "hyperconsciousness of race and its negation" as the "dialectic of white supremacy" in Brazil provides a useful framework for understanding the census results by revealing "how a system that is on the surface devoid of racial awareness is in reality deeply immersed in racialized understandings of the social world."[17] Senator Valencia's remarks may appear anomalous to contemporary Colombia's multicultural "racial grammar," but they register with her constituents and beyond because they draw on commonsense understandings of a Colombian national identity rooted in *mestizaje*.[18]

Referred to by Ronald Stutzman as an "all-inclusive ideology of exclusion," *mestizaje* extends the promise of national belonging even as it preserves racial hierarchies that suppress insurgent expressions of blackness and indigeneity.[19] To sustain its upwardly mobile promise of *blanqueamiento* (whitening), *mestizaje* operates through an opaque sliding scale of creole whiteness.[20] I define creole whiteness as an ideology concerned with achieving colonial-capitalist modernity through the maintenance of class, gender, and racial hierarchies that are historically contingent on enslavement and genocide.[21] Thus, creole whiteness is not exclusively concerned with phenotype or ancestry. By shedding customs associated with blackness or indigeneity—such as language, dress, spirituality, or relationship to the land—people can more readily identify with *mestizaje* and move up the scale of creole whiteness, even as they retain other aspects of their culture.[22] Interpellation based on phenotype, however, continues to play a foundational role in determining the position of a person in relation to their identity as mestizo (i.e., it is less likely for a darker-skinned person to identify and be accepted as mestizo or white by peers and society at large than a lighter-skinned person).

Mestizaje's enduring influence on nation-state formation survived Colombia's multicultural turn. This is evident in Senator Valencia's proposal that counterposes the development of the mestizo nation-state with indigenous political demands. Her Colombia continues to be organized through the terms of colonial-capitalist modernity, which associates aspiring to creole whiteness with progress. In an adaptation of Fanon's memorable phrase from *Wretched of the Earth*, you are Colombian because you are mestizo, and you are mestizo because you are Colombian.[23] The "none" bubble on the 2005 census thus served as a placeholder for the mestizo nation-state by creating a distance between the *colombianos normales* and the *minorías étnicas* (ethnic minorities).[24] Multiculturalism, however, seemed to challenge the basis of *mestizaje* by recognizing "the ethnic and cultural diversity of the Colombian Nation," as written in the 1991 constitution. The ensuing policies that granted collective rights to black and indigenous communities provided a space for people historically excluded by the process of mestizo nation-state formation to advocate for themselves on the basis of difference—not sameness—even though the state's institutions defined the contours of acceptable difference.

For some scholars and activists, the recognition of black and indigenous rights through multicultural policies did not promote equality. They argue that it instead flipped the scale of oppression against mestizos by giving a legal advantage to black and indigenous peoples. In a section of his 2015 book suggestively titled "Colombian Multiculturalism: A System of Interethnic Competition?" Carlos Duarte, a renowned scholar of rural politics in Colombia, program coordinator at the Intercultural Studies Institute of the Javeriana University in Cali, and member of the Working Group on the Rights of Peasants and Other People Working in Rural Areas of the United Nations Human Rights Council, argues:

> In Colombia, the process of *mestizaje* is an inconclusive process, which was effectively truncated after the implementation of the current multicultural State. After the 1991 constitutional process, the pyramid of *mestizaje* was inverted in rural contexts. While historically stigmatized populations can count on important blocks of differential rights (Law 21 and Law 70), the subject of the mestizo-rural campesino, which was developed as a project of the liberal State throughout the twentieth century to modernize the countryside and expand the frontiers of the Nation, was converted into a bearer of a rural third-class citizenship in comparison to the ethnic populations.[25]

Although Duarte does not elaborate on the structure of the pyramid of *mestizaje* that is supposedly being flipped, other scholars have used the metaphor to describe the hierarchy of racial oppression that locates creole whiteness at the top, with black and indigenous peoples constituting the base.[26] By arguing that the "subject of the mestizo-rural campesino [. . .] was converted into a bearer of a rural third-class citizenship in comparison to the ethnic populations," Duarte frames the recognition of black and indigenous rights by the state as a menace to the social standing of mestizo campesinos.[27] This approach simultaneously invests the legislating power of the state with outsized influence and occludes the enduring forms of anti-black/anti-indigenous racism in state institutions and beyond.

Rather than analyzing how multicultural recognition figures into the formation of racial capitalism and settler colonialism, he draws attention to how mestizo campesinos are excluded from public policies. This dynamic is crucial, albeit insufficient, for understanding the conjuncture of Colombian agrarian politics of the last three decades. For example, Law 160 of 1994 created the figure of the peasant reserve zone (*zona de reserva campesina*, ZRC) as a way to provide support for peasant communities by addressing their tenuous legal standing in regard to land tenure and facilitating their integration into regional economies. However, high-ranking public officials have often stigmatized the ZRCs as bastions of the FARC, and previous governments consistently refused to recognize or provide meaningful support for the ZRCs since their inception.[28] In addition to facing institutional obstruction, members of the ZRCs confronted death threats, attacks, and murders at the hands of paramilitary groups in response to their organizing efforts. As of October 2018, the state formally recognized only seven ZRCs throughout the country and was in the process of constituting six more. In December 2022, the Petro administration recognized an additional three ZRCs. Thanks in part to the efforts of the National Association of Peasant Reserve Zones (Asociación Nacional de Zonas de Reserva Campesina, ANZORC), sixty-four more ZRCs function without formal recognition from the government.[29] The ZRCs, along with other community-based entities such as the Agro-food Peasant Territories

(Territorios Campesinos Agroalimentarios) offer an organizational space for rural peasants that do not identify with Afro-Colombian community councils or indigenous *resguardos* and *cabildos*.

Yet mestizo campesinos do not enter into conflict with their black and indigenous counterparts by default, as an interpretation of multiculturalism as a "system of interethnic competition" would suggest. In many parts of the country, black, indigenous, and non-black/non-indigenous campesino claims to land overlap with one another, as well as private sector and state entities interested in exploiting the land. These spaces of overlapping land claims can become sites of intense and occasionally violent conflict in northern Cauca, as evidenced by the clashes in San Rafael in 2011 and Canaima in 2023. However, to call these conflicts "interethnic" implies that the primary reason people are fighting against one another is based on their ethnic or racial background, as if that revealed some inherent or essential incompatibility.[30] While potentially advantageous in the short term for enlisting membership to identity-based organizations, blaming conflicts on the ethnic or racial background of people does long-term damage to the possibility of building solidarity across groups.[31]

This logic stirs resentment and fosters the sedimentation of vulgar identity politics by shifting critique of systems of oppression (i.e., neoliberal multiculturalism) to the effects of those systems (i.e., *traslapes*, or "overlapping land claims").[32] Building on Friedrich Nietzsche's ideas in *On the Genealogy of Morals*, the political theorist Wendy Brown explores how the *"ressentiment"* that animates identity politics represents a "triple achievement: it produces an affect (rage, righteousness) that overwhelms the hurt, it produces a culprit responsible for the hurt, and it produces a site of revenge to displace the hurt (a place to inflict hurt as the sufferer has been hurt)."[33] The emergence of campesino identity politics resuscitated discourses of *mestizaje* that appeared relatively dormant in the aftermath of the multicultural turn following the 1991 constitution. However, this process did not take place just among community-based organizations. Political and economic elites also maneuvered to appropriate expressions of campesino identity politics for their own benefit.

CHANNELING DISCONTENT

In northern Cauca, multicultural policies contributed to competition over land and resources. Black and indigenous communities used the legal framework to acquire resources from the state, attain collective land titles, and employ their right to free, prior, and informed consultation and consent. Bettina Ng'weno—an anthropologist who conducted extensive fieldwork in northern Cauca during the late 1990s—called the budding conflicts with the government "turf wars" that "revolve around the dual concepts of community autonomy and self-governance on the one hand and state territorial authority and national sovereignty on the other."[34] While Ng'weno's definition rightfully places top-down governance in tension with bottom-up self-determination, the turf wars of the twenty-first century in northern Cauca became increasingly complicated by the growing presence of drug traffickers, gold prospectors, left-wing guerrillas, and right-wing paramilitary groups that also competed for control over the territory. The conflicts could no longer be characterized as "society against the state," if they ever could have been to begin with.[35] Illegal actors now permeated almost every aspect of rural life both in collaboration with and in opposition to the government, and efforts to acquire formal recognition from the state resulted in some communities replicating the hierarchical and bureaucratic features of the state within their own organizations.[36] Nevertheless, the perseverance of black and indigenous social movements resulted in the accrual of political power on their behalf. By filing lawsuits and taking direct action, they slowed and even stopped the implementation of development and infrastructure projects, leading major media outlets to refer to the black and indigenous communities' use of free, prior, and informed consultation and consent as a "spoke in the wheel of development."[37] Increasingly, these communities advocated for their participation in the design and implementation of local development projects and national policies with varying degrees of success.

The visibility and strength of black and indigenous political power expressed in organizations like the Black Communities' Process (PCN) and the Çxhab Wala Kiwe Association of Indigenous Cabildos of Northern Cauca (ACIN) threatened the dominance of the traditional political establishment in Chaux, one of the municipalities where I conducted fieldwork in northern Cauca.[38] In the lead-up to the signing of the Peace Accords in 2016, the municipal authorities of Chaux anticipated the disbursement of resources intended to support postconflict development of the region. As one of the municipalities prioritized by the Development Program with a Territorial Focus (Programa de Desarrollo con Enfoque Territorial, PDET) created by the accords, it was slated to receive significant funding and technical support from the Colombian government and international community thanks to its reputation as a hot spot for armed conflict.

On the basis of their understanding of the opportunities available through the Peace Accords, a group of government officials and private sector contractors from the urban center of Chaux designed a strategy to limit the reach of black and indigenous organizations. They created a front organization, ORGANICHAUX, to appeal to disaffected campesinos who did not identify with the municipality's indigenous *cabildos* or Afro-Colombian community councils. Their decision to focus on campesinos was not coincidental.

Historically, the term "campesino"—typically translated as "peasant"—did not hold an explicit racial connotation in Colombia. In fact, throughout much of the twentieth century, black and indigenous rural workers identified as campesinos.[39] However, as a result of consciousness-raising efforts by black and indigenous social movements, black and indigenous peoples began to identify more explicitly as such. By organizing as black or indigenous communities, particularly after the 1991 constitution, they could acquire collective land titles, access affirmative action policies, and participate in government programs intended to address the needs of black and indigenous populations. The people who did not identify as black or indigenous, on the other hand, could not.

ORGANICHAUX attempted to maneuver through the budding tensions between the groups. Beginning in early 2016, they started to meet with various Community Action Committees (Juntas de Acción

Comunal, JAC), the semigovernmental rural development groups that once formed the bedrock of the National Association of Peasant Users (ANUC).[40] Representatives of ORGANICHAUX traveled to isolated sectors of Chaux in privately owned trucks—not the municipal buses that most people used—and encouraged campesinos to join the new organization. According to one campesino who attended their meetings:

> They told the campesinos that they had to get organized because the Havana Accords [Peace Accords] were coming, and it would be easier to capture resources and projects because they were intended [*destinados*] for the campesinos. They also told the people, "You will be able to struggle more strongly against the indigenous [*los indígenas*] because the indigenous are surrounding you." *They started to sell the idea to us leaders that the fight was practically against the indigenous.*
>
> That's basically the idea that they sold to the campesinos, to the leaders, the presidents of the JAC because . . . How can I say it? They are the political group that runs the institutions in Chaux so it is easy for them to convene the JAC and all that.[41]

By stoking racial tensions and extending the promise of development, ORGANICHAUX's backers expected to profit from managing their own nominally grassroots organization that could apply for development projects from the government and other potential donors in the context of the Peace Accords.

The local political and economic elites behind ORGANICHAUX read the political moment correctly in a sense. Throughout the negotiations, the FARC made addressing the root causes of the internal armed conflict a central component of their conditions for laying down arms, and the text of the Peace Accords reflected their focus on agrarian politics as a guerrilla movement with historic ties to the peasantry. The first section of the accords—"Toward a New Colombian Countryside"—laid out the Comprehensive Rural Reform (Reforma Rural Integral, RRI), the centerpiece of the government's strategy for building peace in rural areas in the post–Peace Accord moment.[42] The RRI created a series of rural development programs that ranged from investing in schools to fixing roads after incorporating suggestions from campesino organizations and other parts of the agricultural sector. The land reform itself consisted of implementing a process that was supposed to result in the titling of ten million hectares of land. But the RRI's explicit mandate to "allow Colombia to be integrated into the global economy" sought to ensure that these projects would facilitate the expansion of capitalist relations and not the seeds of revolution. Nevertheless, the Peace Accords named the plight of campesinos directly and provided them with an officially recognized platform for making demands on the state as such.

On the basis of its focus on "regional integration," "national agriculture," and "community-based production," the Peace Accords reflected a distinctly *campesinista* (peasant-based) approach to addressing the problems of the Colombian countryside. Perhaps best summed up in the slogan "La Tierra es de Quien la Trabaja" (literally, the land belongs to those who work it, and similar to the English-language slogan "Land to the Tiller"), *campesinista* politics emphasize the relationship between land ownership and labor (i.e., the peasant who works the land should be the rightful owner, not the off-site landlord).[43] This ideological premise, however, does not reflect the totality of subaltern perspectives on rural land use and ownership, especially when compared to the spiritual and ecological conceptions of territory espoused by some black, indigenous, and campesino organizations. For example, the Planes de Vida (Life Plans) of the Çxhab Wala Kiwe ACIN indigenous organization and the *reglamentos internos* (internal regulations) of some Afro-Colombian community councils in northern Cauca refuse to tie their concepts of territory to conventional forms of private property, resource extraction, productivity, and labor. PCN, for instance, conceives of the territory as a "space for being" (*el espacio para ser*) and thus rejects the notion that they must work the land for it to belong to them. Instead, territory is understood as an integral part of their culture, spirituality, health, and lifeways.[44]

The organizers behind ORGANICHAUX understood the potential for common ground between the aforementioned strain of *campesinista* politics and the capitalist interests in extracting wealth from land and labor. They attempted to manipulate the competing conceptions

of land use in order to intensify the conflicts between mestizo campesinos and the Nasa indigenous people in the municipality.[45] Beyond
capturing funding from projects associated with the Peace Accords,
the local elites asserting control over ORGANICHAUX also wanted to
offset black and indigenous opposition to gold mining projects.

In addition to the creation of front organizations like ORGAN-
ICHAUX, a variety of strategies to undermine the reach of black and
indigenous organizations surfaced throughout the region in the context of the Peace Accords. For example, signs such as the one in figure
3.2 began to pop up in places with deepening divisions between indigenous and campesino communities. The writing on the sign reads "Alto
Miraflores: Pluriethnic and Intercultural Territory" (top center), "With
Respect for Private Property" (bottom left), and "No to the *Resguardo*"
(bottom right). The image in the middle of the billboard illustrates five
phenotypically distinct faces looking in the same direction thereby
evoking the "myths of racial harmony" implicit in mestizo nation-state
formation.[46] This sign and others like it aroused suspicion and became

FIGURE 3.2

Sign stoking racial tensions on the outskirts of Corinto, Cauca
(photo by author, March 2017)

a topic of conversation among my friends and comrades because it did not appear to be associated with any of the social movements in the region. One of my friends eventually took a closer look at the sign and pointed out the website URL displayed in the bottom-right corner: www.ingse.co. Upon reviewing the website, it became clear that the sign was made by a company whose clients consisted primarily of the sugarcane refineries that monopolize land use throughout the valley.

As part of their efforts to gain legitimacy among the campesinos, the urban-based leadership of ORGANICHAUX appointed a long-time community leader from the region as the president of the organization. Their cynical attempts to co-opt the peasantry, however, failed as the campesinos in the municipality became conscious of the forces behind ORGANICHAUX. Around the edges of the meetings convened by ORGANICHAUX, attendees questioned the role of the urban-based leadership and their support for large-scale mining projects.

Contrary to the stereotypes of ignorant peasants, campesino leaders became de facto experts on the Peace Accords through attentively listening to radio programs and seeking out the representatives of national-level campesino organizations like ANZORC and COCCAM, as well as by meeting with representatives of the FARC-EP. Over the course of the four years of negotiation with the government, the guerrilla group released a series of documents that circulated throughout their areas of influence. They also convened meetings and attempted to build their political base. Three documents in particular—(1) "Rural and Agrarian Development for Democratization and Peace with Social Justice in Colombia: 100 Baseline Proposals," (2) "Political Participation for Real Democratization, Peace with Social Justice, and National Reconciliation: 100 Baseline Proposals," and (3) "Antidrug Policies for the Sovereignty and Buen Vivir [Good Life] of the Poor People of the Countryside: 50 Baseline Proposals"—laid out the FARC-EP's analysis of the conjuncture in plain terms.[47] Following the signing of the Peace Accords, the FARC-EP courted community leaders, churches, students, and local government officials more openly. While it would be irresponsible to overstate the connection between the FARC-EP and campesino communities, the FARC-EP's influence on the content of the demands of many community-based campesino organizations is un-deniable. In the case of Chaux, the FARC-EP's influence helps explain why the campesinos in the municipality came to vigorously oppose ORGANICHAUX.[48]

By November 2016, the tensions between the urban leadership of ORGANICHAUX and its campesino base became untenable. Campesi-nos from throughout Chaux criticized the antidemocratic nature of the organization and its support for large-scale mining and development projects bankrolled by multinational corporations. During a public meeting of approximately three hundred people, the president of OR-GANICHAUX—who had a history of organizing in the region and ulti-mately came to understand that he was being used by the forces behind the group—took the stage and endorsed the calls for direct participa-tion from the rural communities in decision-making processes and leadership positions. Before publicly resigning, he directed his atten-tion to the urban leadership of ORGANICHAUX and asked, "What am I doing in an organization that doesn't allow for communities to repre-sent themselves?" Although some people maintained their allegiances to ORGANICHAUX, the president's resignation marked the demise of the organization. However, the opportunities presented by the Peace Accords and the spark of campesino identity politics motivated people to continue organizing as campesinos throughout the region.

CAMPESINO IDENTITY POLITICS IN CHAUX

Following the Popayán march in January 2017, community organizers associated with COCCAM traveled to remote parts of northern Cauca as part of an effort to found community-based Coca Growers' Asso-ciations (Asociaciones de Cocaleros). The organizers—many of them coca growers themselves—shared valuable information about how peasants could influence the programs created by the Peace Accords that were intended to facilitate the transition from cultivating coca to participating in the legal economy.[49] The participatory impulse behind the accords included several stipulations about how the people living in municipalities affected by coca, marijuana, and poppy cultivations could orient each of the regionally based substitution programs. As the lowest rung on the drug-trafficking ladder, however, the peasants that cultivated and harvested the crops were also the most vulnerable to being excluded from direct participation in the substitution programs. Moneyed drug traffickers and front organizations like ORGAN-ICHAUX threatened to minimize their voices in order to acquire the resources available through participating in the government-led programs. Therefore, COCCAM organizers set about forming Coca Growers' Associations village by village to ensure that their unified voice would be included in the formation of the Comprehensive Community and Municipal Crop Substitution and Alternative Development Plans (Planes Integrales Comunitarios y Municipales de Sustitución y Desarrollo Alternativo, PISDA), which formed the basis of the Peace Accords' National Comprehensive Program for the Substitution of Illicit Crops (PNIS). The Coca Growers' Associations—which were not widespread in northern Cauca before the 2016 Peace Accords—sprang up in areas of the region, regardless of whether potential recruits were also part of an Afro-Colombian community council, an indigenous *cabildo*, or a ZRC.

The sudden growth of the Coca Growers' Associations surprised the region's more established black and indigenous organizations such as PCN, ACONC, and Çxhab Wala Kiwe ACIN. COCCAM's clear association with the Patriotic March (Marcha Patriótica) and ANZORC gave rise to suspicion. The three organizations—COCCAM, Patriotic March, and ANZORC—shared spokespeople, and all three entities espoused *campesinista*-style politics that appeared to be in close alignment with the FARC-EP's political platform. These sympathies were evident during the COCCAM launch in Popayán when the FARC-EP's delegation received a standing ovation from the audience; meanwhile, they welcomed the government's representatives with *chiflidos* (hissing). Furthermore, as the FARC-EP backed out of its role in drug trafficking, it advocated for the formation of Coca Growers' Associations. During one meeting I attended in a remote community of Chaux in December 2016, a representative of the FARC-EP encouraged the participants to organize a Coca Growers' Association. Now that the FARC-EP no longer charged the *vacuna*—its tax on coca production—he suggested that the coca growers should use the money formerly dedicated to the *vacuna* to pay for the expenses of the Coca Growers' Association. But the black and indigenous organizations grew concerned that the Coca Growers' Associations represented a covert strategy to undermine their authority in the territories, especially considering that coca drove a considerable part of the municipality's economy.

The distribution of censuses by the Coca Growers' Associations did not help mend the divisions in Chaux. Potential respondents expressed suspicion about how the census would be used, especially given the sensitive information that it collected. The preface to the census stated:

> Colombia has an opportunity to strengthen the foundation for building peace on the basis of the dialogues between the National Government and the FARC-EP. For that supreme good [*bien supremo*] to be successful, it is necessary to change the social investment policies in the historically forgotten campesino communities, such as our municipality, where coca cultivations have become the economic subsistence for the majority of people living in the territory.
>
> We ask for you to please voluntarily fill out this questionnaire with the purpose of collecting the necessary information for the design of policies and programs that guarantee better conditions for the peasantry [*campesinado*] and all of the social sectors.

The census itself consisted of fourteen questions that asked participants to provide their name, location, gender, size of family, level of education, and details about how much coca they grow and at what capacity they were involved in the drug-trafficking chain. The fifth question caused the most consternation in the Afro-Colombian Community Council of Nuevo Amanecer where I lived and worked for a time:

> Culture: Campesino(a)____ Indigenous ____ Afro ____ Others ____

Owing to the volume of *foráneos* who had arrived over the last twenty years, the black population in Nuevo Amanecer no longer made up the majority of inhabitants. The leadership of the community council feared that COCCAM would use the information from the census, specifically in relation to the fifth question, to support efforts to replace the community council with a ZRC or another formation that could potentially challenge their authority.

When the Chaux chapter of COCCAM drafted an open letter to the government in April 2017 declaring that the coca growers throughout the municipality were committed to substituting their crops and participating in the PISDA and PNIS, the black and indigenous organizations reacted sharply. Julio, a leader from the Afro-Colombian Community Council of Nuevo Amanecer, invited me to join him at a meeting at the headquarters of the indigenous *cabildo* in the mountains. The leadership of the Afro-Colombian community councils and indigenous *cabildos* called the meeting to discuss the contents of the COCCAM letter with the campesino leaders from CAMPOCAUCA, the community-based campesino organization that replaced ORGANICHAUX.

The rain picked up on the way to the meeting, making it impossible for Julio and me to discuss our expectations on the way there. He parked alongside the dozens of other motorcycles in the muddy field outside the *cabildo's* meeting hall. Inside, more than a hundred people participated in a community assembly. We waited around the kitchen fire to stay warm until our meeting started, and the cooks served us a stew of boiled beef in red and green plastic bowls. When Álvaro—the governor of the indigenous *cabildo*—found an opportune moment to leave the assembly, he hurried Julio and me upstairs, where the two campesino leaders sat next to another one of the indigenous leaders. Perceiving me as an outsider with connections to powerful people, community leaders often invited me to participate in side meetings where important decisions were made outside the collective. I had grown so accustomed to (and at times flattered by) being invited into these side meetings with leaders that their deeply undemocratic nature did not occur to me until years later.[50] After a round of brief introductions, Álvaro addressed his concerns head-on:

> The black and indigenous organizations have gotten along well because we recognize each other's autonomy, but you [the campesinos] are causing disharmony [*desarmonización*] in the territory—especially

in our *cabildo*. You know what causes the unrest? When we hear that at your meetings people are talking about how the indigenous community is not doing anything in relation to the Peace Accords. We have the audio recordings as proof. So you have organized yourselves as an organization: Tell us what your objective as an organization is!

Jaime, the older of the two campesino representatives, responded to Álvaro:

CAMPOCAUCA has been organizing in towns without denying your struggle. We have a deep history of organizing through the JACs. The 1991 constitution gave power to the indigenous *resguardos* and *cabildos* and the Afro-Colombian community councils. At a certain level, we see that we're at a disadvantage. Basically, it tells us that we're out of place.

There are many people and families that do not identify with indigenous organizations, even though we are all indigenous. We saw that as campesinos we could win over that space. Basically—through Law 160—we wanted to be on the same level. Basically, if the black and indigenous communities could do it, we could too.

We do not think of ourselves as a campesino organization in order to confront indigenous and black people. There is a need for everyone—black, indigenous, and campesino—to participate. The Havana Peace Accords [of 2016] demand that we get organized. We have always had the idea [to get organized] and the Peace Accords gave us that push.

If tomorrow we have to confront the state, then we can do it together as a region. [. . .]

In our meetings we always recognize the historic advantage that the black and indigenous communities have over us. *This historic moment obligates us to be in one of three spaces: indigenous, black, or campesino.* And that is the essential part of identity—to be where I feel comfortable. Those cultural differences will always cause debates, but we do not want conflicts because that does not interest us at all. At no point did we think about taking over your space.[51]

Even so, the representatives of CAMPOCAUCA failed to dispel Álvaro's concerns about the audio recordings and the aspirations of their organization. The indigenous leaders from the *cabildo* were particularly defensive because they had evidence that CAMPOCAUCA was organizing meetings and recruiting members from communities within their realm of influence.

Álvaro pulled the conversation back from reaching outright conflict and spoke about the COCCAM letter. Even in light of the tensions that dominated the beginning of the meeting, he argued that it was easier for the three community-based organizations in Chaux to speak to one another because they were based in the same territory. He told them, "Look, when the big organizations get involved, they fracture our efforts." By big organizations, Álvaro referred to the major regional and national-level black, indigenous, and campesino organizations like COCCAM, ANZORC, Çxhab Wala Kiwe ACIN, PCN, ACONC, and Regional Indigenous Council of Cauca (CRIC). Everyone at the meeting seemed to agree. He went on to discuss the practical aspects of organizing through the Peace Accords and determined that any public statement in reference to the government's coca substitution policy in Chaux should come from the communities, not the "big organizations." The campesinos and Afro-Colombian community council representatives supported Álvaro's idea and kept the fragile peace between them. Instead of publishing a letter signed by the three main organizations (COCCAM, Çxhab Wala Kiwe ACIN, and ACONC), each community would sign the letter by name without mentioning their organizational affiliations.

Before the meeting, my only recollection of CAMPOCAUCA was of seeing around fifty people marching behind their banner at the COCCAM mobilization in January 2017. Their presence in Popayán and our subsequent meeting at the *cabildo* impressed me because—after close to a decade of working with social movements in northern Cauca—I had never heard of CAMPOCAUCA or any other ongoing efforts to organize non-black, non-indigenous campesinos as an explicitly political movement in Chaux. This was in part understandable because ORGANICHAUX and CAMPOCAUCA formed less than eighteen months before the April 2017 meeting. Yet my ignorance also spoke to the "historic moment" mentioned by Jaime during the meeting, which according to him, "obligates [the people involved] to be in one of three spaces: indigenous, black, or campesino." My perspective was circumscribed owing in part to my long-term commitment to working with PCN and other black movements in the region. Given security concerns and competing political agendas in northern Cauca, my allegiances to PCN to a large extent determined whom I spoke with and at what capacity. That meant—although it was never explicitly communicated to me—that associating with certain organizations and individuals could be met with a high degree of suspicion.

Over the course of the following months, however, I became friends with Andrés, one of the leaders of CAMPOCAUCA. We were both in our early thirties and shared an interest in the implementation of the Peace Accords. As a result, we ended up seeing one another fairly frequently at meetings throughout northern Cauca. Unlike some of his colleagues, Andrés respected the autonomy of indigenous territories and looked for ways to create space for dialogue. This was probably possible in part because Andrés was new to the political scene at the time.

Andrés grew up in Chaux and so did his parents and grandparents, which meant that he was not typically interpreted as a *foráneo*. His adolescence was interrupted by the paramilitary invasion of northern Cauca during the early 2000s, when his father was forced to give up three of his cows. The family originally wanted to sell the cows to buy more land so that the children could continue their studies, but—after the paramilitaries confiscated their livestock—Andrés and his father started to grow coca to supplement the lost income. During the Naya Massacre, the paramilitaries arrived ostensibly to clear out the guerrillas, but according to people in Chaux nearly all the victims were civilians. Many of the dead were never registered with the coroner. The witnesses and families feared retaliation for speaking out against their murders or disappearances. Andrés told me about the brother of one of his friends who worked on the local bus line: "He left one day and never came back." Andrés went on to recall how they found his body a couple of weeks later. On another occasion, two trucks full of heavily armed paramilitaries waited outside a village with a list of names in hand.

Unbeknownst to Andrés's family, his father—a community leader in his own right—was on the list. The paramilitaries stopped all of the people transiting on the dirt road and reviewed their IDs. Another man with the same name as his father was pulled off the bus. Andrés remembered the man whom the paramilitaries mistakenly identified as his father as a hard-working evangelical campesino who "never got into it with anyone." They later found his decapitated body strewn on the side of the road. The cadavers gave force to a saying that gained notoriety at the time: "Snitches die in the street" (Los sapos mueren en la carretera). The wanton paramilitary violence pushed Andrés to leave Chaux in search of a job and a semblance of security. "I wanted to see them [the paramilitaries] eliminated," he told me with uncharacteristic severity.

Like many young men in the region, Andrés made his first trip to the Naya River basin as an adolescent around the time of the paramilitary invasion despite his parents' pleas. The Naya region was infamous for its expansive coca fields and remote location on the western flank of the Andes, which separate the Pacific coast from the rest of the country. He left on foot with three of his friends, and for the next four years he and his buddies would periodically make the multiday trek to Naya over the mountains.[52] They got to play at being real men in a masculine rite of passage. Andrés did not gloat about unsavory details or even mention if he partook in these activities, but other guys that I met relished telling me stories about how they would need to borrow money for penicillin shots after spending all their cash at the brothels. The FARC-EP tried to recruit Andrés and his friends in Naya after telling them all about their struggle to "change Colombia." A couple of his friends joined the guerrillas because they shared Andrés's disdain for the paramilitaries, but Andrés ultimately did not.

His last trip to Naya ended abruptly. The *patrón* (boss) accused Andrés of having an affair with his wife and pulled a gun on him. Andrés fled Naya and kept a low profile working as a *raspachín* (coca picker) in other parts of Cauca because his former *patrón* put out a hit on him through the local FARC-EP front. When he finally returned to Chaux, Andrés worked on his family's farm and spent his free time gambling and going to cock fights. One night at the bar, he intervened in a fight to defend one of his friends. After Andrés spoke with the police, the other guy in the fight accused Andrés of being a *sapo* (snitch) and told the FARC that he was selling out the guerrillas to the police in Chaux.

In spite of Andrés's pleas to the contrary, the local leader of the FARC-EP paid Andrés a visit. That month, the FARC-EP had already murdered several people in the area as part of a campaign to "cleanse the region of paramilitary collaborators and informants." Andrés was certain that the FARC-EP leader was going to kill him outside the pool hall where he was summoned to the meeting. As they walked along the road, it appeared that the *gatillero* (trigger man) was going to make his move, and Andrés spoke up to tell them it was a big mistake. The FARC-EP leader said it was too cold outside to talk and that they should go over things at his home. Throughout the night, Andrés emphatically repeated that the accusations against him were false. In an effort to catch him in a lie, the FARC-EP leader said that they had video evidence of him talking to the police and taking money. Andrés remained resolute and denied the charges that he was a snitch. The FARC-EP leader told him, "We checked out your entire farm looking for caches, weapons, and money, but we didn't find anything. I recommend that you concentrate on growing your crops and starting a family. Don't ever go back to Naya because they want to kill you over there."

Andrés wept the next morning and gave himself over to God. He joined one of the evangelical churches, stopped gambling, and uprooted the little coca he had. Within a couple of years, he got married and started working at a new job in the legal economy that required him to travel around the municipality. Andrés reflected on how he developed an interest in political organizing because of his experiences working the job in the midst of the coca boom:

> I got to know the municipality through that job. Every day I went house by house, and I saw how drug trafficking and the mafia devoured the communities. It started to fill me with sadness to see how things were degrading. You would arrive in one of the towns, and the schools were

in dismal shape. Totally abandoned. Around here there's a lot of development compared to other parts of the municipality. There are other zones where people are living under inhumane conditions. They don't have latrines. Everyone sleeps, cooks, and everything else in a one-room house! So that had me thinking about the accords, and that's why I told the local leaders, "Look, the accords are talking about restructuring the countryside!" [. . .]

I was in the same line of work at [that job] and—because I lived in a town that was characterized as one of the most violent zones in the municipality because of drug trafficking and supposedly being guerrilla collaborators—the army targeted me . . . the National Army. They carried out three attempts in a row, and that made me think a lot because I wasn't even a leader. [. . .]

I got used to walking from house to house as part of my daily routine. There are some homes that are more rural than others around here. It can take up to forty minutes or an hour to get from one house to another. So I always listened to the news and heard about what was being agreed to. I followed every advance [in the peace negotiations] on the radio because it concerned me. I thought to myself, When is the army going to stop attacking people? When are we going to be able to live peacefully in the countryside? So I waited to see when they would finally sign that blessed final accord. I told the leaders, "Look, this is a good opportunity for the development of the communities so that they can live peacefully and get involved with that issue of [coca] substitution."

The situation was really sad. For example, I would visit homes once a month and there would be friends or young people hanging out there. I would arrive the next month, and they would either be in mourning or on their way to the cemetery to bury someone. I would ask, "But what happened?" "Oh, they killed him." "But why?" "Well it looks like they snitched on the mafia and gave information to the army. The mafia found out and had them killed." Situations like that continued to happen constantly. [. . .] So, yeah, that affected the history around here because that's what the mafia was doing. Every once in a while they would justify deaths for X or Y reason. At the end of the day, you never knew if it was the mafia that killed them or what, but there were deaths upon deaths. So that's why for me that issue of substituting the crops has become one of the struggles that needs to be taken on here. It has taken so many lives here and it continues to do so. That's why as leaders we have pushed hard for it.

Despite the ongoing peace negotiations, the continued combat between the guerrillas and the military did not provide him or the other inhabitants of Chaux with reprieve from the violence. In April 2015, the FARC-EP attacked a nearby military outpost, killing ten soldiers and injuring more than twenty. The hostilities bled over into the civilian population with widespread accusations of snitching on all sides: military, guerrillas, drug traffickers, paramilitaries, and inhabitants of the towns affected by the conflict. "Deaths upon deaths."

Throughout Andrés's adult life, he witnessed how coca simultaneously became the basis of many people's livelihoods and a motivating force behind the surge in violence.[53] According to him, the FARC-EP's ideology "started to disappear and they began to depend on drug trafficking" when they reinstalled themselves in the region in the middle of the first decade of the 2000s, after the paramilitary invasion. That did not stop the FARC-EP from pressuring the municipal governments to spend more resources on infrastructure projects that should benefit the local population. However, according to him, the FARC-EP gradually shifted away from their support for peasant struggles to be more in sync with the aspirations of the drug traffickers. Their legitimacy as a force for social change among the peasant population declined substantially as they settled scores for the mafia and allowed cocaine production to take on a more prominent role in the community. Chaux no longer was a place to just grow coca leaves. Over the course of a decade, cocaine-producing laboratories (*cristalizaderos*) appeared in the area, and *foráneos* settled into their own enclaves. "They only talk about money," Andrés said in reference to the *foráneos*. People from Andrés's generation stopped caring about school and traditional festivities. CAMPOCAUCA even had to implement its own gun control initiative because so many people showed up to parties with revolvers.

While the deleterious impacts of drug trafficking served as an incentive for some campesinos like Andrés to join CAMPOCAUCA, resentment toward the indigenous *cabildo* motivated other sectors of the peasantry to join. Individuals like Jaime acknowledged that they may have descended from indigenous people but they refused to associate with the indigenous organizational structure such as the *cabildos*. For them, their refusal to participate in the indigenous organizations made them campesino and not indigenous, regardless of whether their last names or phenotype would lead an onlooker to assume otherwise. Two widely held perceptions contributed to campesinos' disidentification with indigenous *cabildos* and *resguardos*: (1) the imposition of indigenous spirituality in the schools and (2) corrupt management of community resources by indigenous authorities.

The expansion of evangelical churches throughout northern Cauca directly conflicted with the expressed position of significant sectors of the indigenous movement to embrace Nasa cosmology.[54] As a result, schooling became one of the central points of contention between the evangelicals and the *cabildos*. Because indigenous communities have the legal right to dictate curricula in the schools under their purview, the indigenous authorities in northern Cauca included language lessons in Nasa Yuwe and courses in Nasa spirituality. For the growing evangelical population, this was tantamount to indoctrination or heresy, and they attempted to enroll their children in schools outside the *cabildos* by using the resources available through the municipal government. Another frequent complaint about the *cabildos* was corruption. The campesinos argued that the leadership of the *cabildos* stole money and extended favors to friends. Taken together, these two issues represented an impingement on the autonomy of campesino culture as it took on an increasingly distinctive form.

CAMPOCAUCA's meteoric growth in membership from sixty members to over six hundred within a year depended on their ability to articulate a compelling political platform for defending the rights of campesinos. The core of the platform revolved around the central demands of participating in the implementation of the Peace Accords and obtaining official recognition from the state as campesinos. The campesinos framed their political aspirations as campesinos in relation to land tenure, education, and political participation. According to Andrés, "We don't want the state to give us anything. We just want to be recognized." However, advocating for campesino rights more often appeared to be a tit-for-tat strategy that attempted to keep up with the indigenous model for rights-based political organizing. For example, Andrés also argued for campesino quotas along the lines of the indigenous model:

> They have special quotas [for being accepted to universities] and their students can get training if they want it. But if you are not indigenous then you do not have a right to that quota. Right? So how are we supposed to go to the university? By getting to work with the machete on a farm or working as a day laborer picking coffee? A campesino who produces coffee around here can save at most four million pesos [approximately US$1,300] in a year, and that's a lot. With four million you can't pay for a university education.

The campesinos, therefore, defined their approach to social change through the politics of recognition that increasingly reflected the problematic notion of multiculturalism as a "system of interethnic competition,"[55] which in turn reified the state's recognition policies as the hegemonic terrain for asserting political power. Although concerns about their historic marginalization and precarity continued to inform the programmatic concerns of CAMPOCAUCA, many campesinos turned to the organization out of desire to forge a space of their own and counteract what they perceived as the imposition of indigenous politics and spirituality.

MAKING PEASANTS COUNT

CAMPOCAUCA's strategy fit in with broader efforts to achieve collective recognition on behalf of the *campesinado* in Colombia. Because of their association with the National Federation of United Agricultural Workers (Federación Nacional Sindical Unitaria Agropecuaria) and ANZORC, CAMPOCAUCA could plug into regional and national networks that pressured the Colombian government to recognize the *campesinado*. Their demands for official recognition also reflected international efforts to pass the UN Declaration on the Rights of Peasants and Other People Working in Rural Areas. Even the FARC-EP argued for the recognition of the *campesinado* as a differential subject in their document "Rural and Agrarian Development for Democratization and Peace with Social Justice in Colombia: 100 Baseline Proposals." The fifth proposal of the FARC-EP's document recommended the following:

> Political recognition of the *campesinado* and all of their rights, as well as defining their territories. The campesino territories should have the same reach as the other forms of collective territories guaranteeing the diverse forms of peasant property, both individual and collective. [. . .] These territories represent a form avoiding the concentration of property and take on two forms: first, the peasant reserve zones [ZRCs] and, second, the zones of peasant food production. All of this should be accompanied by state-sponsored measures that dignify and politically recognize the campesinos and campesinas, which should begin with the signing onto the UN Declaration on the Rights of the Peasants.[56]

These diverse efforts to advocate for peasant recognition reflected the hegemony of the recognition-based politics symptomatic of the multicultural turn.

One of the most important campaigns for recognition in Colombia was an effort to include the category of campesino in the 2018 National Census. The campaign, "For the Peasantry to Count, It Must Be Counted," hinged on a sixty-four-page lawsuit filed November 23, 2017, by the renowned human rights lawyer Rodrigo Uprimny on behalf of 1,758 campesinos. The efforts to organize support for the lawsuit brought together distinct sectors of the peasant movement, including ANZORC, ANUC, and National Agrarian Summit (Cumbre Agraria Nacional). The lawsuit accused the government of "violating the fundamental right to material equality" by the "unjustified omission of questions that inquire into the differential cultural identity of the peasantry [*campesinado*] and their socioeconomic situation in the XVIII National Census of the Population and the VII Housing Census in 2018."[57] During interviews with participants, I learned that Dejusticia, the legal clinic cofounded by Uprimny, conducted interviews with experts on campesino issues to prepare the lawsuit but not with experts from black and indigenous organizations whose bases would likely have been considered campesino thirty years earlier. Despite the supposedly colorblind approach to the category of the *campesinado* in the policy discourse, this oversight served as another reminder of the racial assumptions about what constituted a campesino.

Ultimately, the campaign failed to get inclusion of the category of campesino in the 2018 census, but it left legal precedent for its inclusion in future censuses. It also resulted in a memorandum by the Colombian Institute of Anthropology and History (Instituto Colombiano de Antropología e Historia) that provided observations about how to reach a more concrete definition of the *campesinado* and recommendations for future census questions to ensure the participation of campesinos.[58]

The growing mobilization around campesino inclusion in censuses resonated among CAMPOCAUCA's membership in Chaux. For example, Andrés referred to the experience of one of CAMPOCAUCA's members with a census worker as exemplary:

> Look, the census is of transcendental importance for our organization because in Chaux the indigenous people just got another win by gaining recognition as a *resguardo*, which means that now they will receive direct money transfers from the state. So the issue of counting how many indigenous, *afros*, or other populations exist [is very important], but there are major errors in the ways in which they are conducting the census. I don't know if I am mistaken in what I am going to say, but—according to people who participated in the census—the people conducting the census have done a very mediocre job. They arrive somewhere and ask very little. They simply look at the person's physical features and assume that they belong to X population.
>
> For example, one *compañera*, who is a very good leader from CAMPOCAUCA and lives in the urban center of Chaux, participated in the census. When they were about to wrap up, she asked, "You're not going to ask if I am campesina or indigenous?" "Oh yes, that's there."

"And what did you mark?" "Well, we already marked you as an indigenous." She replied, "But why? Why did you mark me as indigenous if I am a campesina?" They said, "No, well campesina doesn't appear here, and that is why we marked you as indigenous." So she responded to them and told them to take her off where it says indigenous and that they needed to find another box. She says that they eventually found her a box that says "none of the above," and they put her in that box. Simply "none of the above" because there is not a box that recognizes that we are campesinos . . . That's something that the DANE [Departamento Administrativo Nacional de Estadística (National Administrative Department of Statistics)] has not wanted to do.

So if we are successful in making sure that the Supreme Court implements the sentence that forces the DANE, the Ministry of Interior, and others to count the *campesinado* [peasantry], then that will be a huge success for us because we had to sue the government. We had to sue the government to ensure that we are a part of it and that we would be counted so that we could begin to demand our rights [*para empezar el tema para la exigibilidad de derechos*].

If at some point we are counted and they determine that there are [for example] one million campesinos, then imagine how that will influence public policies. [. . .] At some point the government needs to allocate a budget to attend to our population, which will be recognized by the UN and international entities like the Latin American Coordinator of Peasant Organizations [Coordinadora Latinoamericana de Organizaciones Campesinas] and Vía Campesina that are also doing important work, and Colombia, too. We hope that now with the increase in congressional representatives from more alternative political parties that we can move forward because we have been talking about this for a long time.

We have always been invisibilized, and they have not wanted to recognize us.

The response of Andrés's *compañera* regarding the census question about her ethnicity represented an important shift regarding the cultural politics of identity in Colombia. For many scholars, the move to identify as either black or indigenous represented a strategic move to acquire benefits from the state that potentially challenged the tenets of mestizo nation-state formation. That also led to campesinos linking up with black and indigenous organizations to assert rights, as discussed in chapter 2. However, her decision to reject the imposition of indigenous identity reversed the trend toward what the anthropologists Margarita Chaves and Marta Zambrano call "reindianization." In "From *Blanqueamiento* to *Reindigenización*" they argue, "Becoming indigenous again is a deliberate reversal of deindianization, a process by which indigenous collectives divested themselves of their own identity in response to outside pressures [. . .]. Significantly, they question fixed ethnic categories and also reverse mestizaje's directionality: from a privileged path to whitening to an enabling road for becoming indigenous."[59] By racializing (or "ethnicizing" in Colombian terms) the category of campesino, Andrés's colleague advocated for her recognition on the basis of being different from those who claim difference—that is, *not* being indigenous. However, in what might be considered a potent expression of Costa Vargas's "hyperconsciousness of race and its negation,"[60] most campesino organizations and their sympathizers go to great lengths to insist that campesino identity is cultural and decidedly *not* ethnic. Nevertheless, campesino resistance to being interpellated as indigenous signals a reappraisal of *mestizaje* on behalf of campesinos confronting their exclusion from the multicultural rights regime.

THE PROBLEM WITH RECOGNITION

After a workshop on the Peace Accords in a rural community of northern Cauca, a coca grower from Naya followed up with me about a concern via WhatsApp. He asked me, "Under the peace process, should I get in as a campesino or through a *cabildo*?" In addition to revealing a pragmatic impulse that can shape the practice of self-identifying in Colombia, his question pointed to a significant gap between the analysis of experts that propose clean categorizations based on cultural or racial difference and the lived experiences of campesinos from diverse cultural and racial backgrounds. The best answer that I could give him at the time was a cop-out: "That's a good question. That depends on your situation and how you identify."

The armed conflict and the expansion of coca cultivations brought people from different backgrounds and parts of the country into contact with one another under conditions of extreme precarity and violence. For black and indigenous communities, the possibility of accessing a set of differential rights made it possible to assert a semblance of self-determination and autonomy through the state, even if the government rarely recognized or implemented those legal rights. For mestizo campesinos, on the other hand, the opportunities to redress grievances were less clear. Some sought refuge in Afro-Colombian community councils or indigenous *cabildos* and *resguardos*, as evidenced in Nuevo Amanecer. Others developed relationships with campesino organizations and attempted to build on the limited wiggle room afforded by Law 160 of 1994 or created new entities altogether. With the opportunities provided by the 2016 Peace Accords, campesinos in Chaux seized the opening and, by doing so, exposed some of the tensions exacerbated by neoliberal multiculturalism. The emergence of campesino identity politics therefore revealed an important shift in the course of neoliberal multiculturalism. Instead of embracing indigeneity or blackness, campesinos tacitly mobilize through the discourse of *mestizaje*.

Although describing multiculturalism as a system for interethnic competition displaces critique from the structure of neoliberal multiculturalism to its effects, it provides a glimpse into how multiculturalism is enacted and felt in Chaux as a form of rivalry. One of the consequences of shifting the strategy and tactics of political struggle toward gaining recognition from the settler colonial state is that it reinforces the forms of belonging and promises of protection established by the state's recognition policies.[61] Adherence to the state's definitions of racial difference creates fodder for racist resentment between the supposed beneficiaries of recognition. Therefore, the emergence of campesino identity politics also reveals what the political theorist Judith Butler calls the "hegemony of the juridical subject."[62] The contradictory relationship between peasants and the state whereby peasants desire redress from a state that is actively facilitating their destruction through capitalist development is not something new: it was one of the principal reasons why the FARC was able to draw so many people from the peasantry into its ranks over the years. The difference with the emergence of campesino identity politics is that—instead of articulating a class-based demand as they did in the past—the new campesinos are making a cultural-cum-racial demand for recognition that aligns with the project of mestizo nation-state formation.[63] Without an explicitly anti-racist orientation that challenges the basis of racial capitalism and settler colonialism, this strategy promises to deepen divisions across marginalized peoples and facilitate the deepening of colonial capitalist relations through the medium of recognition.

4   ¡TOD@S SOMOS PRIMERA LÍNEA?

Preliminary Notes on the 2021 Uprising in Cali

> We are not the ones from before. We are the ones from now on.
> —Graffiti on a destroyed bus stop in Cali,
> Colombia, June 2021

Somebody named Camilo,paso aguante CALI spoke into a webcam from a nondescript room. His white skin contrasted with the black hoodie and black bandana covering his face: "We—the youth—accomplished in thirty days what the armed guerrillas were unable to do in thirty years. It's time to realize that the sociopolitical situation that we are in cannot be addressed by the corrupt politicians. Politics is about decision-making and—we the youth—made a decision to give our lives to better the country."[1] A little over one month after Colombia's longest uprising on record, Camilo,paso aguante CALI expressed the insurgent energy of the moment. I am still intrigued by what he meant by accomplishing more than the guerrillas. Perhaps the uprising and its barricades earned popular support in a way that the FARC never could. Maybe he thought the revolution was finally here. His rejection of the status quo, however, was absolute.

What started on April 28, 2021, as a seemingly routine demonstration against the imposition of neoliberal policies quickly became an
expansive revolt against the rule of law. People throughout Colombia
challenged state violence and capitalist exploitation by becoming un-
governable for nearly three months. According to one widely cited
report by the Ministry of Defense, between April 28 and June 27, there
were over 14,175 actions related to the uprising in 860 of Colombia's
1,101 municipalities.[2] Instead of entrusting politics to professionals,
people took to the streets and reclaimed their neighborhoods. The insurgent energy of the revolt seemed to catch everyone by surprise,
including the participants in the protests turned rebellion.

As Cali became the epicenter of the uprising, people described the
intense repression they faced in relation to the state's counterinsurgency war. According to Vice President Francia Márquez Mina, who
was living in Cali at the time and put her presidential campaign on
hold to draw attention to the uprising, "I will never be able to explain
what we lived through during the first two months of the strike. It was
like four or five times worse than what we lived through in Suárez
when they killed [former FARC Commander] Alfonso Cano and the
helicopters were bombarding from above. It was like five times worse
than that. There were helicopters here as if there was a war going on."[3]

Many other people I knew from my work in northern Cauca—from
former FARC guerrillas to black and indigenous activists—also got
wrapped up in the uprising in one way or another. Nearly five years
had passed since the signing of the 2016 Peace Accords, and the optimism around the potential for peace had declined significantly under
the right-wing Duque administration (2018–2022). The uprising simultaneously became an outlet for an accumulation of frustrations and
opened spaces to challenge the forms of domination and state violence
that people continued to confront.[4]

In this chapter, I reflect on some of the contradictions and opportunities that unfolded during the 2021 uprising in Cali. I am particularly
interested in exploring the potential for solidarity and transformation, as well as the pitfalls of representative politics, in the context of
popular revolt. Racism, as will become clear, served as a significant

obstacle to expanding the struggle for liberation during the uprising. Along with revealing the centripetal force of state-centric politics even during moments of widespread resistance, the uprising also offered glimpses into how the practices of the rebellion signaled the potential of incipient alternatives to the forces of oppression.

FROM CITY BLOCKS TO RESISTANCE POINTS

The National Strike Committee (Comité Nacional del Paro, CNP)—a coalition of trade unions and established social movements—called for a strike on Wednesday, April 28, 2021, explicitly targeting the Duque administration's proposal to instate neoliberal tax reforms and other policies related to COVID-19.[5] In keeping with the more expansive approach to striking prevalent throughout much of Latin America, this meant more than a work stoppage.[6] People from all sectors of society were invited to converge and express their discontent with the government's policies. Early that morning, however, there were already signs that the CNP was not calling the shots.[7] In Cali, a group of Misak indigenous people from Cauca tore down a statue commemorating Sebastián Belalcázar, a Spanish colonizer from the sixteenth century.

Seven months before the onset of the 2021 revolt, the Misak toppled a different statue of Belalcázar in Popayán during another uprising.[8] The spark for that uprising was a murder, not a tax reform. On September 9, 2020, police killed Javier Ordóñez, a mestizo taxi driver in Bogotá, and dozens of police stations were burned down by September 21.[9] During the riots that broke out in Bogotá, the police fired live ammunition at demonstrators, murdering at least a dozen people.[10] In hindsight, that rebellion—which itself emerged out of a series of intensifying mobilizations throughout the country—served as one of many rehearsals for 2021.[11] President Duque made it clear which side he was on during the 2020 uprising in Bogotá by dressing up in a police uniform and placing his hand over his heart for a photo op outside a charred police station in the nation's capital.

These memories must have rushed back into popular consciousness in Cali on April 28, 2021. The state doubled down on force shortly after

Belalcázar fell. Under the conditions of the dialectic of state violence, the Duque administration wagered that force could quell the unrest and restore the rule of law. Former President Álvaro Uribe endorsed the strong-arm tactics in an April 29 tweet saying, "The Army being on the streets is urgent and better than recording the news of murder and vandalism."[12] By framing the participants in the uprising as vandals, the policy makers and pundits sought to deny the uprising of any political orientation. As a result, the military and police did exactly what billions of dollars in training and weapons—much of which came from the United States—were intended to do: exact violence. According to Campaña Defender La Libertad: Asunto de Tod@s, 28 people were murdered and 1,435 people were injured in Cali alone during the 2021 National Strike.[13]

Even after government officials resigned and the Duque administration retracted the tax reform that instigated the uprising, the demonstrations continued. State violence kept people in the streets and demonstrated the need to move beyond the forms of ritualized protests that tended to result in piecemeal concessions from the government. The authority of entities like the CNP, which originally called for the protests, faded—if they ever held sway on the participants to begin with. Many of the participants in the uprising like Camilo,paso aguante CALI rejected the politics of representation expressed by organizations, leaders, and social movements that claimed to speak for them. They sought to break out of a familiar format whereby their dissidence was diluted by outsiders. Instead of communicating through interlocutors, they wanted to speak and act on their own behalf.

In its contempt for the powers that be, the uprising manifested a desire for transformation through contestation, even if it lacked demands that were legislatively coherent through a liberal, rights-based framework.[14] For the Argentine militant-research group Colectivo Situaciones, this "insurrectional negation" should be thought of as a "positive no"—that is, not "merely a negative reaction, but a gesture of self-affirmation that permits the exercise of negation."[15] The Zapatistas might call this "a revolution that makes revolution possible."[16] The refusal to make legible demands did not betray some underlying confusion or preconscious angst typically associated with crowds of unruly masses.[17] Instead, the act of refusal itself embodied the potential for self-determination beyond the strictures of the state and capital.[18]

The *primera línea* (front line) exposed the hollow promises of the colonial-capitalist social contract. With shields made of scrap metal and facial coverings meant to protect them from bullets, tear gas, COVID-19, and surveillance, they assumed a heroic status within the rebellious political conjuncture by setting up blockades and resignifying public space in what became known as the *puntos de resistencia* (resistance points). Dozens of resistance points took shape in Cali during the uprising. The neighborhood of Loma de la Cruz (Hill of the Cross) became Loma de la Dignidad (Dignity Hill), Puerto Rellena (Full Port) became Puerto Resistencia (Resistance Port), Calipso (Calypso) became ApoCalipso (Apocalypso), the Puente de Mil Días (Bridge of a Thousand Days) became the Puente de Mil Luchas (Bridge of a Thousand Struggles), and so on.[19] These resistance points did not aim to take control of governmental buildings or squares. Instead, they tended to materialize in and around some of the city's most impoverished neighborhoods and important intersections (figure 4.1).[20]

The *primera línea* derived its strength from the mutual aid and solidarity networks emerging around the resistance points. While the real front line may have been the groups of predominantly young men with shields and Molotov cocktails facing off with cops, they were not alone.[21] Behind them were groups of people providing them with supplies like rocks and *papa bombas* (potato bombs) or other artisanal explosives, along with others who built up the barricades with materials they found on-site. Brigades of volunteer paramedics provided medical attention to the injured demonstrators, and *ollas comunitarias* (communitarian kitchens) offered free food to hungry neighbors and participants in the uprising. One of the most iconic aspects of the resistance points were the "popular libraries" built atop the ashes of burned down police stations. In addition to holding space in the face of immense repression, the participants also organized political workshops, artistic activities, community gardens, and popular assemblies in the resistance points as expressions of how they intended to decide

FIGURE 4.1

Puerto Resistencia Popular Library (photo by author, July 2021)

their agendas for themselves. Veteran activists in Cali insisted that the *primera línea* did not invent the tactics deployed during the uprising. The uprising did, however, give these potentially disparate activities form in time and space.

The resistance points reclaimed the things that the capitalist state took away from people: health, education, nourishment, joy, and security. Behind the barricades, people struggled to sustain the conditions for life and dignity.[22] For Camilo,paso aguante CALI, "The *Primera Línea* is any person that from their position, from their power, from their capacity, from their qualities, contributes their best for a social change, for a dignified life." This expansive definition of *primera línea* challenged more macho appraisals of the front line as a space to exclusively engage in street fighting with the cops. It corresponded to a slogan that took off in the context of the uprising: "Tod@s Somos Primera Línea" (We Are All Front Liners).

This more expansive approach to the *primera línea* promised to create space for a transgressive catch-all category that transcended the usual barriers to unity. It brought the barricades into everyday life. After all, doesn't capitalism undermine everything and everyone's well-being? Couldn't we all—in a sense—become front liners?

THE ÑERO REBELLION

After closely following the uprising from the United States, I arrived in Cali in late June 2021. Although some of the most intense confrontations had passed, several resistance points around the city continued to face repression in their struggle to build "something else."[23] For the next month, I visited resistance points and chatted with friends involved in local organizing efforts. They introduced me to their friends and so on and so forth. A friend of mine who taught anthropology at a university in Cali recommended that I speak with somebody named William to get a firsthand understanding of the uprising.

Within a couple of hours of getting in touch, William and I met up in downtown Cali. We spent the afternoon on the steps of the Dignity Hill resistance point hanging out with his friends, who included a veteran of the M-19 guerrilla movement, his girlfriend, and three guys from Medellín who traveled to Cali for the National Popular Assembly (Asamblea Nacional Popular, ANP). The ANP was supposed to be a major convening of social movements, organizations, communities, front liners, and anyone else who supported the uprising but did not feel represented by the CNP. Beginning on July 16, participants in the ANP occupied the campus of Universidad del Valle after the local government refused to provide them with a permit. Many of the ANP's organizers were associated with the Peoples' Congress (Congreso de los Pueblos)—a broad coalition of social movements and organizations from throughout the country founded in 2010—and they hoped to spark a new network of resistance with the collectives that took shape during the uprising. On the basis of my experience at the working groups and plenaries at the ANP, however, the proceedings were heavily influenced by the agenda of the Peoples' Congress despite the calls for mass participation and an emphasis on horizontality.[24] The guys from Medellín still seemed excited about the potential of the uprising, but they were frustrated with the organizers of the ANP for hanging them out to dry. The organizers called off the demonstration planned for July 20, Colombia's Independence Day, amid threats of repression and agreed to vacate the campus of the Universidad del Valle. By canceling the protest and leaving demonstrators without a place to sleep, the organizers of the ANP confirmed the suspicion of the guys sharing a joint on the steps of the Dignity Hill resistance point: conventional political platforms could not be trusted because they negotiated on their own behalf and exposed people to the same vulnerabilities as always.

After they left to catch their bus to Medellín, William and I continued the conversation over beers outside a heavy metal bar at the base of Dignity Hill. William, a light-skinned mestizo, used his fingernails to etch a map onto a black wall. As he animated the wall with his hands, he described the multiple facets of the rebellion in Cali. Every line and circle signified a different actor or interest: a neighborhood, a front line, a political party, an *oficina de cobro* (organized crime syndicate), a police lieutenant, a resistance point, a nongovernmental organization. The crosscutting lines and curves represented the mutually reinforcing elements of the uprising. With each new strike of his fingernail against the wall appeared a new need, desire, or conflict. They all contributed to the explosion and were influenced by it. In fact, the most popular way of referring to the uprising in Spanish was as an *estallido* (explosion). William said there were *"millones de micropoderes"* (millions of micropowers) participating in the uprising, each one jockeying for more power.

I asked him several questions aimed at understanding what motivated people to participate in the uprising. Many people whom I had spoken with over the course of the preceding weeks were wary about the potential of a revolt in the absence of a clear political orientation. These skeptics tended to come from explicitly leftist political platforms and "critical sectors."[25] William, in contrast, was a gangbanger turned school teacher, and a few of his students got arrested during the uprising. His neighborhood, Siloé, was profiled in an Amnesty International report after three people were killed and dozens were injured during a police offensive there on May 3. I impatiently asked him, "Who were these people?" "What did they want?" "Was there any truth to the rumors about gang participation in the resistance points?"

William listened to my hurried questions. He said that the poor folks on the front lines of the uprising may not have known much about this or that public policy, but he was sure about at least one thing, "Yo a los ricos los odio" (I hate the rich). He went on to tell me how he had hated the rich since he was eight years old because they looked at him differently. He said:

> "I wanted to destroy everything. There's the answer to what you don't understand: my rage, my impotence, my . . . How do you say that fucking word? When you think the worst of yourself? It's not impotence—it's rage."

For him, this mix of "rage" and "impotence"—but primarily rage—was fundamental for understanding why the *chirrete* participated in the uprising (figure 4.2).[26]

Puerto Resistencia resistance point (photo by author, July 2021)

Typically, the word *chirrete* derogatorily refers to "junkies," "scum," or "lowlifes." There was also another word that people used to talk about the participants in the rebellion: *ñero,* short for *compañero*—that is, comrade, buddy, friend—but *ñero,* like *chirrete,* is used to disrespect "street people," "hoodlums," and the "homeless." Yet when I asked William to define who were the *chirrete,* he said, "They are the lowest of the low for society, but they are what most represents society. That micropower [the *chirrete*] is the greatest force in society. It is the greatest force in Colombia."[27]

At first glance, it might seem that William may have been invoking the latent power of the working class. The *ñeros* and *chirrete,* however, do not neatly fit into the box of the working class because they are not, strictly speaking, workers or wage laborers. At the time of the uprising, Cali had the country's second-highest unemployment rate (21.4 percent), and nearly half (48.9 percent) of the city's working population worked in the informal sector.[28] Decades of neoliberalism and war had taken their toll and pushed people into the precarity that predominates in Colombia and throughout much of the world.[29] Instead of having access to formal employment, the urban masses—many of whom had been forcibly displaced from rural communities to cities by violence—made do with the scarce opportunities available to them.[30]

Despite the pivotal role of the people who might be considered *ñeros* and *chirrete* in the uprising, not everyone drew inspiration from their participation. Throughout my time in Cali during June and July of 2021, I noticed a bump in the usage of the term "lumpenproletariat" among some of my friends and contacts who considered themselves leftist or progressive. Until the uprising, "lumpenproletariat" was a term that I read in books, but it did not come up in conversation. However, with the protagonism of the uprising exceeding the grip of the leftist establishment, the term became a way to discount the strategy and tactics of the unaffiliated. Many of these same people from the leftist establishment, however, took a markedly different approach to the participants in the uprising less than a year later during the Petro campaign and after his election. Instead of denigrating the *chirrete* and *ñeros* as lumpenproletariat, they celebrated the youthful participants in the uprising as the *muchachada* (the youth) and praised them for making change possible. Yet the circulation of lumpen discourse continued to play an important role in distinguishing the supposedly serious protesters from the unruly masses.

Marx's writings on the lumpenproletariat were relatively brief but damning nonetheless.[31] In *The Manifesto of the Communist Party*, Marx and Engels famously referred to the lumpenproletariat as

> the "dangerous class," the social scum, that passively rotting mass thrown off by the lowest layers of the old society, may, here and there, be swept into the movement by a proletarian revolution; its conditions of life, however, prepare it far more for the part of a bribed tool of reactionary intrigue.[32]

This unsavory characterization of the lumpenproletariat served as a pretext for many self-proclaimed radicals and progressives to disregard people like William and his neighbors. As a "dangerous class," the lumpenproletariat were considered a weak link in revolutionary organizations because they were perceived as corruptible and unreliable.

The irony of this conscious disavowal of the lumpenproletariat is that people like William and his neighbors have been at the center of uprisings around the world. Who flooded the streets during the rebellions that shook the status quo in Argentina, Tunisia, Greece, the United States, Sri Lanka, and elsewhere? Was it just—or even primarily—wage laborers and the card-carrying members of trade unions, political parties, and other established social movements?[33] Beyond the members of these organizations, the protagonists in twenty-first-century uprisings tend to emerge from the masses of disenchanted, disenfranchised, and disaffected people surviving in the ruins of capitalism.

Anarchists and other anticolonial militants have taken an alternative approach to these "dangerous classes." Mikhail Bakunin, for example, idealized them as "the flower of the proletariat,"[34] and the Black Panther Party named its funk band the Lumpen. Many twentieth-century radicals searching for a more generous reading of the lumpenproletariat drew from *The Wretched of the Earth* by Frantz Fanon. In part of his chapter "Spontaneity: Its Strength and Weakness," Fanon moved

beyond the limitations of Marxist dogma and explored the potential of
the lumpen in the colonized world:

> It is within this mass of humanity, this people of the shanty towns, at
> the core of the *lumpenproletariat,* that the rebellion will find its urban
> spearhead. For the *lumpenproletariat,* that horde of starving men, up-
> rooted from their tribe and from their clan, constitutes one of the most
> spontaneous and the most radically revolutionary forces of a colonized
> people. [. . .] The constitution of a *lumpenproletariat* is a phenomenon
> which obeys its own logic, and neither the brimming activity of the
> missionaries nor the decrees of the central government can check its
> growth. This *lumpenproletariat* is like a horde of rats; you may kick
> them and throw stones at them, but despite your efforts they'll go on
> gnawing at the roots of the tree. [. . .] The *lumpenproletariat,* once it is
> constituted, brings all its forces to endanger the "security" of the town,
> and is the sign of the irrevocable decay, the gangrene ever present at
> the heart of colonial domination.[35]

Although Fanon's words inhere the lumpenproletariat with revolutionary agency, it might be better to do away with the lumpen prefix
altogether.[36] The moralistic weight and sociological neatness of the category hinders the possibility of understanding the dynamic position of
the so-called lumpenproletariat within capitalist relations.[37] By framing the lumpen in terms of their dubious moral-cum-political character, vanguardists and the intelligentsia lock them into an underclass
within the working class, as if the working class did not also carry the
possibility of mercurial political convictions.

The lumpen prefix, then, should be understood as a way to establish difference. It separates the ideal type of revolutionary from the
undesirable, and this separation is often imbued with racism and an
allegiance to a revolutionary formula based on a problematic politics
of representation.[38] In July 2021, Juan David Quiñones, an activist in his
twenties from a majority black neighborhood in eastern Cali, told me:

> Above all, that term "lumpen" is very pejorative to me because they
> circumscribe it to blackness. It's as if—for people on the left—lumpen/

eastern Cali/black are the same. So I even feel that they are using the narrative and discourse of the elite in Cali. They are reproducing it in one way or another, but they are reproducing it at our expense.

By linking the racist trope of lumpen terminology on the left to racist elite discourses, Quiñones crucially opened up space to understand how these divergent ideologies coalesce around the racialization of so-called bad protesters.[39]

Throughout the uprising, it was common to hear mainstream pundits talk about the shadowy forces presumably behind the rebellion. By resurrecting the Cold War threat of internal enemies and outside agitators, they pointed the finger at gangs, guerrilla groups, drug traffickers, and vandals. It seemed impossible for them to imagine—at least publicly—that the people holding down the resistance points might be the domestic worker in their home, their child's schoolteacher, or a nurse from their health clinic. The ignorant masses must have been duped by outsiders.

The not-so-sub-text of their anxiety built on fears of a vengeful and racialized other. In this context, the arrival of the primarily indigenous Minga in Cali on May 1 triggered a wave of racist hysteria among the region's elites, colloquially known as the *gente de bien* (a sardonic and, depending on the person, presumptuous wordplay of "good people" and "rich people"). Beginning in the early 2000s, the indigenous organizations of southwestern Colombia along with their allies from black and peasant social movements organized Mingas of Social and Communitarian Resistance (Mingas de Resistencia Social y Comunitaria), mobilizations based on the indigenous concept of collective labor.[40] The Mingas with a capital *M* became a crucial strategy for rejecting neoliberalism and the destruction of the commons, and the Mingas earned their reputation as an instantly recognizable symbol of resistance in Colombia.[41] Even so, some of my interlocutors understood the Mingas' arrival in Cali as a calculated attempt by the indigenous organizations in Cauca to gain an upper hand in negotiations with the government by undercutting the bargaining power of the CNP's strike committee in Bogotá.[42]

The Minga's reception at the resistance points, however, was glowing. The front liners welcomed them with open arms and quickly incorporated the Indigenous Guard into the violent clashes with police.

The potential of this nascent intercommunal solidarity across regional, organizational, and racial lines amplified elite fears about the uprising.[43] In May, *gente de bien* were caught on camera shooting at the participants in the Minga alongside police officers in a wealthy neighborhood.[44] The videos demonstrated the enduring strength of paramilitarism and the lengths to which *gente de bien* would go to preserve their version of law and order. During the following weeks, the elites scrambled to use all the tools at their disposal to undermine the protests in Cali: official bans on interdepartmental travel aimed at preventing indigenous people from coming to Cali, pledges to fund development projects in impoverished neighborhoods, propaganda campaigns stigmatizing the protests, and the blunt force of the state's (para)military apparatus.

Even so, people remained undeterred and continued to struggle. They said, "Perdimos tanto que hasta perdimos el miedo" (We lost so much that we even lost our fear). This popular response to state violence opened up a world of possibilities. Outside the heavy metal bar, William knew why the *ñeros* participated in the uprising. He said, "Me hace sentir importante en la vida" (It makes me feel important in life).

The front liners—from whatever position they inhabited in society—struggled to take back the dignity that was denied to them. By embracing the idea that "Tod@s Somos Primera Linea," they shirked the lumpen prefix and embraced their common relation to capital and the state as *(compa)ñeros* in struggle (figure 4.3). Beyond resurrecting a squabble over Marxist terminology, they challenged a logic that sought to deny agency to the most marginalized people in society. In doing so, they overflowed the constraints typically ascribed to them.[45] Still, the impediments to liberation did not magically disappear because of the insurgent energy budding in the uprising.[46]

FIGURE 4.3

We Are All Front Liners (photo by author, July 2021)

"500 YEARS STRUGGLING ON THE FRONT LINE"

Vicenta Moreno of the Casa Cultural Chontaduro (Chontaduro Cultural House)—a black cultural center in the Aguablanca neighborhood of eastern Cali—spoke to a crowd of mostly black women after meeting with the Inter-American Human Rights Commission of the Organization of American States in the midst of the rebellion in June 2021: "All of the youth from our neighborhoods are on the Front Line of Death (la Primera Línea de la Muerte). They always have been and even more so now that our territories have been stigmatized because it is said that only vandalism occurs there."[47] Moreno and her friends at Chontaduro challenged the routinization of anti-black violence in the city, but their protests were often ignored by their white-mestizo counterparts. Frustrated by the disavowal of anti-black state violence, Moreno decried how murdered black youth were understood as the "*muertos que merecen morir*" (the dead who deserve to die), while others were considered "*muertos políticos*" (political deaths).⁴⁸ Why were some of the murders that occurred during the uprising considered political, while others were not? What was at stake in reducing some deaths to common crime (*delincuencia común*), especially when those deaths occurred in predominantly black communities?

Throughout the course of the uprising, the contributions of black people to the struggle and anti-black violence were sidelined in the dominant portrayals of the events in Cali.⁴⁹ Many black activists whom I spoke with pointed out the following contradiction: the longest urban rebellion in Colombian history took shape in the city with one of the largest black populations in Latin America, but black participation and critiques of racism during the uprising seemed to be erased from the narrative of resistance. Who, then, was included and excluded from the affirmation that "we are all front liners!"?

In *¡Venceremos? The Erotics of Black Self-Making in Cuba*, Jafari Allen plays with the punctuation of another slogan—"¡Venceremos!" (We Shall Overcome!)—to examine the enduring forms of racism and heteropatriarchy in revolutionary Cuba. Allen's simultaneous questioning and affirming of the slogan helps us reflect on the challenges and possibilities that emerged in Cali. Concrete expressions of racism throughout the uprising confirmed the enduring influence of what Aníbal Quijano called the "coloniality of power," or the process whereby racism, patriarchy, and other forms of colonial oppression continued in contemporary power relations.⁵⁰ Although the rebellion in Cali pushed against this form of power in important ways, it was not free from it.

One black activist whom I spoke with preferred to remain anonymous. Her frustration with the racist politicking at the resistance points was palpable:

> How many of the lives lost during the strike were of black bodies? Because they were never visibilized. Nor were they visible as spokespeople at the resistance points either. In Puerto Resistencia, which had a large

black presence, black folks were never up front as spokespeople making demands or dialoguing with institutions. They were never there. It was always white or mestizo people up front taking over and making decisions in the spaces of power. Meanwhile, we black people are instrumentalized or—as always—end up in the most fatal positions risking our lives so that they can continue moving forward with their struggle.

According to her, these tensions were especially marked in the relationship between the predominantly black resistance point of AfroResistencia (Afro-Resistance) and the Cali Resistance Union (Unión de Resistencia Cali, URC). The URC was supposed to serve as a coalition of spokespeople from the resistance points throughout the city, but some black activists were criticized as opportunists by members of the URC when they asserted leadership roles.[51]

These dynamics, however, were not limited to debates about formal representation of the resistance points at the URC. Esther Ojulari, who coauthored a report with Harrinson Cuero Campaz, "Ethno-Racial Analysis of Excessive Use of Force by State Agents in Cali," told me about one of her experiences presenting the report at a meeting in Cali in June 2021. Their report revealed the racial identities of the people subjected to state violence during the uprising because the state did not officially keep race-specific data. Ojulari and Cuero found that black people and black communities were "disproportionately" attacked by police and other agents of the state.[52] The report concluded with the following warning: "This is an urgent situation [that], if necessary measures are not taken, runs the risk of becoming a genocide."[53] After Ojulari's presentation at the meeting, a mestiza woman from a victims' organization confronted her and criticized her for being divisive by bringing up anti-black violence in a moment when people were coming together. The mestiza woman told Ojulari, "We are all human and we all suffer the same!"

For some black activists, this racism masquerading as colorblindness was expressed in the most enduring symbol of the uprising in Cali: the *Resiste* statue. On June 13, 2021, thousands of people gathered to celebrate the inauguration of a twelve-meter fist in the middle of the Puerto Resistencia resistance point. The fist held a plaque with the word "RESIST" painted in the colors of the Colombian flag, and shields commemorating the martyrs of the front line adorned the base of the statue (figure 4.4). In his June 2021 article for the Mexican newspaper *La Jornada,* the Uruguayan political theorist Raúl Zibechi celebrated *Resiste* as an "antimonument":

> It was very different and even antagonistic to the monuments built by the colonial and patriarchal culture of the dominant class. It was a collective, communitarian, and anonymous creation made by those from below for those from below. Therefore, while monuments have a sculptor that receives benefits, *Resiste* was built by the people and is dedicated to the people. Meanwhile, the monuments from above are dedicated to white men, mostly violent and genocidal soldiers that receive the pathetic name of "heroes." [. . .] The *Resiste* antimonument showed all of the colors of life in contrast to the weak uniformity of the monuments from above.[54]

FIGURE 4.4

The *Resiste* monument in Puerto Resistencia (photo by author, July 2021)

The fanfare around *Resiste* overshadowed criticism regarding the original color of the fist in a city with such a large black population. Instead of interpreting it as an antimonument, some of my friends from black social movements saw *"ese puño blanco"* (that white fist; see figure 4.4) as evidence of racism on the left.[55]

Taken together, these experiences revealed the limits of inclusion in the slogan "We Are All Front Liners!" In another article, "Colombia: 500 Years Struggling on the Front Line in Defense of Human Dignity," Cuero Campaz and Ojulari traced the importance of black resistance throughout Colombian history. In the conclusion, they focused on Simon Bolívar, the hero of Colombia's wars for independence from Spain, and his deeply problematic relationship with the participation of black soldiers in his ranks. For them, the living legacy of his "genocidal pretensions" demonstrated the following:

> The history of independence and the current war teaches us that the representatives of the colonial economic project, the right wing, and the elite are not the only ones that utilize excluded people as cannon fodder in their "liberation" struggles—so do many of those that say they struggle for the freedom of the people and the rights of the excluded.[56]

Although the uprising created the conditions to think about and create new possibilities, it still confronted the reality of Colombia's deeply embedded racial hierarchies.

MEDIOS LIBRES

By the end of July 2021, the plaza at the foot of the monument in Puerto Resistencia had already become a place to sell handicrafts commemorating the revolt and the site of intense struggles to defend the legacy of the uprising.[57] It was not long before people on social media started floating the idea of forming a political party named after the *primera línea*. With the 2022 elections looming, political party operatives attempted to capitalize on the uprising at the ballot box, but they were not the only ones. The gangs also took advantage of the moment to strengthen their position, and the mainstream media milked it for sensationalist stories.

The multiple interests in exploiting the uprising made it difficult for the resistance points to persevere in their struggles for self-determination.[58]

My friend René Nariño was disappointed in the outcome of the uprising after actively participating in the Dignity Hill resistance point. We met at the FARC's fifty-third anniversary celebration in Cauca shortly after he was released from prison in 2017 thanks to the Peace Accords. René eventually made his home in Cali and continued to engage in political organizing with other ex-combatants who no longer identified with the FARC's political party. Reflecting on his experiences at the Dignity Hill resistance point, he told me, "For a moment, we felt as though we were in Chile, but then we remembered that we are in Colombia, *hermano* [brother]." With the Constitutional Assembly on the horizon after Chile's 2019–2020 uprising, René initially thought the uprising in Colombia might be an opportunity to build an alternative to the reigning political system. However, for him, the adventurist core of the *primera línea* ended up doing the bidding of the ruling class by privileging violent confrontations with the police at the expense of building a political base for transformation. He insisted that I not romanticize the *primera línea*.[59]

On July 20, René sent me the location where the Olla Rodante (a mobile communitarian kitchen) was cooking rice and fish left over from the ANP.[60] People had blocked traffic in the area around Dignity Hill to celebrate the uprising on Colombia's Independence Day. On my way to see René, I heard some loud pops in the distance. Two elderly women at the demonstration warned me that the confrontations ahead of us were getting more intense and that I needed to be careful. Just as I caught a glimpse of René serving food, a flood of people ran toward me after an explosion. Instead of continuing toward the Olla Rodante, I turned around and joined the crowd running away from the police. We looked for ways to break off from the Quinta, the main avenue near Dignity Hill. At first, I went to the left, but some guy saw me with a camera and warned me that it was safer to go in a different direction. I returned to the Quinta, where the front liners were setting up for a confrontation with the police about sixty meters ahead. I tried to cross to the other side of the street and saw the Anti-disturbance Mobile Squad (ESMAD) tanks and cops.

FIGURE 4.5

Confrontations with the state on July 20, 2021 (photo by author, July 2021)

The ESMAD shot tear gas at us, and I was scared that they would use live ammunition. I ran up a side street toward the neighborhood of San Antonio and stumbled to the ground. Feeling clumsy and the need for more agility, I put away my camera (see figure 4.5 for my last photo from the July 20 confrontations on the Quinta). The rhythms of the riot determined the pace of the crowd. The ESMAD would shoot tear gas at a crowd assembling on the Quinta, and people would disperse onto the side streets. After the smoke cleared enough, we would go back to the Quinta to hold space. The unspoken pact in the movement of the people going back and forth onto the street evinced a refusal to be bullied by the state.

The demonstrations around the city were festive until the police showed up. I had spent much of the day until that point covering the activities at Puerto Resistencia for *Colombia Reports* (an independent English-language news outlet), and it felt more like a block party than a riot. People were sharing food, playing music, and hanging out with friends. During the confrontations on the Quinta, I thought back to a

conversation with someone from the URC about the discreet agreements that they tried to reach with the mayor's office in anticipation
of the July 20 demonstrations, whereby the URC had basically tried to
push the mayor to keep the police out of the way of the gatherings to
avoid unnecessary conflict. Because of that conversation, I thought
that maybe the ESMAD would use restraint to avoid a major alterca-
tion. They did not, and neither did the front liners.

The fighting intensified, as did the tear gas. At one point, it felt as if
the ESMAD was moving down the Quinta with more force. I sprinted
up another side street, where I encountered a front liner who seemed to
have just escaped a beating. I asked him what happened, and—gasping
for breath—he told me that the ESMAD shot a tear gas canister at his
chest, but thankfully, his backpack was on his chest, which softened
the blow. He lifted his shirt to show me the marks from the impact
caused by the tear gas canister.

As I turned the corner onto the next block, I saw a lot of people
coughing. A neighbor (an elderly white man) intentionally left his hose
running outside his house. Several people came to the entrance of his
home and rinsed their eyes and faces. Others pleaded for milk to flush
the tear gas because they believed that milk worked better than water.
On the Quinta, the protests escalated: people set things on fire, front
liners broke slabs of concrete sidewalks into smaller pieces that were
easier to throw at cops, small bands played live music to keep up the
spirit of the crowd, and—perhaps most bizarre of all—we were close
enough to the Dignity Hill resistance point to hear a heavy metal ren-
dition of a Silvio Rodríguez song as the ESMAD fired tear gas and other
projectiles at the crowd.

It would be wrong to interpret the crowd as fearful or timid about
confronting the cops. It would also be wrong to characterize it as a
horde of angry young men—the participants represented a diversity of
ages, races, and genders. In addition to breaking up the concrete and
sharing the hose, other tactics of revolt became clear. For instance, I
was somewhat puzzled by how and why motorcycles could get so close
to the front lines until I saw them stop at a relatively safe distance
and allow a front liner to syphon gasoline into a beer bottle to make

a Molotov cocktail to throw at the ESMAD. After nearly three months of protest, some of the front liners had learned to shape-shift into resourceful urban insurrectionary groups.

I would guess that the ESMAD, too, learned their own lessons from facing off with the crowds. That day, they shot something that sounded like live ammunition that sent everyone running. Although I still haven't heard about any deaths resulting from the confrontations on July 20, there were plenty of injuries. After one of those rounds from the ESMAD that sounded like gunfire, several people around me ran scared, and I joined them. I did not want to risk getting hit by live ammunition. Still, many people stayed despite the state's disregard for restraint. Eventually, the barricade made it to my doorstep, and I saw bloodied people get carried off in an ambulance from my friend's apartment a few blocks from the Dignity Hill resistance point. Later that night, one of the windows in the apartment was smashed by a rock hurled during the confrontations between the front liners and the police (figure 4.6). Many of the neighbors on the block congregated on

FIGURE 4.6

ESMAD firing at front liners during a confrontation on July 20, 2021 (photo by author, July 2021)

the rooftops to catch their breath and get a break from the clouds of tear gas pouring into their homes.

The riot on July 20 was one of the last gasps of the 2021 uprising in Cali. The experience was crucial for me because it revealed the forms of solidarity that can emerge when confronting state violence. No textbook, activist handbook, or theoretical treatise could have prepared me for navigating the interdependence, fear, and courage that I felt that afternoon. In those moments, I understood the emancipatory potential of affirming "Tod@s somos primera línea!" even as I witnessed how quickly it broke down outside that space and time. In this sense, the uprising created what the CrimethInc Ex-Workers' Collective calls "spaces of encounter" or what the Situationist International might have called "situations."[61] These shared moments of revolt disrupt capitalist alienation and imbue people with self-determination by bringing them together under intensely immediate conditions. The uprising in Cali provided opportunities for people to meet one another and build relationships that at times exceeded the constraints of capitalist modernity and the divisions that separate us—albeit with major setbacks, such as those examined in this chapter.

In tandem with the onset of the uprising, an alternative media collective named Medios Libres began publishing firsthand updates that circulated through their Telegram channel and online. Their updates challenged the perspectives emanating from Colombia's conservative mainstream media outlets and provided a glimpse into the insurgent energy of the uprising. In "Dignified Rebellion and Social Organization," they affirmed, "The Colombian people are tired of not being heard, tired of futile marches that arrive at the great centers of power and end up in the manipulative hands of powerbrokers who negotiate the nonnegotiable."[62] By charting out a space for transgressive and revolutionary politics, Medios Libres expressed the multiple meanings of their name (figure 4.7).

Medios Libres has at least two translations or interpretations in my estimation. The first—Free Media—reflects a familiar concept among independent media platforms like *Colombia Reports* that provide an alternative to the corporate-controlled media conglomerates.

FIGURE 4.7

Mural with the words "autonomy," "organization," and "mutual aid" at the Puerto Resistencia Popular Library (photo by author, July 2021)

The second—and the most relevant one for these preliminary notes—is Free Means. Instead of the ends justifying the means, freeing the means of struggle reflects an openness to possibility and liberation through prefigurative politics. It is a reflection of how the ends—that is, the transformations we seek—will become legible only through struggle and are contingent on the forms of struggle that take shape. Medios Libres' coverage of the uprising made space for understanding how militant tactics (e.g., barricades, street fighting, looting) coalesced with the mutual aid efforts of communitarian kitchens, libraries, health clinics, and so on. For example, one flyer that I saw at an *olla comunitaria* (communitarian kitchen) in Cali was titled "Beneath the Cement, the Earth!" (¡Bajo el Cemento la Tierra!), encouraging militants to turn the terrain of rebellion into a site of liberation.[63] According to this logic, the cement could be transfigured into a weapon against alienation, capitalist modernity, and the destruction of the planet. The participants in the Cali rebellion unearthed the potential for freedom here and now with the means accessible to them: the earth itself. Somewhat surprisingly, the "Beneath the Cement, the Earth" flyer appeared at an *olla comunitaria* in a quiet residential area that felt more like a tranquil farmers' market, not at the barricades on the front lines of a rebellion against state violence. Medios Libres—like the authors of the flyer and the aspiration implicit in affirming "Tod@s Somos Primera Línea"—sought to break with the rule of law and respectability politics that upholds the state and capitalist relations.

Yet the revolt did not transform into a proliferation of resistance points that overturned the system. As the rebellion moved beyond the one-month mark, several of the blockades around the resistance points faltered. People needed to attend to their homes, and the threat of state violence materialized in the murder of dozens of demonstrators and the arrest of many more. The solidarity networks that emerged around the resistance points during the uprising provided essential needs for people, but they weren't enough to withstand the violence. Government officials also initiated a plethora of disarticulated negotiations at the local level in a well-worn strategy to pacify expressions of resistance.[64] As a result, some leaders and collectives bought into the system—probably hoping to achieve some kind of concession after all of the effort. Some sought power by leaning into racism and patriarchy.

Others did not.

The front liners of the rebellion—from whatever position they inhabited in society—did just that: rebel. They forged unexpected relationships and created space for unanticipated forms of socialization beyond the state and capital, and—as a result—the legacy of the 2021 uprising is still up for debate.[65] As of 2024, the 2021 uprising remained widely attributed with creating the conditions for the election of Colombia's first "progressive" government.[66] I suggest that the uprising did more than this. As the longest uprising on record, it also exposed a "general crisis of the State" by revealing the cracks in ruling-class hegemony and its politics of representation more broadly.[67] This crisis was not limited to the conservative or reactionary sectors of Colombian society—it also included significant sectors of the left that attempted to dismiss or contain the groundswell of struggle for popular power by deploying the worn and often racist trope of the lumpen and other analogous terms. Yet as the authors of *Policing the Crisis* succinctly argue, "You cannot resolve a social contradiction by abolishing the label that has been attached to it."[68] In this case, the social contradiction relates to the enduring power of racism and the state to undermine the potential of struggles for liberation. Nevertheless, the ugliness of the uprising's limitations reflected the weight of Colombia's colonial past and present more than some sort of ineluctable future. That can be addressed only by struggle, and the fact of the uprising demonstrates that the potential for transformation remains open.

CONCLUSION
THE DOING OF DISSIDENCE

I often ask myself:
Why are we forgotten
if legally we have rights,
and we are all Colombian women?
Who mourns our lives?
Who mourns our people?
Who mourns our dead women?
Who is hurt?
—Song composed by Elena Hinestroza of the Chontaduro
Cultural House[1]

———

We indigenous people are everywhere in the territory. If you're listening
to us, I greet all of you. I invite you to defend the territory, the cabildos,
our children, and our language because hard times are coming, and they
are surveilling us to see who speaks up so that they can silence that person.
They have already decided all of this.
If you're listening, I invite you to defend the territory.
—Fredy Campo Bomba, June 2018, Indigenous Reservation of Pioyá[2]

They will kill us, but thousands will be born.
—Banner at Javier Oteca's funeral[3]

MINGAS HACIA ADENTRO

"The community must act! We must fulfill the mandates of the community!" Sandra Liliana Peña Chocué implored the people of the Laguna Siberia Indigenous Reservation in Sa'th Tama Kiwe at a meeting in early 2021.[4] As governor of the *resguardo*, she understood the dangers of opposing the powerful drug traffickers, many of whom were coca-growing settlers from other parts of the country.[5] However, the risk of allowing them and their coca crops to stay was greater, and the community had collectively decided to confront them. A man at the meeting warned her that taking action would have "consequences." She persevered despite the threats that ensued. According to one of her friends, Peña Chocué was "very tough, but alone" (*muy berraca pero sola*). Her friend was not referring to her personal life. Peña Chocué's solitude expressed itself politically because she struggled for an uncompromising form of autonomy that placed her at odds with the state, drug traffickers, and even some indigenous organizations.

On March 17, 2021, her community organized what has become known as a *minga hacia adentro* (inward *minga*) in the community of La Isla. The word *minga* typically refers to a form of collective labor in the Andes. This shorthand definition, however, falls short of evoking the depth and potential of a *minga*. According to Manuel Rozental of Pueblos en Camino:

> It is collective labor for a common purpose. The *Mingas* do not have owners. They belong to the collectives that participate in them. Their remuneration is the completed objective and, above all, sharing in community. The *Minga* is a party, an opportunity to share, exchange, consolidate community ties, weave society. The *Minga* is a custom and a miracle, a tradition and a unique and unrepeatable event. The

strength of the people is multiplied. What appears impossible in the eyes of each individual becomes reality through collective work.[6]

In the last twenty years, *Mingas* became synonymous with large-scale indigenous-led demonstrations from Cauca that tended to culminate in high-stakes negotiations with the government. The *mingas hacia adentro*, however, are not oriented toward negotiations with the state. They are focused on creating the conditions for autonomy and self-determination inside communities by taking action within the territory.[7] Crucially, they embody a form of self-criticism and communal reflection that expresses itself in collective action.

In La Isla, this meant pulling together some forty members of the Indigenous Guard from twelve of the twenty-seven communities in the reservation to participate in a self-organized coca eradication effort. Almost as soon as they arrived in La Isla they heard gunshots. Notwithstanding the potential for retaliation, the *minga hacia adentro* uprooted six hectares of coca and burned down coca seedbeds. Peña Chocué unapologetically participated in the activities instead of watching from afar.

As expected, the owners of the coca crops and seedbeds were furious. Even with the uptick in threats against her, Peña Chocué remained in the territory and continued organizing. She expressed her frustration with the leadership of other indigenous communities and regional indigenous organizations: "You talk about unity, but you did not arrive [to join us]." Despite the lack of support from the other indigenous organizations, the community began preparing a second *minga hacia adentro* in the community of Caimito.

On April 20—eight days before the beginning of the 2021 National Strike—Sandra Liliana Peña Chocué was murdered before she could participate in another community-based effort to assert autonomy. Somewhat lost amid the turmoil triggered by the countrywide rebellion that started on April 28, Peña Chocué's murder reverberated throughout Cauca. The Regional Indigenous Council of Cauca subsequently called for a *minga hacia adentro* to investigate and prosecute the perpetrators of her murder through the indigenous judicial system.

With the quickly escalating situation in Cali, however, the *minga hacia adentro* transformed into a *minga hacia afuera* (outward *minga*).

In a pivotal expression of solidarity, the indigenous movement from Cauca brought hundreds of people in *chivas* (the colorful open-air buses that transport people and goods throughout the hills and mountains of northern Cauca) to the budding rebellion in Cali. Based on their long history of resistance and mobilized by righteous indignation stemming from Peña Chocué's murder, the indigenous movement provided crucial support to the resistance points in Cali in terms of strategy, tactical know-how, and bodies on the ground. Years later, the protagonists at the resistance points throughout Cali still fondly remembered the *Minga*'s vital role in breathing life into the process.

One of the members of the Indigenous Guard that joined the front liners at the Resistencia Luna resistance point in Cali in May 2021 was deeply familiar with Peña Chocué's struggle. In the original version of this manuscript, I intended to preserve his anonymity out of concern for his safety. I met with him—Fredy Campo Bomba—at my friends' home in Cauca in July 2022 while his daughter skated around us in pink rollerblades. My friends introduced us because I was trying to learn more about Peña Chocué's life and the circumstances surrounding her murder. He was part of the community-led effort to investigate and capture those responsible for Peña Chocué's murder. Over the course of a couple days, Campo Bomba generously shared his reflections on the *mingas hacia adentro*, Peña Chocué's life, and his experiences during the 2021 uprising in Cali. We also celebrated his daughter's birthday alongside family and friends. Almost exactly one year later—on July 26, 2023—Fredy Campo Bomba was murdered in front of his wife and children at the age of thirty-five.

Despite the numerous threats against him during his short life, Fredy Campo Bomba continued to struggle. He reflected the resolute perseverance of his community of Pioya, which was known to some as the heart of the Nasa peoples' resistance. The people of his community in Sa'th Tama Kiwe mandated that they would not permit traditional political parties, armed groups, or drug trafficking within their territory. In Nasa Yuwe, they called these phenomena *Wee Wala*, or the "'the big sickness,' which comes from outside and sickens, confuses, dirties, kills, and threatens our destruction."[8] Like Sandra, like Fredy, like so many others, they affirmed, "We cannot be complicit."

AUTONOMY AS A FORM OF LIFE

Sandra Liliana Peña Chocué and Fredy Campo Bomba did not find peace in an agreement signed by warring parties. They were killed because they refused to be enclosed by the colonial capitalist project that endures. Sandra and Fredy put into practice the words of Cristina Bautista Taquinás, yet another indigenous governor from Cauca murdered in 2019 for confronting the insidious effects of the drug trade in her community: "If we shut up they kill us. If we speak out, they still do. So, let's speak out!" This tragically prescient quote became a slogan for social movements and activists throughout Colombia after she was killed. I remember seeing a portrait of Cristina alongside those words on a large banner hung from the stage at a music festival that I attended at the Puerto Resistencia resistance point in July 2021. In a way, her quote and the Indigenous Guard, along with the red and green colors of Cauca's indigenous movement, came to represent the moral value of dignified martyrdom for many Colombians desiring change during the uprising (figure C.1).

Time and again my friends and comrades in black and indigenous organizations have insisted that they do not want more martyrs. They want freedom. In *Crack Capitalism*, John Holloway argues, "The key to our emancipation, the key to becoming fully human is simple: refuse, disobey. *Resolve to serve no more, and you are at once freed. Nothing more difficult*, however."[9] Difficult indeed, particularly under the conditions of genocidal state formation. Black and indigenous activists in Colombia have long denounced how the violence facing their communities amounts to "ethnocide," but that is not the end point of their praxis.

Communities in Colombia and throughout Abiayala continue to struggle for life, autonomy, and self-determination not just despite existential threats but also because of them.[10] A moment shared with people in struggle—even amid tragedy—points to actually existing life.

FIGURE C.1

Entrance to the Toez Indigenous Reservation (photo by author,
January 2017)

It also reveals the potential of and need for liberation beyond the colonial-capitalist state. In an effort to name this "activity that is self-deter-
mined or at least pushes towards self-determination," Holloway lands
on *doing*. To do so, he distinguishes between "two antagonistic types of
doing": one associated with the compulsion to work under capitalism
and another enacted by our desire for liberation.[11] This second form of
doing becomes the site for breaking with the rule of state and capital
in our lives. By emphasizing activity, this approach to emancipation
hinges on praxis—that is, the productive tension between theory and
struggle.

The doing of dissidence, then, is the practice of autonomy. Unmoored from a revolutionary framework, the term autonomy risks
becoming a catch-all concept that could just as easily include the aspirations of proponents of rugged individualism and right-wing liber-
tarianism. That is clearly not the perspective of this book. For critics
of autonomy from the left, such as the former FARC guerrilla quoted in

chapter 1, autonomy is a "minority trap" devoid of transformative potential beyond the "reduced space" of an indigenous reservation or an Afro-Colombian community council because it undermines the potential of building universal class consciousness. Setting aside the problems with the FARC's approach to vanguardism that were addressed in chapter 1, the so-called minority trap is undoubtedly a risk for struggles that delimit autonomy to a narrowly legalistic framework or what the Çxhab Wala Kiwe Association of Indigenous Cabildos of Northern Cauca called "authorized autonomy."[12] Under neoliberal multiculturalism, autonomy has largely become understood as a right that can be protected by the state. There are a whole host of laws in Colombia and elsewhere that define the legal parameters for so-called autonomy and create a bureaucracy for upholding them, thus paving the way for what Modibo Kadalie calls "state creep."[13] But state-centric approaches to autonomy can hardly be called autonomy at all. Instead of presenting a challenge to the system, these forms of authorized autonomy reify it and facilitate the expansion of capitalist relations and state formation.

While autonomous struggles may surface in a reduced space—be it an ephemeral encounter behind a barricade or a planned meeting in a legally recognized collective territory—that does not encapsulate their scope. If capital—and the state as its agent—must expand through overlapping processes of colonization and accumulation, then autonomy in a reduced space is not viable because the space is always subject to enclosure.[14] To be realized, autonomous struggles must confront the alienating expressions of coloniality through what the Zapatistas succinctly manifest as "one no, many yeses" in their unequivocal rejection of capitalism and simultaneous solidarity with struggles that share this repudiation. It is thus impossible for autonomous struggles to remain confined to a reduced space in the political economy of colonial capitalism. The major limitation to the prevailing critique of autonomy from the left is that it insists on seeing autonomy from the perspective of a state: autonomy, according to this logic, must be made legible through the practices of sovereign states such as borders, policing, exclusion, and bureaucracy (figure C.2).

FIGURE C.2

"Do you see me? Do I see you?" at the Loma de la Dignidad resistance point (photo by author, July 2021)

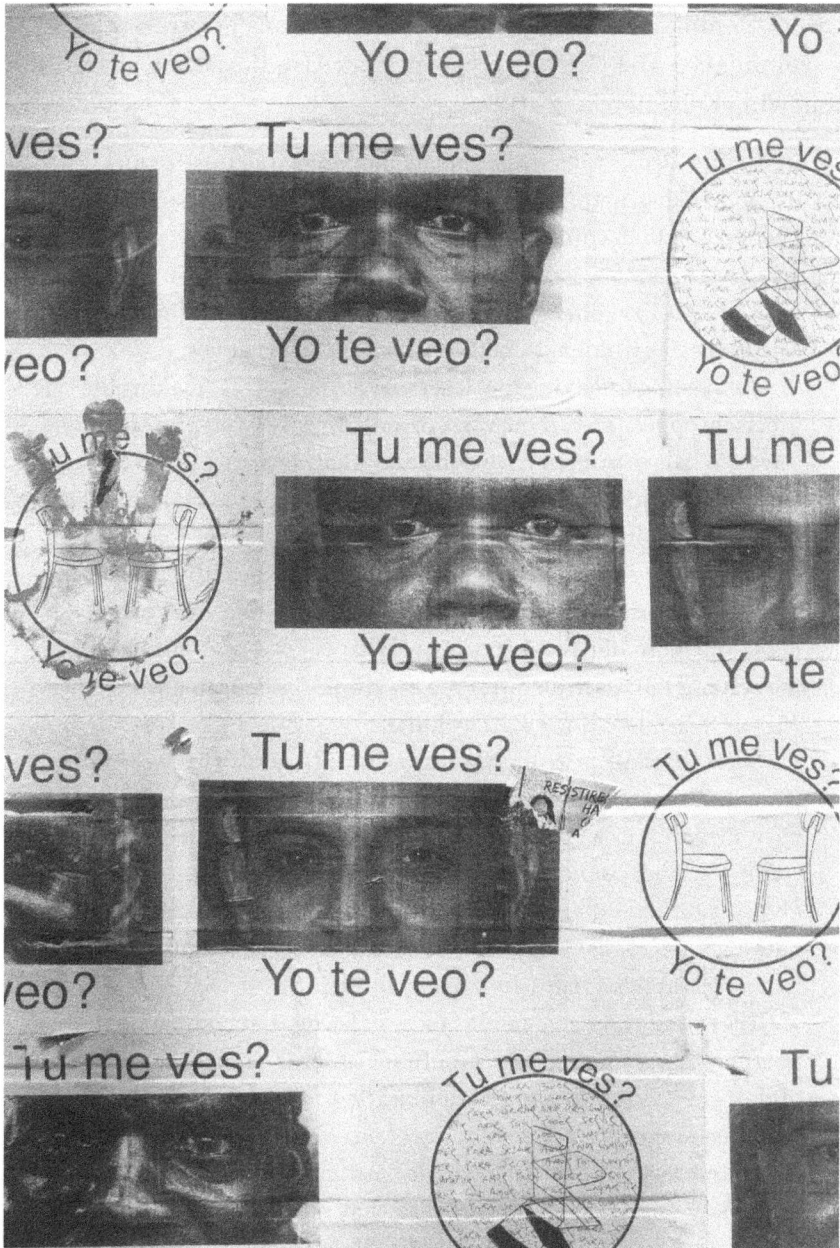

Instead of understanding autonomy as the formation of ministates, the transgressive potential of the concept is better understood as a form of life expressed in everyday practice.[15] At the 2016 International Forum on Feminicides of Ethnic and Racialized Groups in Buenaventura (Colombia), Elba Mercedes Palacios Córdoba of Otras Negras . . . y ¡Feministas! and Colectivo Sentipensar Afrodiaspórico shared the following reflection:

> Resistance, for us, Black and Indigenous women in this country, and for women in general, is an everyday issue. It is not an issue of "today I get up and I am going to resist," or "today I am going to resist until 3:30," or "tomorrow I am going to start resisting at nine in the morning." No. It is like different issues present themselves all the time that orient the task of doing something, creating alternatives.
>
> Re-existing is making life, it is everydayness. This "making life" is precisely opposite to all the ways of making death that present themselves. What we women have done and what we are called to do each day is to *make life*. First, to construct ourselves daily, to make our lives have meaning in a society that sees us as nonhuman, as objects. Also, that every day shows us models of the good, the beautiful, the desirable, and we are increasingly distant from it. When we try to make ourselves more like those models of what is good or desirable, what the systems tells us to imitate, then we are objectified, and we distance ourselves from *making life*. They kill us.
>
> Since they kill us in many ways (as Vicenta says), what we, coming from different spheres, do every day is *make life*. We make our lives have meaning in a society that racializes us, in a society that constantly reminds us that we are Black women, that uses cultural norms and institutional means to impoverish our lives. [. . .] Rather than naming the ways the capitalist world system seeks to impoverish us, it must be said that there are ways of re-existing.
>
> There are two basic modes of re-existing that complement one another for us, coming from different localities, from different ways of doing. The first is understanding the process that oppresses us and this implies a detailed reading of our history, of where we come from, and why your everyday life is so difficult. [. . .] The other part, besides understanding the process that oppresses us in multiple

ways, is organizing modes of resistance that are oriented toward looking for new spheres. This process has always been negated by objectification and the historical dehumanization of Black women in this country.

Therefore, looking for other spheres of making life, we search, organizing ourselves, putting in practice all of those historically negated practices. We show ourselves, and we surprise ourselves with all that we are able to do. What we have experienced gives us strength to keep doing other necessary tasks and to keep advancing in re-existence; to keep understanding why the everyday pushes us forward in an unstoppable process. Since the so-called colonial era in Colombia, from the subjugation of slavery, we have been developing all types of capacities that have not been studied, have still not been recognized, and part of the task of resistance is to recognize all the achievements that have been made historically in order to be here today and to exist as a people. We are a people that resists and that names itself in ways that are different from how they have named us. We want to participate like we are here: resisting in our everyday lives.[16]

Re-existir, or to re-exist, is to create the conditions for autonomy. As Palacios Córdoba suggests, this must be rooted in the doings of everyday life.

In 2022, Vilma Almendra Quiguanás of Pueblos en Camino shared a saying with me that Kurdish women shared with her: "As autonomies advance, the state retreats." For a moment during the 2021 rebellion in Cali, for example, this seemed to be the case. The retreat of the state did not just relate to the realm of military confrontation in the material world. It was also a retreat of the state that inhabits us (i.e., the cop in our heads). In this sense, struggles for autonomy challenge forms of alienation and respectability politics by enacting the potential to do what some black communities in Colombia call *sentipensar* (feeling-thinking).[17] This embodied praxis of autonomy is rooted in a primordial connection with the earth, our ancestors, and future generations.[18] Autonomous struggles exist—or better yet, re-exist—in an ecology of resistance against and beyond capital and the state. From the formation of resistance points during the uprising in Cali to the inward *mingas* in Cauca, people in struggle recognize the centrality of this interconnectedness in their visions of autonomy, even if they appear to be captured at each turn.

ACKNOWLEDGMENTS

"THE SPIRIT OF THE COMMUNITY" referred to in the closing words of the preface grounds the ideas that pass through this book. From the beautiful, shared moments to the bitter disagreements, I am deeply grateful for all the individuals and collectives in Colombia that opened their doors and hearts to me over the years. Writing acknowledgments is a frustratingly incomplete endeavor, primarily because I cannot in good conscience name so many of the people who made this work possible because of the risks that they continue to endure. I dedicate this book to all of them and particularly the people of the pseudonymous Afro-Colombian Community Council of Nuevo Amanecer, whose hospitality and care I will not forget.

This book benefited tremendously from the steadfast encouragement, patience, and critical engagement of Daniel Campo Palacios. *Gracias por todo, compa.*

I am very grateful to my friends Ajamu Baraka, Sofía Garzón Valencia, Brian Hicks, Alex Liebman, Robert Rouphail, Shreyas Sreenath, and Shreya Subramani for their generous comments on drafts of this manuscript over the years.

This book is based on the collective reflections and practices of projects that I have had the privilege of accompanying or being a part of over the years. Thank you to all my *compas* from the Afro-Colombian

Solidarity Network, Colombia Freedom Collective, Black Communities' Process (PCN), Pueblos en Camino, and Woodbine, among others. Yellen Aguilar Ararat, Vilma Almendra Quiguanás, Adelmo Carabali, Roosbelinda Cárdenas, Kevin Caron, Felipe Castiblanco, Harrinson Cuero Campaz, Sheila Gruner, Joseph Jordan, Jeanne Lieberman, Marilyn Machado, Alysia Mann-Carey, Francia Márquez Mina, Paul McLennan, Esther Ojulari, Camilo Pérez-Bustillo, Matt Peterson, Sara Quiñonez, Charo Mina Rojas, Ofelia Rentería Carabali, Carlos Rosero, Manuel Rozental, Gimena Sanchez, Jose Santos Caicedo, Albenis Tique, and Janvieve Williams Comrie all deserve special mention for their invaluable support. The project also took shape through conversations, solidarity work, and friendship with the late Manuel Matos. The final version would have surely been improved by his constructive feedback.

My colleagues at the University of Texas at Austin provided me with encouragement and crucial mentorship since the early stages of my research. My coadvisers, Charlie Hale and Christen Smith, inspired me to be creative and embrace my political and ethical commitments as a scholar—I am immensely thankful for their guidance and example over the years. In Austin, I also had the great fortune of building community with students, faculty, and staff that continue to shape the ideas that I work through in the book. I am particularly grateful to Maya Berry, Claudia Chávez Argüelles, Lina del Castillo, Alejandro Flores, Ted Gordon, Juliet Hooker, David Hutchinson II, Sarah Ihmoud, Marianela Muñoz Muñoz, Luciane Rocha, Joseph Russo, Daniel Perera, Tathagatan Ravindran, and Elizabeth Velásquez Estrada. I was also very lucky to have the opportunity to work closely with and learn from Jonathan Hartlyn, Louis Pérez, and Lars Schoultz as an undergraduate at the University of North Carolina at Chapel Hill.

I am profoundly appreciative of the generous mentorship from Kiran Asher, Margarita Chaves Chamorro, Arturo Escobar, Matt Meyer, Joanne Rappaport, Axel Rojas, and Victoria Sanford over the years—their support has been vital to making this book a reality. The following people have also been crucial to strengthening this project: Pedro Arenas, Martha Balaguera, Attilio Bernasconi, David Gow,

Michael Birenbaum Quintero, Gwen Burnyeat, Pamela Calla, Christopher Courtheyn, Adam Isacson, Nikola Garcia Johnson, Diana Gómez Correal, Jameelah Imani Morris, Jean Jackson, Sam Law, Alex Miller, Mariana Mora, Mario Murillo, Hector Nahuelpan, Oscar Pedraza, Nancy Postero, Laura Quintana, Patricia Richards, Erica Williams, and Coletta Youngers.

Working with students at Lehman College, Spelman College, Morehouse College, and Emory University sharpened many of the ideas included here. I am especially thankful for the support from my colleagues at Lehman College who created a warm environment for finishing this book, especially William Harcourt-Smith, Sarah Ohmer, Ryan Raaum, Stephanie Rupp, and Christa Salamandra. The graduate students at the Colombian Studies Group in New York provided a stimulating space to think through many aspects of this manuscript, particularly Oscar Aponte, Juan Corredor García, Aura Angelica Hernández Cárdenas, and Alejandro Jaramillo.

This book benefited tremendously from feedback from a wonderful community of committed scholars and intellectuals. Comments from John Holloway, Ellen Moodie, Manuel Rozental, and Maite Yie Garzón on the near final version of the manuscript at the City University of New York Gittell Public Scholar Book Manuscript Workshop strengthened the book considerably. I am especially grateful to Ruthie Gilmore, David Harvey, Peter Hitchcock, and Mary Taylor for inviting me to join the Center for Place, Culture and Politics at the Graduate Center as a faculty fellow in 2023/2024, where our cohort's committed praxis pushed me to think harder about every aspect of this book. Chapter 1 benefited from the careful review of the South Asia Research Group at Emory University facilitated by David Nugent and Gyan Pandey. Feedback from María Clemencia Ramírez and others at the Rodeemos el Diálogo series organized by Gwen Burnyeat and Andrei Gomez-Suarez, as well as my cohort at the Afro-Latin American Research Institute's Mamolen Workshop at Harvard University, was crucial for developing the ideas included in chapter 2. Kendra McSweeney and Laura Sauls helped me think more deeply about the role of illicit economies. The organizers and participants at the Yale Agrarian Studies Colloquium provided stimulating feedback that sharpened chapter 3. Chapters 3 and 4 also benefited from the careful attention of my peers at CUNY who participated in the Faculty Fellowship Publication Program. Support from Lehman College, the Professional Staff Congress–City University of New York Research Award, Inter-American Foundation, National Science Foundation, Social Science Research Council, and University of Texas at Austin made much of this research possible. Parts of the introduction are derived from "'Disenchanted with the State': Confronting the Limits of Neoliberal Multiculturalism in Colombia" (*Latin American and Caribbean Ethnic Studies* 15, no. 4 [2020]: 368–390). An earlier version of chapter 2 was published as "The Coca Enclosure: Autonomy against Accumulation in Colombia" (*World Development* 137 [January 2021]). I am also very appreciative of the generous feedback from the anonymous reviewers and the support of my editor at Stanford University Press, Dylan Kyung-lim White.

My family motivated and comforted me throughout the experience of studying, researching, and writing this book. In Colombia, my cousins, aunts, and uncles always invited me to stay longer. Back home, my parents and siblings provided me with unflinching support over the years, despite the anxiety that I may have caused.

Finally, Lis was with me through it all, even when she was far away. During the most trying parts of this process, she reassured me. More often, she dared me to grow and to experience, and I could not be more grateful for that. Now, everything takes on new meaning with our little ones. I love you all.

LIST OF ACRONYMS

ACIN	Association of Indigenous Cabildos of Northern Cauca (Asociación de Cabildos Indígenas del Norte del Cauca)
ACONC	Association of Afro-Colombian Community Councils of Northern Cauca (Asociación de Consejos Comunitarios del Norte del Cauca)
AGC	Gaitanista Self-Defense Forces of Colombia (Autodefensas Gaitanistas de Colombia)
ANP	National Popular Assembly (Asamblea Nacional Popular)
ANUC	National Association of Peasant Users (Asociación Nacional de Usuarios Campesinos)
ANZORC	National Association of Peasant Reserve Zones (Asociación Nacional de Zonas de Reserva Campesina)
ASOMINUMA	Peasant Association of the Mira, Nulpe, and Mataje Rivers (Asociación de Juntas de Acción Comunal de los Ríos Mira, Nulpe y Mataje)
AUC	United Self-Defense Forces of Colombia (Autodefensas Unidas de Colombia)
CCO	Joint Western Command (Comando Conjunto de Occidente)
CNP	National Strike Committee (Comité Nacional del Paro)

COCCAM	National Coordinating Committee of Cultivators of Coca, Marijuana, and Poppy (Coordinadora Nacional de Cultivadores y Cultivadoras de Coca, Amapola y Marihuana)
CRIC	Regional Indigenous Council of Cauca (Consejo Regional Indígena del Cauca)
ELN	National Liberation Army (Ejército de Liberación Nacional)
ESMAD	Anti-disturbance Mobile Squad (Escuadrón Móvil Antidisturbios)
FARC-EP	Revolutionary Armed Forces of Colombia–People's Army (Fuerzas Armadas Revolucionarias de Colombia-Ejército del Pueblo)
FENSUAGRO	National Federation of United Agricultural Workers (Federación Nacional Sindical Unitaria Agropecuaria)
ICANH	Colombian Institute of Anthropology and History (Instituto Colombiano de Antropología e Historia)
JAC	Community Action Committees (Juntas de Acción Comunal)
MAQL	Quintín Lame Armed Movement (Movimiento Armado Quintín Lame)
PCN	Black Communities' Process (Proceso de Comunidades Negras)
PDET	Development Program with a Territorial Focus (Programa de Desarrollo con Enfoque Territorial)
PISDA	Comprehensive Community and Municipal Crop Substitution and Alternative Development Plans (Planes Integrales Comunitarios y Municipales de Sustitución y Desarrollo Alternativo)
PLMT	Mother Earth Liberation Process (Proceso de Liberación de la Madre Tierra)
PNIS	National Comprehensive Program for the Substitution of Illicit Crop (Programa Nacional Integral de Sustitución de Cultivos de Uso Ilícito)

RRI	Comprehensive Rural Reform (Reforma Rural Integral)
UNDMO	National Unit for Dialogue and the Maintenance of Order (Unidad Nacional de Diálogo y Mantenimiento del Orden)
URC	Cali Resistance Union (Unión de Resistencia Cali)
ZRC	Peasant Reserve Zone (Zona de Reserva Campesina)

NOTES

Preface

1. The FARC incorporated "People's Army" (Ejército del Pueblo) into their official name after their Seventh Conference in 1982. Throughout the book, "FARC-EP" refers to the guerrilla group between 1982 and 2016, even though the group is more commonly referred to as "FARC." The only exceptions to this include direct quotes from interviews, written statements, or references to the FARC before 1982. By referring to them as the FARC-EP throughout the text, I aim to dispel confusion between the FARC-EP, the FARC's political party after the Peace Accords, and the groups that retained the FARC nomenclature after 2016.

2. *Compa* is short for *compañero/a/x*. It can be used as a term of affection for another person who accompanies you in life and struggle.

3. Ruth Wilson Gilmore's approach to "rehearsals" has been instructive for my thinking about these kinds of experiments.

4. See Berry et al. (2017).

5. Wolford (2010, 11). According to Wolford, "We tend to study the ideal members, the coherent messages, and the brightest media stars. We do not focus on the ambivalent or half-hearted members; social movements are usually read sympathetically as organizations of ideologically committed members for whom the act of joining the movement and participating in movement activities is inherently transformative" (11).

6. See chapter 4.

7. Berger 1984, 18.

8. See Marcos (1994).

Introduction

1. Throughout the book, I use the word "dissident" in a way that diverges from popular usage of the term in Colombia in the aftermath of the 2016 Peace Accords. As of 2024, the word is primarily used as an adjective to describe factions that broke off from the FARC-EP or claim to be its successor following the Peace Accords. These armed groups continue to assert violence in many of the communities where I have lived and worked, and their political program in words and practice conflicts with the orientation of this book. None of these groups self-identify as "dissidents"—they claim to be a continuation of the FARC-EP's political project. My use of the term in no way should be confused with sympathy for them. I interpret the popular usage of "dissident" as an effort to constrain the political imagination by moralizing and stigmatizing an approach to politics that emerges from a critical consciousness. Instead of conceding our language to the normative thrust of dominant politics, I want to reclaim the value of dissidence as an organizing principle.

2. *Víctimas de la masacre* 2020.

3. See Benjamin (1996) for a generative discussion on the relationship between law-preserving and law-making violence.

4. See Skinner (1989) for a useful genealogy of "state"; Wallerstein's chapter on "Absolute Monarchy and Statism" in volume 1 of *The Modern World-System* is particularly helpful for understanding the early stages of state formation (2011); and Holloway (1994) provides crucial analysis of how the social relations of state and capital are intertwined.

5. See Arias Vanegas (2007), Echeverri (2016), Lasso (2007), and Rojas (2001) for critical approaches to early Colombian state formation and its relationship to race. See chapter 3 for more on my approach to "creole whiteness."

6. Rivera Cusicanqui (2010) analyzes "the process of forced citizenship" as a feature of the Western civilizational model (58).

7. Petro and Márquez, 2022, 6, 50.

8. Petro 2021, 20.

9. Petro (2022). He explicitly reiterated this approach during a speech at the Economic Reactivation Forum two years after taking office (Petro 2024).

10. Notably, most analysis of this trope rightfully places emphasis on the absence of the state. However, as noted in Petro's statement, there is a widespread belief that the absence of capitalist development is also responsible for violence and so-called backwardness. For more on the trope of state absence in Colombia, see Ballve (2021) and Serje (2011).

11. Burnyeat and Johansson (2022) provide a useful overview of approaches to social contract theory. Burnyeat's article in the same special issue (2022) offers an insightful analysis of how the officials under the Santos

administration sought to enact a "liberal social contract" in the aftermath of the 2016 Peace Accords with the FARC-EP.

12. I intentionally use the term "men" here with the racial and gender implications that it carries (see Wynter 2003).

13. Rousseau 2002, 169.

14. For rigorous appraisals of this beyond a specifically Latin American context, see Bhandar (2018), Harris (1993), and Moreton-Robinson (2015).

15. Friede (1969) includes an insightful history of the development of the *resguardo* system in Colombia. Twinam (2015) provides an overview of academic debates on *gracias al sacar*. Barragan (2021) offers a critical analysis of the abolition of slavery in Colombia and its implications for the meaning of freedom. See Rivera Cusicanqui (2012) for more on her use of "conditional inclusion" in relation to multiculturalism. Arias Vanegas (2007) offers an in-depth look at how Colombia's founders interpreted racial difference in the nineteenth century. The deeply colonial aspects of this approach to state formation are also evident, for example, in the explicit civilizing mission of Law 89 of 1890 on how "the savages should be governed." See Rappaport (1994, 26–28) for more on the significance of Law 89 of 1890.

16. Todorov 1982, 174.

17. Neocleous 2014, 29.

18. This points to the need for engaging with settler colonial theory in a Latin American context. I am not suggesting that it should be deployed as a totalizing framework that replaces other useful concepts, such as internal colonialism and coloniality of power, that have been astutely developed by scholars in the region (which I also engage with in this book), but settler colonial theory offers particularly useful insights for understanding how state formation and the development of colonial capitalism are part of a continued form of settlement on the land of peoples that continue to exist and resist. I develop some of these ideas more explicitly in chapter 2. For more on the relevance of settler colonialism in the Latin American context, see Castellanos (2020), Gott (2007), Loperena (2017, 2022), Speed (2017), and Ybarra (2018). For a particularly insightful analysis of Mapuche resistance to settler colonialism and pacification in Chile, see Antimil Caniupan, Nahuelpan Moreno, and Curaqueo Mariano (2020).

19. *El Tandil, Una Masacre* (2018). See Pateman (1988) and Mills (1997) for an analysis of how the social contract is rooted in patriarchy and white supremacy. Quijano (2000) and Lugones (2008) theorize the enduring power of patriarchy and white supremacy in their writings on the "coloniality of power."

20. Delgado Montenegro (2023) is a clear and important exception to this trend.

21. See Oslender (2016, esp. chaps. 4 and 5) for a careful analysis of the formation of community councils in the Pacific region of Colombia. Asher's ethnography of that moment also provides powerful insights into how "the processes of black cultural organizing, state policies, and global development interventions in the Pacific were mutually constituting one another" (2009, 29).

22. See Gros (1999), Warren and Jackson (2003), Van Cott (2000), and Yashar (2005) for contrasting perspectives on the rise of multiculturalism in Latin America. I share Hooker's approach: "The impetus for the adoption of group rights for subordinated racial and cultural groups most often comes from the struggles for justice of such groups, while the immediate reasons dominant groups might agree to consider such demands will vary and may include concerns about the stability of the political community, international pressure, and so on" (2009, 157).

23. Paschel 2016, 82.

24. Taussig 2018, 4, 3.

25. For more on the limits of neoliberal multiculturalism, see Anthias and Asher (2024), Coulthard (2014), Dest (2020), and Hale (2005).

26. Delgado Montenegro 2023, 17.

27. See Comisión de la Verdad (2022, 430–436, "En Nariño, 'las razones por las que matan a los líderes son por defender el territorio'") for more on the history of the Afro-Colombian Community Council of Alto Mira and Frontera, as well as the FARC-EP's relationship with the Peasant Association of the Mira, Nulpe, and Mataje Rivers (ASOMINUMA). Lemaitre (2011) also contains some important background on the history of the community council.

28. Comisión de Seguimiento 2010, 4; UNHCR 2017.

29. Cárdenas (2024) provides an incisive and revelatory ethnography of the multifaceted approach to black activism in Colombia; see especially her chapter 1 for analysis of the process in the neighboring Afro-Colombian Community Council of Bajo Mira and Frontera.

30. See chapter 2 for a more expansive analysis of coca-growing settlers in northern Cauca.

31. CONPA 2015.

32. Smith 2016b, 31.

33. *Ranchera* is a genre of music from Mexico that is associated with drug trafficking in Colombia.

34. See Sabogal (2019) and Cárdenas (2024) for more on the struggle of the Ethnic Commission in the context of the negotiations between the Colombian government and the FARC-EP.

35. For more on the FARC-EP's approach to vanguardism, see chapter 1.

36. Rebollo 2012.

37. See Zambrano (2012) for full speeches by Iván Márquez and Humberto de la Calle, the Santos administration's chief negotiator. Márquez defected from the peace process and became one of the leaders of Segunda Marquetalia, one of the most important armed groups to splinter from the FARC-EP in the aftermath of the 2016 Peace Accords.

38. Gómez Correal 2017, 15.

39. Interview with a participant at the "Intercambio negociaciones de paz y los derechos de los pueblos: Las experiencias de Guatemala, Mexico y Colombia. Diciembre 15 al 18 de 2014." For scholarly engagement on the limits of peace accords in Guatemala and El Salvador, see McCallister and Nelson (2013) and Moodie (2010).

40. Bermúdez Liévano (2015). According to the report from the Truth Commission, "The armed imposition by the FARC-EP on [ASOMINUMA] resulted in the stigmatization of ASOMINUMA as the political wing of the guerrillas and caused multiple human rights violations by the National Army, which have undermined its process. Just like in the black communities, [ASOMINUMA] was victim to threats, homicides, and forced displacement by the Daniel Aldana and Mariscal Sucre columns of the FARC-EP" (Comisión de la Verdad 2022, 434).

41. Bermúdez Liévano (2015). See CONPA (2015) for additional background on the murder of García.

42. FARC-EP 2015.

43. Movilización de Mujeres (2018). For more on the group, see Dest (2020).

44. CAJAR 2009.

45. PCN 2018.

46. For a thorough ethnographic analysis of the multiple and competing approaches to peace in Colombia, see Courtheyn (2022, esp. chap. 4).

47. See King (1963) and Galtung (1969), for example.

48. Aranguren Molina 2001, 96.

49. Aranguren Molina 2001, 96.

50. Gordon and Smith 2010, 5.

51. Negotiation Table 2017, 135.

52. "FARC-phobia" refers to the anti-FARC sentiment among many bureaucrats responsible for implementing the Peace Accords. The term came up during conversations with people who worked at the agencies. They described colleagues engaging in apparently marginal acts of protest, such as ignoring an email or not signing a document, in order to block progress of the Peace Accords. This serves as another reminder of how "peace is not signed, peace is built," in the words of Lederach's interlocutors in Montes de María (2023, 15–17).

53. For de Zubiría Samper, the malleability of the concept made the "'instrumentalization' of the social mobilization for peace by government objectives" likely (2022, 42).

54. Richmond (2006) uses the term "state-centric" peace to describe the "orthodox" and "conservative" variants of "liberal peace" (300). The Colectivo Contrainformativo Sub*Versión also critiques the 2016 Peace Accords as "state-centric" in *For War, Nothing* (2023, 40–45).

55. Ministerio del Interior 2022.

56. Wolfe 2006.

57. PLMT 2016, 33.

58. PLMT 2024.

59. *LA MINA (Video Clip)* (2014).

60. Personal communication with Michael Birenbaum Quintero, ethnomusicologist and author of *Rites, Rights, and Rhythms: A Genealogy of Musical Meaning in Colombia's Black Pacific* (2018).

61. DuBois 1935, 67.

62. Perry (2013), Colectivo Otras Negras y . . . ¡Feministas! et al. (2021), Goett (2017), Morris (2023), and Loperena (2022) provide generative reflections on black women's struggles for autonomy in Brazil, Colombia, Nicaragua, and among the Garifuna in Honduras.

63. Movilización de Mujeres Afrodescendientes por el Cuidado de la Vida y los Territorios Ancestrales 2014.

64. In 2022, the Petro administration officially renamed the anti-riot police. Formerly known by its acronym, ESMAD (Escuadrón Móvil Antidisturbios), in the era of Total Peace, the anti-riot police became the National Unit for Dialogue and the Maintenance of Order (Unidad Nacional de Diálogo y Mantenimiento del Orden, UNDMO).

65. *Permaneceremos—We Shall Remain* 2015.

66. Simpson 2017, 35, 242–245.

67. See "An Intimate History of Slavery of Freedom" in Hartman (2019).

68. Hartman's *Scenes of Subjection* (1997) is crucial to my use of the term "subjection" and its relation to the "subject." Judith Butler (1997) also explores this aspect of subjectivity.

69. Rozental and Almendra (2013). Pueblos en Camino (Peoples on the Path) "weaves resistances and autonomies of peoples and processes." It is not a closed collective, institution, or organization. For more information, see https://pueblosencamino.org/?p=53.

70. This is the contradiction at the source of the "autonomy/inclusion dialectic" that I explore in "Disenchanted with the State" (2020). Some of this material also appears there, albeit with a different emphasis.

71. Holloway's distinction between "power-to" and "power-over" is particularly helpful for understanding how the state relation is one of dominance rather than freedom (2010a).

72. Gutiérrez Aguilar 2017, 89–90.

73. Dinerstein 2015, 9.

74. The concept of "critical consciousness" runs through the work of Paulo Freire.

75. Raquel Gutiérrez Aguilar's call to "generate a 'common sense of dissidence'" resonates with my approach to thinking through dissident peace (2009, 172). This has also been echoed by Paley (2021).

Chapter 1

1. See Scahill (2013, chap. 49) for a description of the raid on Bin Laden's compound.

2. For a series of homages to Cano written by former FARC combatants, see Angel (2016).

3. In *Contingency, Hegemony, Universality*, Butler, Laclau, and Žižek call this "the trope of a 'knowing' vanguard subject" (2000, 3).

4. The FARC made this explicit with their decision to incorporate "People's Army" (Ejército del Pueblo) into their official name after their Seventh Conference in 1982.

5. Johnson (1965). For an analysis on the origins and uses of the "hearts and minds" aphorism, see Dixon (2009).

6. See Mao's *On Guerrilla Warfare* (1937, chap. 6) for a reference to this analogy.

7. See Brittain (2010, esp. chaps. 1 and 2) for a largely sympathetic overview of the FARC's evolution.

8. FARC 1964 and FARC-EP 1993.

9. Cano, n.d.

10. For example, in the first elections, in 2018, after the Peace Accords, the FARC's political party claimed less than 0.5 percent of the vote.

11. In the prologue to *Basta Ya! Colombia: Memories of War and Dignity*, the former Director of the National Center for Historical Memory Gonzalo Sánchez suggests that "especially since the mid-1990s, the unarmed population became progressively involved in armed projects not by consent or social adhesion, but by coercion and victimization" (National Center for Historical Memory 2016, 15). The first chapter of the General Report by the Historical Memory Group is also titled "A Prolonged and Degraded War: Dimensions and Methods of Violence." There was undoubtedly an intensification of violence in the 1990s, but describing it as "degradation" suggests that there was a fall from grace in the course of the war.

12. The term "failed state" represents a normative approach to state formation because it implies that its opposite—a functioning state—would be innately better or more desirable.

13. The Patriotic Union political party was founded by the FARC-EP and the Colombian Communist Party in 1985. Its members were subjected to systematic assassination, attacks, and threats.

14. *Cabildos* (councils) are a form of indigenous authority legally recognized by the Colombian government. However, some communities exercise their role as *cabildos* even if they are not formally recognized by the state. In 2011, Nasa communities in northern Cauca moved away from the *cabildo* model of indigenous authority, which is strongly associated with state administration, to one of "traditional authorities," or *autoridades tradicionales*, such as the *kwe kwe ne'j we'sx* (Campo Palacios 2020, 126–127). *Resguardos* (reservations) are a specific form of indigenous territorial recognition with origins in sixteenth-century Spanish legal code. According to Joanne Rappaport in *The Politics of Memory*, "The *resguardo* converted indigenous tribute into a State patrimony by isolating the Indians from Spanish and mestizo elements, including their *encomenderos*, by granting the Indians some measure of self-government so as to be able to live peacefully in sedentary communities, and by awarding *encomiendas* by virtue of participation in the colonial administration instead of as recognition of conquest activities. In other words, the *resguardo* was part of the [Spanish] Crown's attempt to centralize and increase control of its overseas possessions" (1998, 48). On paper, *resguardos* currently recognized by the Colombian state are endowed with inalienable rights to the land and entitled to direct money transfers from the state.

15. James, Lee, and Chaulieu reached a similar conclusion regarding vanguardism in *Facing Reality* ([1958] 1974, 86–87). Subcomandante Insurgente Marcos (2003) of the Zapatista Army of National Liberation (Ejército Zapatista de Liberación Nacional) also harshly criticized vanguardism in his response to a letter from the Basque separatist organization Euskadi Ta Askatasuna (ETA).

16. According to Gros (1991, 119), "There is nothing more removed from a social movement than a guerrilla movement that is defined by the conquest of power." After describing how both conservative and revolutionary forces attempt to manipulate social movements, he goes on to enumerate nine critiques from indigenous organizations about why "the guerrillas and indigenous communities cannot coexist without frictions" (120, 122–123). The list remains remarkably relevant more than thirty years after its publication.

17. For more on the Bojayá Massacre, see Vergara-Figueroa (2018) and Grupo de Memoria Histórica (2010, 59–64).

18. Gramsci 1971, 3–23.

19. The concept of communion is central to Freire and Guevara's approach to relating to the people. See *Pedagogy of the Oppressed* for Freire's discussion

of Guevara's approach to establishing relationships with the peasantry during the Cuban Revolution (2000, 170–171).

20. Lenin 1964, 422.

21. Gramsci 1971, 189.

22. The 2012 volume by the Casa de Pensamiento de la Çxhab Wala Kiwe ACIN includes several of the correspondences between the FARC-EP and the Çxhab Wala Kiwe ACIN from 2011 and 2012, some of which are cited here. Archila (2013) also includes a helpful analysis of these letters.

23. FARC 1964.

24. Riochiquito, a predominantly indigenous town in northeastern Cauca bordering Huila, figured prominently in the FARC's origin stories as a site of solidarity with indigenous peoples and base building for the FARC after the U.S.-supported attack on their base in Marquetalia in 1964. See Trujillo, *Páginas de su vida* (1965), and Arenas, *Diario de la resistencia de Marquetalia* (1972).

25. This tendency is entrenched in the tradition of the Latin American left, and it calls to mind the attitude of numerous guerrilla and liberation movements toward indigenous, black, and other racialized peoples. See, for example, Peñaranda Supelano (2015, chap. 2).

26. Mariátegui (2011, 142, 149, 152), each page with a quotation from, respectively, 1924, 1926, and 1928.

27. Casa de Pensamiento de la Çxhab Wala Kiwe ACIN 2012, 29.

28. See, for example, Rappaport's work on the importance of historical memory in Cauca's indigenous movements (1993, 1998, 2005).

29. CRIC (1981, 149–170). For more on the tensions between indigenous politics and campesino politics, see chapter 3.

30. Rivera Cusicanqui 1987, 169.

31. "Culture" and "autonomy" were added to the CRIC's organizing principles of "unity" and "land" in 1973 and 1982, respectively. Campo Palacios's unpublished report "Los cambios conceptuales de los principios organizativos del CRIC: Unidad, Tierra, Cultura, Autonomía y Resistencia" offers an in-depth analysis of the politics and conditions of the CRIC's organizing principles. See CRIC (2022, 129–138).

32. For more on the MAQL, see Peñaranda Supelano (2015).

33. The Vitonco Resolution, among many other primary sources related to indigenous struggles for peace, can be found in ONIC (2002, 8).

34. FARC-EP 1987.

35. For example, this is clear in the context leading up to the Çxhab Wala Kiwe ACIN's 1999 "Declaration of the Territories on Coexistence, Dialogue, and Negotiation" and the CRIC's Ambaló declaration of 1986 and Jambaló resolution of 1999, which are referred to in Casa de Pensamiento de la Çxhab Wala

Kiwe ACIN (2012). See ONIC (2002) for the original documents by the CRIC (Ambaló is on p. 43 and Jambaló is on pp. 12–16).

36. Casa de Pensamiento de la Çxhab Wala Kiwe ACIN 2012, 20.

37. The history and ongoing struggle of the Peace Community of San José de Apartadó serves as another example of an organizational process rejecting militarization by the state and other armed actors. See Courtheyn (2022).

38. Casa de Pensamiento de la Çxhab Wala Kiwe ACIN 2012, 18.

39. The account that posted the video on YouTube has since been terminated, and the video is unavailable.

40. FARC-EP CCO 2012

41. FARC-EP CCO, 2012.

42. Casa de Pensamiento de la Çxhab Wala Kiwe ACIN 2012, 30.

43. Casa de Pensamiento de la Çxhab Wala Kiwe ACIN 2012, 28.

44. See chapter 4 for more on the "lumpen question."

45. FARC-EP 2017, 38.

46. Some former FARC-EP combatants went on to found the Autonomous Working Group for Reincorporation (Mesa Autonoma de Reincorporacion), which includes the former Comunes Party Senator Victoria Sandino. See Jaramillo (forthcoming) for more on the group.

47. Scott 1998.

48. See Almendra (2017), Campo Palacios (2020), and Dest (2020) for more on this.

49. PLMT 2016, 41.

Chapter 2

1. The anthropologist Margarita Serje's analysis of the so-called frontiers of Colombia as "spaces of projection" is particularly important for my approach to thinking about *colonización* (2011, 23).

2. For more on the institutional and legal history of programs related to colonization in Colombia, see Plazas Díaz (2019).

3. Ramírez (2022) provides a thorough genealogy of the term *colono* in Colombia beginning in the nineteenth century. See her "Colonización dirigida y colonización espontánea o forzada" (39–43) for more on the failure of these programs and the importance of informal forms of colonization.

4. See Gutiérrez-Sanín (2022) and Ramírez (2022) for two recent examples.

5. Ballvé (2018) analyzes the concept of the "narco-frontier." Midnight Notes Collective (1990) argues that the concept of enclosures remain a crucial analytic for thinking through the expansion of capitalism and resistance to it.

6. Scott 2009, 4.

7. Colectivo Darién (2021) and Rocio Valdivia and Okowí (2021) also explore the relationship between settler colonialism and drug trafficking in

Latin America. Although this chapter focuses on coca cultivations in northern Cauca, recent reports suggest that analogous processes of enclosure occurred with the expansion of extensive marijuana cultivations in the region, see Corporación Ensayos (2020) and Espitia Cueca and Majbub Avendaño (2024). For example, Espitia Cueca and Majbub Avendaño specifically address the arrival of marijuana-growing settlers from other parts of the country (2024, 20). This coincides with my own preliminary findings in relation to the expansion of marijuana in the region.

8. Das and Poole 2004, 8.

9. UNODC 2017, 29.

10. See, for example, Ramírez's (1981) article in *Estudios Rurales Latinoamericanos*.

11. LeGrand 1989, 10.

12. LeGrand, 29

13. Jimeno 1983, 65.

14. Molano 2006, 16. See Serje (2005, 193–203) for an instructive critique of Molano's approach to colonization.

15. The Colombian experience is not unique. See Nahuelpan Moreno (2012), Rivera Cusicanqui (2012), and Smith (2016) for more on Chile, Bolivia, and Brazil, respectively. For more on the aspirational qualities of state formation, see Tate (2015b).

16. In that sense, the margins are what Serje (2011, 23) calls "spaces of projection." These spaces of often-violent conflict are inherent to internal colonialism (González Casanova 2006) and embody Harvey's notion of a "new imperialism" (2004) that expands through "accumulation by dispossession" and maps onto the "coloniality of power" that sustains hierarchies based on race, gender, class, and sexuality (Lugones 2008; Quijano 2000). The predicament in northern Cauca related to the influx of coca-growing *colonos* is also premised on the material conditions that contributed to their arrival and, in particular, the U.S.-financed drug war.

17. These dynamics are also reflected in the exponential growth of coca crops in the region of Catatumbo near the border with Venezuela.

18. Tate 2015a, 31.

19. See Tate (2015a, 47), particularly chapter 1, "Domestic Drug Policy Goes to War," for an overview of how popular culture and policy makers in the United States turned international drug policy into a domestic issue and paved the way for Plan Colombia. Paley (2014) also provides incisive analysis of the relationship between the drug war, U.S. foreign policy, and imperialism.

20. UNODC 2008, 13.

21. Tickner (2007) and Nkrumah (1966).

22. For more on the extensive ties between sectors of the Colombian political establishment and paramilitary groups, see López Hernández (2010) and Romero (2007).

23. Mejía 2016, 9.

24. Paley 2014.

25. McSweeney et al. (2017) offers a revelatory glimpse into the relationship between drug trafficking and land grabs in Latin America.

26. Banco de la República de Colombia, n.d.

27. Observatorio de Drogas de Colombia 2024.

28. UNODC 2017, 14.

29. See Gilmore and Gilmore (2016) for more on the interplay between organized abandonment and organized violence under racial capitalism in the era of neoliberalism.

30. PCN 2017.

31. Two hundred million pesos was the equivalent of about US$70,000 at the time.

32. For more on making pacts with the devil, see Nash (1979), Taussig (1980), and Edelman (1994).

33. Ciro (2020) provides a useful ethnographic analysis of how and why people cultivate coca despite its status as an illicit crop in Caquetá.

34. According to Caicedo Fernández, "The local production [of coca] not only engrained [the communities] in the cocaine production chain, it also brought the people into a distinct form of socializing" (2017, 75). Her analysis of the *foráneo*-led land grab in the Afro-Colombian Community Council of Pureto is reflective of the processes of dispossession resulting from coca production in Nuevo Amanecer and other parts of northern Cauca. However, unlike her analysis of Pureto, the Afro-Colombian Community Council of Nuevo Amanecer did not develop a strategy to confront the *foráneos*, due in large part to the grave risks to their security.

35. In the original Spanish, "¿Quién paga por los platos rotos?"

36. Scott's definition of "moral economy" is useful for understanding how Julio interprets the transformations in Nuevo Amanecer (1976, 3).

37. *Cambio de mano* is a form of labor exchange, whereby communities, families, or individuals take turns working for one another. It often includes the host family providing breakfast and lunch for the visiting workers. As the practice changed over time, hosts may also offer a payment in exchange for the labor. In Nuevo Amanecer, *cambio de mano* is strongly associated with the coffee harvest. However, depending on the price of coca, people may opt to work for a flat rate (without lunch) on coca fields.

38. Berlant 2011.

39. See Villaraga Sarmiento (2018) for a more extensive overview of the history of the Naya Massacre. See chapter 3 for an additional description of the Naya Massacre.

40. Contravía 2008.

41. See Friede (2010, 38–42) for more on the historical uses of coca to ward off hunger.

42. EZLN 2016, 270.

43. See Marx (1990, vol. 1, part 8) for more on Marx's approach to "primitive accumulation."

44. Williams 1961, 64–66.

45. See Vargas Meza (2020) for a critical analysis of the initial implementation of the PNIS program and its relationship to peace building.

Chapter 3

1. According to the UNODC "2024 World Drug Report" (2024, 21), Colombia remained the primary producer of coca in the world.

2. *El Tiempo* (2017). See Ramírez (2011, esp. chap. 5) for more on Díaz's role during the coca protests of the 1990s.

3. For more on how the politics of victimhood informs aspects of subject formation in contemporary Colombia, see Cárdenas (2018).

4. I draw on Mallon's use of "peasant nationalism" here. In *Peasant and Nation*, she builds a framework for analyzing nationalism in a way "that account[s] for the active participation and intellectual creativity of subaltern classes in processes of nation-state formation" (1995, 3).

5. For debates regarding the definition of "peasant," see Edelman (2013), as well as Bernstein and Byers (2002), Mintz (1973), Shanin (1987). For more on the definition of campesino in Colombia, see Castilla Salazar (2015), Duarte (2015), Forero Álvarez (2010), Montenegro (2016), Velasco (2014), and Yie Garzón (2018). For an excellent historical analysis of peasant issues in Colombia, see LeGrand (1986).

6. Forero Álvarez 2010, 9.

7. Congreso de Colombia 2023.

8. Ramírez 2011, 10.

9. Proclama del Cauca 2015b.

10. IEI 2017. See also Campo Palacios (2020, 76). According to Institute of Interethnic Studies data from 2017, the ethnic population of northern Cauca was 48 percent Afro-descendant, 30 percent indigenous, and 22 percent campesino.

11. @PalomaValenciaL, March 16, 2015.

12. Proclama del Cauca 2015a.

13. According to Rappaport, "By the late twentieth century Colombia was envisioned as a mestizo nation, even if few Colombians identify themselves individually as mestizos and racial ascriptions tend to be assigned to particular geographic regions" (2014, 3).

14. In Colombia as in much of Latin America, racial difference is typically discussed in terms of ethnicity or culture. This is the source of significant debate among activists and scholars (Hooker 2020, 29; Paschel 2013). For the purposes of the discussion in this chapter, I at times replicate the dominant terminology around ethnicity to demonstrate how racism is downplayed in the discourse of ethnicity. The 2005 census did not, however, explicitly use either "race" or "ethnicity." The thirteenth question on the 2005 census asked, "According to your culture, people, or physical features, are you or do you recognize yourself as: (1) Indigenous?; (1.1) Which indigenous peoples do you belong to?; (2) Rom?; (3) Raizal from the archipelago of San Andrés and Providencia?; (4) Palenquero from San Basilio; (5) Black [*Negro(a)*], Mulatto [*mulato(a)*], Afro-Colombian [*afrocolombiano(a)*] or Afrodescendant [*afrode-scendiente?*]; (6) None of the above?" For a thorough analysis of black struggles around the census, see Paschel (2013).

15. I thank Daniel Campo for the observation regarding *ciudadanos rasos*.

16. See Wade (1993) for more on the relationship between perceptions of race and geography in Colombia. Appelbaum (2003) and Paschel (2016) also provide crucial insights into Colombian racial formation.

17. Costa Vargas 2004, 443.

18. For more on "racial grammar," see Bonilla-Silva 2012.

19. Stutzman (1981). Silvia Rivera Cusicanqui relatedly defines "Andean colonial *mestizaje*" as a "brutal process, which accepts only to exclude and affirms with the condition of denial" (2010, 133).

20. A crucial aspect of this sliding scale is the slippage within *mestizaje*. For Christian Gros, "The current process of ethnogenesis in Latin America does not generate the creation of closed categories. The 'boundary' is permeable and its geometry is variable. It opens and closes according to the contexts in which the individuals and groups are situated (moments, situations, and places)" (1999, 17). For Rappaport, "The central question before us is not 'Who is a mestizo?' or 'What is a mestizo?' but '*When* and *how* is someone a mestizo?' That is, we should move our gaze away from the condition of the individual, toward the context of the meaning" (2014, 4).

21. In Colombia, creole (*criollo*) typically refers to the American-born people of Spanish descent, particularly before the twentieth century. See Arias Vanegas (2007) for more on the contradictions, tensions, and problematic continuities implicit in the formation of a creole identity.

22. This reflects what de la Cadena refers to as the "de-indianization" of indigenous mestizos in Peru (2000).

23. The original quotation from *The Wretched of the Earth* is "You are rich because you are white, you are white because you are rich" (1963, 40).

24. There is a striking resonance here with Rappaport's analysis of the Colombian historian Victor Álvarez's concept of "none of the above" in relation to the category of mestizo in the sixteenth and seventeenth centuries (Rappaport 2014, 13).

25. Duarte 2015, 41.

26. According to Wade, "In Iberian colonies, a socially stratified pyramid emerged, with Europeans at the apex, black slaves and *indios* (indigenous people) at the bottom and an ambiguous and contestable set of intermediate categories in the middle" (2008, 179).

27. Morris's analysis of "mestizo victimhood" in Nicaragua resonates with the logic of this argument (2023, 134–141).

28. Fajardo 2014, 153–162.

29. C. Ávila 2018.

30. Carolina Rocío Fernández Tovar analyzes the conflict in San Rafael in her master's thesis, "Ustedes y Nosotros: Finca San Rafael un conflicto ¿'interétnico'?" (2014). See also Dest (2022).

31. Balibar develops a similar argument in "Is There a 'Neo-Racism'?": "In fact, what we see is a general displacement of the problematic. We now move from the theory of races or the struggle between the races in human history, whether based on biological or psychological principles, to a theory of 'race relations' within society, *which naturalizes not racial belonging but racist conduct*" (1988, 22; emphasis in original).

32. In her rigorous ethnography of campesino struggle in southwestern Colombia, Yie Garzón also discusses the importance of resentment in shaping campesino subject formation (2018, 256–257).

33. Brown 1993, 401. Fassin (2013) offers an instructive distinction between "resentment" and "*ressentiment*."

34. Ng'weno 2007, 24.

35. See Clastres (1987).

36. See Campo Palacios (2020) for an excellent ethnography of the extent of this process in northern Cauca.

37. *Semana* (2012) and *El Espectador* (2013).

38. Chaux, ORGANICHAUX, CAMPOCAUCA, Julio, Álvaro, and Jaime are pseudonyms I use for security concerns.

39. CRIC (1981) includes insights into the relationship between indigenous organizing and peasant organizing in Cauca. See Restrepo (2013) for more on the history of black peasant organizing in the twentieth century. Note that the

language of black peasants is evident in books like Mina's *Esclavitud y Libertad en el valle del rio Cauca* (2011).

40. See Zamosc (1986) and Rivera Cusicanqui (1987) for excellent overviews and analysis of the ANUC in the early 1970s, as well as their decline. The ANUC continues to exist as an expression of the peasant movement but with decidedly less influence. The local chapter of the ANUC is a part of the Interethnic and Intercultural Commission of Northern Cauca. In this municipality in particular, however, the primary national-level organization that works with self-identified campesinos is ANZORC.

41. My emphasis.

42. Negotiation Table (2017, 9, 10, 11).

43. Silvia Rivera Cusicanqui argues that in Bolivia "under the slogan of 'land to the tiller,' the [land] reform imposed the parcelization of the common lands in both the *ayllus* and the *haciendas* and consolidated the rights of the recently migrating settler population, which had been brought as part of a deliberate effort by the landowners to break ethnic solidarity" (2010, 95). In recent years, some campesino organizations and intellectuals have moved toward emphasizing a less extractive relationship with the land in their public statements. For more information on these shifts, see Montenegro (2016, 80–85) and Velasco (2014, 149–151).

44. For an in-depth analysis of PCN's approach to territory, see Escobar (2008).

45. This should be understood in relation to Bhandar's analysis of how "the colonial encounter produced a racial regime of ownership that persists into the present [. . .]. Thus not only was property law the primary means of appropriating land and resources, but property ownership was central to the formation of the proper legal subject in the political sphere" (2018, 4).

46. See Lasso (2007) for how this concept is an important analytic for understanding racial formation during the wars for independence from Spain.

47. FARC-EP, n.d.a., n.d.b., n.d.c.

48. See chapter 1 for more information on the FARC's relationship with communities in northern Cauca.

49. See chapter 2 for more on coca cultivations in the region.

50. I am grateful to John Holloway for raising this point to me.

51. My emphasis.

52. A paved road now connects northern Cauca to the Naya thanks to financing from the illicit drug trade. Before 2024, it was accessible only by foot or mule.

53. See chapter 2 for more information on the expansion of coca throughout northern Cauca.

54. Evangelical churches proliferated throughout northern Cauca in recent years. In the community of approximately six hundred people where I conducted research, the majority of the people worshipped at one of three evangelical churches compared to the one Catholic Church, which operated out of someone's home.

55. Duarte 2015.

56. FARC-EP, n.d.a., 23.

57. Uprimny 2017.

58. The full title of the booklet edited by Saade is *Elementos para la conceptualización de lo "campesino" en Colombia* (2018).

59. Chaves and Zambrano 2006, 10, 11.

60. Costa Vargas 2004, 443.

61. Coulthard (2014). According to Wolfe, "Assimilation can be a more effective mode of elimination than conventional forms of killing, since it does not involve such a disruptive affront to the rule of law that is ideologically central to the cohesion of settler society" (2006, 402).

62. Butler 1997, 101.

63. For the Bolivian case, Silvia Rivera Cusicanqui analyzed an analogous phenomenon as "mestizo citizenization" (*ciudadanización mestiza*) (2010, 92).

Chapter 4

1. *Juventud y Protesta Social* 2021.

2. Ministerio de Defensa (Colombia) 2021.

3. See chapter 1 for a firsthand description of the raid that culminated in the murder of Alfonso Cano.

4. Uprisings, as an unpredictable and particularly militant form of socialization and resistance, evade definition. Too often, though, distinguishing uprisings from other forms of revolt by their supposed spontaneity denies the conditions that made the revolt possible and disavows the agency and knowledge of the participants. Although the trigger for an uprising might be clear—for example, a fraudulent election, another instance of police violence, or a new tax on the poor—the end of an uprising is less obvious. Its lessons bleed into commonsense understandings of enmity and possibility, for better or for worse.

5. Gaviria Díaz (2023) provides a useful analysis of the foundations of the CNP in the lead-up to the 2019 National Strike, as well as an analysis of its role in calling for and negotiating with the government during the 2021 National Strike.

6. In Colombia, there is a long history of civic strikes that go beyond the traditional definition of a strike. For example, the 1977 Civic Strike serves as one of the principal reference points for this form of protest in Colombia, and

the 2017 civic strikes in Buenaventura and Chocó were the first major public demonstrations following the signing of the 2016 Peace Accords (see Cuero Campaz, Dest, and Ojulari 2021). Crucially for my thinking about the potential expressed in the 2021 uprising, Gago draws attention to how "feminisms, through the strike, contest the boundaries of what is defined as a strike, contest the boundaries of what is defined as labor and, therefore, the working class, opening the category back up to new experiences and demonstrating its historically exclusionary meaning" (2020). Although I would not venture to call the 2021 uprising a feminist strike, there were certainly elements of the feminist strike present throughout it, such as the *ollas comunitarias* (communitarian kitchens) (see, e.g., Almendra Quiguanás 2024 and Marrugo Gómez 2024).

7. For many critics of the uprising, the absence of a representative authority was understood primarily as an obstacle (see, e.g., González 2021).

8. Azuero Quijano (2023) includes a helpful discussion of the toppling of monuments during the 2021 uprising.

9. See Vega Cantor (2021) for a thorough overview of the 2020 riots in Bogotá.

10. A. Ávila 2021.

11. Tracing the lineage of the 2021 uprising has become increasingly relevant to scholars, activists, politicians, and other critics. While there is broad consensus that the 2019 National Strike and the uprising in Chile served as immediate and important influences on the 2021 National Strike, there is debate about how other mobilizations, uprisings, riots, and protests informed the unfolding of the 2021 National Strike. The volume edited by Celis Ospina (2023) includes insightful analyses on the historical antecedents of the 2021 uprising. Medina Pineda, for example, argues that his concept of the "*muchedumbre política*" (political crowd) is central to understanding the 2021 uprising because it built on the "the persistence of the phenomenon of rebellion in Colombia over the course of 128 years" beginning with the Bogotá Riots of 1893 (2023, 41).

12. Amnesty International 2021, 18.

13. Amnesty International, 23, 24. For additional context related to violence during the uprising, see reporting by Temblores, Indepaz, and PAIIS (2021) that documented seventy-three murders between April 28 and June 26, 2021. According to these numbers, Cali would have constituted more than one-third of the murders during the uprising.

14. For Lefebvre, "contestation arises out of a latent institutional crisis. It transforms this crisis into an open crisis which challenges hierarchies, centers of power, and the bureaucratization which has infected the entire society. [. . .] It surges beyond the gap that lies between the realm of limited economic

trade-union demands and the realm of politics, by rejecting the specialized political activity of political machines" (1969, 68, 69).

15. Colectivo Situaciones 2002, 65, 67.

16. Subcomandante Marcos 2005, 93.

17. There is no shortage of literature that is critical of uprisings on these terms (e.g., Le Bon 2002).

18. According to Archila Neira and García Velandia's analysis of police reports during the uprising, "The multitude, despite its ire, did not attack indiscriminately. Without justifying it, we should recognize that it oriented its direct action against precise targets, especially material and symbolic goods that represented the structures of domination and oppression. Schools and hospitals were not, strictly speaking, the targets of the social explosion [. . .]. They were the banks, the large retail chains, police buildings and vehicles, and security cameras" (2023, 98).

19. Puerto Resistencia traces its history at least as far back as the National Strike of 2019. *Rellena* is also a style of blood sausage typical of the region.

20. Hekatombe (2021) includes a map of the resistance points in Cali. See Liebman (forthcoming) for an analysis on the expressions of the uprising in rural areas around Cali. Clover also explores this shift to what he calls "circulation struggles" during uprisings in *Riot. Strike. Riot* (2016).

21. Londoño (2021) offers a description of the various layers of a resistance point.

22. See Johnson (2023) for how these processes manifested during the Chilean uprising in 2019–2020.

23. Hartman 2019, 46.

24. Again, the work of Colectivo Situaciones is useful here. In their analysis of the *piquetero* movement in Argentina, they explore how the politics of representation can instrumentalize the assembly model: "The assembly ceases to be an organ of thought and becomes a place for the legitimation and reproduction of the relations of representation" (Colectivo Situaciones and MTD de Solano 2002, 102). The CrimethInc Ex-Workers' Collective makes a similar point in *From Democracy to Freedom* (2017). Relatedly, Bernes argues, "The problem is that the 'organized minority' takes its own motives—and its capacity for sacrifice, discipline, self-abnegation—as evidence of the structure of motivation in general, and as such will frequently turn to pedagogical or pastoral supplement in order to compel the support of the larger revolutionary mass and install in them its own motives [. . .] this is bound to fail, and in fact sets in motion a number of counterrevolutionary processes" (2019, 199). On a different but related register, Nunes (2021) provides a useful critique of dogmatic approaches to horizontality that frame it in "sovereign terms" (163–164).

25. Juris (2008) describes the category of "critical sectors" in the alterglobalization movement as "anticapitalist groups that organize within grassroots assemblies but favor centralized coordination, viewing the 'sovereign' assembly as the primary decision-making body and expression of unity" (76).

26. See Quintana (2021), Lorde's essays "The Uses of Anger" and "Eye to Eye" from *Sister Outsider* (1984), and the proceedings of the Zapatista Army of National Liberation's Festival de la Digna Rabia (http://enlacezapatista.ezln .org.mx/category/2009/) for more on the political potential of dignified rage and anger.

27. "Esto es lo mínimo para la sociedad pero es lo que más representa la sociedad. Esa microfuerza es la mayor fuerza de la sociedad—es la mayor fuerza de Colombia."

28. The unemployment rate in Cali for this time period was exceeded only by Quibdó (21.9 percent), the capital of the majority black department of Chocó on Colombia's Pacific coast (DANE 2021a, 2021b).

29. Colombia has historically been one of the most dangerous places in the world to be a trade unionist. According to the Escuela Nacional Sindical, 3,300 trade unionists were murdered in Colombia between 1973 and 2019. The vast majority of murderers of trade unionists remain in impunity. In 2020, Colombia had the lowest unionization rate in Latin America at 4 percent (Pardo 2020).

30. Gago's *Neoliberalism from Below* (2017) provides a useful analysis of the relationship between neoliberalism and popular economies, particularly in the informal sector.

31. See Sakai (2017) for a provocative and insightful examination of the lumpen question.

32. Marx and Engels, 118. In *The 18th Brumaire of Louis Bonaparte*, Marx enumerated some of the occupations he associated with the lumpenproletariat: "vagabonds, discharged soldiers, discharged jailbirds, escaped galley slaves, swindlers, mountebanks, *lazzaroni*, pickpockets, tricksters, gamblers, *maquereaux*, brothel keepers, porters, literati, organ grinders, ragpickers, knife grinders, tinkers, beggars—in short, the whole indefinite, disintegrated mass, thrown hither and thither" (2021, 64).

33. The UK-based journal *Endnotes* offers a critical analysis of the workers movement in the twentieth century. For an analysis of the decline in workerism, see Dauvé (2019).

34. Bakunin 1872, 287.

35. Fanon 1963, 129–130.

36. This is not a novel argument. Mattick pointed out the following in his 1935 article "The Scum of Humanity": "The communist groups to the left of the official parliamentary and trade-unionist labor movement have given

such broad bounds to the concept that 'Lumpenproletariat' has become a term of abuse, is made to cover all those elements which, in virtue of their class situation, would naturally be counted among the proletariat but which perform some service or other for the ruling class" (11). In his 1972 article "Frantz Fanon and the Lumpenproletariat," Worsley advocated that it was "high time to abandon the highly insulting, inaccurate and analytically befogging Marxist term lumpenproletariat which is so commonly used" (208). In her 2023 article "The Lumpenproletariat and the Politics of Class," Weeks framed the terms of the debate the following way: "Whether it was ever legitimate, the distinction between proletariat and lumpenproletariat cannot survive the transition from the industrial model of the Fordist employment contract, Taylorist work process, and Keynsian ideal of gendered separate spheres of waged production and household based reproduction to the postindustrial period's post-Fordist, post-Taylorist, neoliberal hodgepodge of increasingly precarious labor contracts, rise of service labor, and more extensive confounding of what is productive and what is reproductive" (2023, 331–332).

37. Bonefeld's reminder about the dangers of sociological definitions of class is helpful in this regard: "Class is not a group of people to whom sociologists assign particular characteristics which, in turn, allows social pigeonholing in terms of ascribed class character. Rather, class needs to be approached as a relation of struggle in and against domination that denies social self-determination" (1992, 102). See also Nasioka (2020).

38. See chapter 1.

39. The terminology of "bad protester" is particularly prevalent in the United States, but it is analogous to the use of "vandals" or "terrorists" in Colombia. In *Policing the Crisis* (1978), Hall et al. provide a thorough analysis of the discourse around mugging and explore the deployment of lumpen terminology in relation to black communities and struggles in the United Kingdom during the late 1970s (particularly in the final chapter, "The Politics of Mugging"). Quiñones's insight is particularly helpful for understanding the relevance of this trope in other parts of the black diaspora.

40. See the conclusion for a more expansive definition of *mingas*.

41. See Campo Palacios and Dest (2020).

42. For example, one of the participants in the Minga interviewed by Martínez expressed her dismay with the conduct of some of the other participants in the Minga: "When we arrived in Cali it was a very beautiful feeling because I realized that we were not the ones who mobilized—it was them. We arrived five days later after everything had already been done. It bothered me that some people arrived to, like, assume the roles of protagonists. I said, 'The

indigenous are assuming the role of protagonists [*sacar protagonismo*] from something that does not belong to them'" (2023, 112).

43. See Newton (2018) for more on "intercommunalism."

44. One of them—Andrés Escobar—was elected to the city council in Cali in 2023.

45. See Holloway's *Hope in Hopeless Times* (2022), particularly the final part, for more on his concept of "richness overflowing" (6).

46. This melting away of difference appears in much of the literature about crowds and uprisings. For example, Canetti suggests that "as soon as a man has surrendered himself to the crowd, he ceases to fear its touch. Ideally, all are equal there; no distinctions count, not even that of sex. The man pressed against him is the same as himself. He feels him as he feels himself. Suddenly it is though everything were happening in one and the same body. This is perhaps one of the reasons why a crowd seeks to close in on itself: it wants to rid each individual as completely as possible of the fear of being touched" (1978, 15–16). This, however, represents a gross oversimplification as the following section demonstrates, particularly in relation to the forms of racist and patriarchal oppression that took shape during the course of the uprising.

47. Asociación Casa Cultural el Chontaduro 2021.

48. For a powerful ethnography of anti-black violence and disavowal in Brazil, see Smith 2016. Moreno's words also evoke Mbembé's definition of "necropolitics" (2003).

49. Betty Ruth Lozano Lerma (2022) crucially raises the issue of sexual violence perpetrated by both the state and "comrades in struggle" during the 2021 uprising in Colombia (426–427). For example, according to a report, there were twenty-eight instances of sexual violence and nine instances of gender-based violence at the hands of police and military forces during the course of the uprising (Temblores, PAIIS, and INDEPAZ 2021, 11). I join Lozano Lerma's call for "a broader vision" of the uprising based on an intersectional approach (2022, 426). For another insightful and provocative analysis of racism during the uprising, see "Fatal Blow" by Alves (2021). His article and this chapter cover similar ground and reach similar conclusions albeit through different emphases. Whereas Alves approaches the question of anti-blackness through Afro-pessimism, I am primarily concerned with thinking through the racist dynamics of the uprising through class struggle and contingency. Hall's analysis of race as "the modality in which class is lived" (Hall et al. 1978, 394; Hall 1980, 341) and Gilmore's definition of racism as "the state-sanctioned or extralegal *production* and exploitation of group-differentiated vulnerability to premature death" (Gilmore 2007, 28; my emphasis) are particularly relevant to my approach.

50. See Quijano (2000) and Lugones (2008) for more on the "coloniality of power."

51. There were clearly exceptions to this tendency within the URC, as it did include some black representatives from various resistance points. For a more celebratory take on the URC, see Maldonado Tovar (2021).

52. I place the word "disproportionately" in quotes here because of its widespread use in the report and in much nongovernmental organization literature about racism and discrimination in Colombia. However, I also want to emphasize that there is no such thing as a "proportionate" level of state violence against black communities.

53. Ojulari and Cuero Campaz 2021, 20.

54. Zibechi 2021.

55. This is reflective of the critique that Alves's interlocutors raise about the peace process as "that white peace, that deadly peace" (2019). In April 2024, debates about how to represent the uprising on the monument continued as it underwent a renovation. These debates included—but were not exclusively based on—the question of race, and the shade of the fist was darkened during subsequent renovations.

56. Cuero Campaz and Ojulari 2021.

57. Political and economic elites in Cali have tried several times to dismantle the monument since its construction in 2021. For example, in June 2023, the city government conducted a sweep of the market at the base of the monument. At the time of writing in 2024, the *Resiste* statue and the market at its base remain the most visible markers of the 2021 uprising. All the burned-down police stations were reclaimed by the state, and there have been ongoing disputes related to representations of the uprising in street art throughout the city.

58. These developments in Cali affirm the following assertion by the Zapatistas in *Critical Thought in the Face of the Capitalist Hydra*: "The System does not fear social explosions, as massive and bright as they may be. If a government were to fall, there's always another one waiting on the shelves as a replacement and as another imposition. What terrifies the system is the perseverance of rebellion and resistance from below" (EZLN 2016, 159). Lefebvre also reflected on this process in the aftermath of the student rebellions of 1968 in France as "authorities feverishly engaged in filling the void they have created" (1969, 53).

59. René's warning reflects important insights from the concluding sentences from *Policing the Crisis* that bear repetition: "This is certainly *not* an argument for failing to do political work in this area. But it constitutes a powerful reminder that we should not mistake a proto-political consciousness for organized political class struggle and practice. It sets up a necessary warning about any strategy which is based simply on favouring current modes of

resistance, in the hope that, in and of themselves, by natural evolution rather than by break and transformation, they could become, spontaneously, another thing" (Hall et al. 1978, 397).

60. Olla Rodante literally translates to the "rotating pot." During the uprising, the Olla Rodante collective organized politically engaged events with music, theater, and free food for anyone. In 2024, they continued to organize these spaces.

61. According to CrimethInc, "In place of formal sites of centralized decision-making, we propose a variety of *spaces of encounter* where people may open themselves to each other's influence and find others who share their priorities. Encounter means mutual transformation: establishing common points of reference, common concerns. The space of encounter is not a representative body vested with the authority to make decisions for others, nor a governing body employing majority rule or consensus. It is an opportunity for people to experiment with acting in different configurations on a voluntary basis" (2017, 72).

62. Medios Libres 2021.

63. The flyer expressed the commitment of several organizations in Cali to "liberate Mother Earth." "Beneath the Cement, the Earth" is likely a nod to the slogan associated with the Situationist International and 1968 in France: "Beneath the Paving Stones, the Beach."

64. For García and Garcés, "The local dialogues with unorganized social subjects ha[ve] become the best weapon of the government to ignore the emergency demands created by the national and regional organizations [such as the CNP]" (2021, 50).

65. One friend from Cali provided me with feedback on these preliminary notes in May 2024 and shared a saying that he had recently heard: "No hay nada que envejezca peor que la literatura sobre el estallido" (Nothing ages worse than writing about the uprising). This saying speaks to the difficulties of writing about uprisings. It also demonstrates how the living legacy of the uprising remains open. As analyses of the uprising in Cali and elsewhere continue to be churned out, I am often reminded of the disparaging quote from *The 18th Brumaire of Louis Bonaparte* in reference to the French peasantry: "They cannot represent themselves, they must be represented" (Marx 2021, 110). This quote is often used to cudgel people into state-centric forms of struggle when there is not a legible leadership structure, but I hope that these preliminary notes move in another direction. Instead of representing the uprising as a closed event, this chapter attempts to contribute to the ongoing debates about how uprisings open terrain for struggle.

66. I place "progressive" in quotation marks to emphasize the looseness of the term. This is in keeping with Mezzadra and Gago's use of the term in their 2017 article "In the Wake of Plebeian Revolt." According to Mezzadra and Gago, Latin American uprisings against neoliberalism "opened up the spaces within which the emergence of new 'progressive' governments in several countries became possible." Along with this potential to open space, they argue that the uprisings hold a 'veto power' [. . .] against any 'return' of those neoliberal policies" (Mezzadra and Gago 2017, 484). In 2024, the "veto power" of the participants in the 2021 uprising in Colombia has yet to be expressed. Instead, many formations that took shape during the uprising tend to be some of the most vociferous defenders of the Petro government's policies.

67. For Gramsci, the "general crisis of the State" emerges when "social classes become detached from their traditional parties. In other words, the traditional parties in that particular organizational form, with the particular men who constitute, represent, and lead them, are no longer recognized by their class (or fraction of a class) as its expression [. . .]. These situations of conflict between 'represented and representatives' reverberate out from the terrain of the parties (the party organizations properly speaking, the parliamentary-electoral field, newspaper organization) throughout the State organism, reinforcing the relative power of the bureaucracy (civil and military), of high finance, of the Church, and generally of all bodies relatively independent of the fluctuations of public opinion. How are they created in the first place? In every country the process is different, although the content is the same. And the content is the crisis of the ruling class's hegemony, which occurs either because the ruling class has failed in some major political undertaking for which it has requested, or forcibly extracted, the consent of the broad masses (war, for example), or because huge masses (especially of peasants and petit-bourgeois intellectuals) have passed suddenly from a state of political passivity to a certain activity, and put forward demands which taken together, albeit not organically formulated, add up to a revolution. A 'crisis of authority' is spoken of: this is precisely the crisis of hegemony, or general crisis of the State" (1971, 210).

68. Hall et al. 1978, vii.

Conclusion

1. Colectivo Otras Negras . . . y ¡Feministas! et al. 2021, 12.

2. Pueblos en Camino 2023.

3. See figure 0.1 in the introduction.

4. Sa'th Tama Kiwe is the Nasa ancestral territory that overlaps with the settler municipality of Caldono, Cauca. See Map 0.1.

5. See chapter 2 for more on coca-growing settlers.

6. Rozental 2009, 2.

7. According to Collazos Cayapu, Soto Pito, and Campo Palacios, "To look from within you must deeply know what is happening inside the territory and what is being confronted outside. It is to take on our issues with malice [*malicia*]. That is, above all, an invitation to delve and search, to find a path that allows us to overcome the malaise that the institutionalization of struggle has generated among us" (Collazos Cayapu, Soto Pito, and Campo Palacios 2022, 21). See also the third section of Yie (2018).

8. Asociación de Cabildos Ukawe'sx Cxhab 2020.

9. Holloway 2010b, 6–7; emphasis in original.

10. Abiayala or Abya Yala means "land in full maturity" or "saved territory." During the latter half of the twentieth century, the Guna term "Abiayala" or "Abya Yala" was increasingly adopted by indigenous movements struggling for self-determination as a way to refer to the region more commonly known as the Americas. See Keme (2018) for a more in-depth history of the struggles around reclaiming Abiayala.

11. Holloway, 84.

12. For an extensive critique of authorized autonomy, see Almendra (2017, 260–270).

13. Kadalie 2020.

14. Colectivo Situaciones and MTD de Solano 2002, 167–168.

15. In the words of Ross, "These are local experiments that refuse to be defined by a localist chauvinism" (2024, 7).

16. Colectivo Otras Negras . . . y ¡Feministas! 2021, 134–135.

17. See Escobar (2008, 2020) for more on the significance of *sentipensar* in black movements. There are also resonances with Ross's analysis in *Communal Luxury*. She argues, "Solidarity grows through increasing liberty, not through constraint or obligation. Personal autonomy and social solidarity do not oppose each other but instead reinforce each other" (2015, 124).

18. For Raquel Gutiérrez Aguilar and Huascár Salazar Lohman, "Transformation does not consist—principally or exclusively—in finding an abstract horizon in the future but in the systematic flow of actions in resistance and of struggles in the present that defend and amplify the concrete possibilities for reproducing life—human and non-human—in their totality" (2015, 17).

BIBLIOGRAPHY

Allen, Jafari. *¡Venceremos? The Erotics of Black Self-Making in Cuba*. Durham, NC: Duke University Press, 2011.

Almendra Quiguanás, Vilma. *Entre la emancipación y la captura: Memorias y caminos desde la lucha nasa en Colombia*. México: Pensaré Cartonéras, Pueblos en Camino, En cortito que's pa'largo, Grietas Editores, 2017.

———. "Ollas comunitarias: Avivando las llamas de la memoria y la rebelión." *Pueblos En Camino*, April 30, 2024. https://pueblosencamino.org/?p=9881.

Alves, Jaime Amparo. "'Esa Paz Blanca, Esa Paz de Muerte': Peacetime, Wartime, and Black Impossible Chronos in Postconflict Colombia." *Journal of Latin American and Caribbean Anthropology* 24, no. 3 (November 2019): 653–71.

———. "Fatal Blow: Urbicidal Geographies, Pax Colonial and Black Sovereignty in the Colombian City." *Environment and Planning D: Society and Space* 39, no. 6 (2021): 1055–72.

Amnesty International. "Cali: In the Epicenter of Repression—Human Rights Violations during the 2021 National Strike in Cali, Colombia." London, UK: Amnesty International, 2021.

Ángel, Gabriel. "Retratos de Alfonso Cano." *Resumen Latinoamericano* (blog), November 4, 2016. https://www.resumenlatinoamericano.org/2016/11/04/retratos-de-alfonso-cano-i/.

Anthias, Penelope, and Kiran Asher. "Indigenous Natures and the Anthropocene: Racial Capitalism, Violent Materialities, and the Colonial Politics of Representation." *Antipode*, July 15, 2024, 1–22.

Antimil Caniupan, Jaime, Héctor Nahuelpan Moreno, and Jakelin Curaqueo Mariano. "'We Can No Longer Endure This Cruel Tyranny': Colonialism, Racism, and Mapuche Resistance in Neoliberal Chile." In *Black and Indigenous Resistance in the Americas: From Multiculturalism to Racist Backlash*, edited by Juliet Hooker, 67–91. Lanham, MD: Lexington Books, 2020.

Appelbaum, Nancy P. *Muddied Waters: Race, Region, and Local History in Colombia, 1846–1948*. Durham, NC: Duke University Press, 2003.

Aranguren Molina, Mauricio. *Mi confesión: Carlos Castaño revela sus secretos*. Bogotá, Colombia: Editorial Oveja Negra, 2001.

Archila Neira, Mauricio. "Cartas van, cartas vienen." *Cien Días*, no. 79 (June–August, 2013): 21–25.

Archila Neira, Mauricio, and Martha Cecilia García Velandia. "Novedades y continuidades del estallido social del 28A." In *Estallido social 2021: expresiones de vida y resistencias*, edited by Juan Carlos Celis Ospina, 67–106. Bogotá, Colombia: Siglo Editorial, Universidad del Rosario, 2023.

Arenas, Jacobo. *Diario de la resistencia de Marquetalia*, 1972. https://mronline.org/wp-content/uploads/2014/01/Diario_Marquetalia-1.pdf.

Arias Vanegas, Julio Andrés. *Nación y diferencia en el siglo XIX colombiano: Orden nacional, racialismo y taxonomías poblacionales*. Bogotá, Colombia: Universidad de los Andes, 2007.

Asher, Kiran. *Black and Green: Afro-Colombians, Development, and Nature in the Pacific Lowlands*. Durham, NC: Duke University Press, 2009.

Asociación Casa Cultural el Chontaduro. *Palabras de Vicenta Moreno después del encuentro de organizaciones del pueblo negro afrodescendiente en Cali con la Comisión Interamericana*, 2021. https://www.facebook.com/casaculturalelchontaduro/videos/palabras-de-vicenta-moreno-despu%C3%A9s-del-encuentro-de-organizaciones-del-pueblo-ne/757408488273661/.

Asociación de Cabildos Ukawe'sx Cxhab. "Pronunciamiento público frente al Wee Wala en el Territorio Ancestral Sa'th Tama Kiwe de Caldono-Cauca," July 8, 2020. https://pueblosencamino.org/?p=8651.

Ávila, Ariel. "La prueba reina: La brutalidad policial y la necesaria renuncia del ministro." *Semana*, September 17, 2021. https://www.semana.com/opinion/articulo/la-prueba-reina-la-brutalidad-policial-y-la-necesaria-renuncia-del-ministro/202029/.

Ávila, Carolina. "Zonas de reserva campesina: 64 oportunidades para proteger el medio ambiente." *El Espectador*, October 8, 2018, sec. Paz y Memoria. https://www.elespectador.com/colombia-20/paz-y-memoria/zonas-de-reserva-campesina-64-oportunidades-para-proteger-el-medio-ambiente-article/.

Azuero Quijano, Alejandra. *El paro como teoría: Historia del presente y estallido en Colombia*. Barcelona, Spain: Herder, 2023.

Bakunin, Mikhail. "The International and Karl Marx." In *Bakunin on Anarchy*, edited and translated by Sam Dolgoff, 286–320. New York, NY: Vintage Books, 1872. https://www.marxists.org/reference/archive/bakunin/works/1872/karl-marx.htm.

Balibar, Etienne. "Is There a 'Neo-Racism'?" In *Race, Nation, Class: Ambiguous Identities*, translated by Chris Turner, 17–28. New York, NY: Verso, 1988.

Ballvé, Teo. *The Frontier Effect: State Formation and Violence in Colombia*. Ithaca, NY: Cornell University Press, 2020.

———. "Narco-Frontiers: A Spatial Framework for Drug-Fueled Accumulation." *Journal of Agrarian Change* 19, no. 2 (2018): 211–24.

Banco de la República de Colombia. "Inversión directa," n.d. https://www.banrep. gov.co/es/estadisticas/inversion-directa.

Barragan, Yesenia. *Freedom's Captives: Slavery and Gradual Emancipation on the Colombian Black Pacific*. Cambridge, UK: Cambridge University Press, 2021.

Benjamin, Walter. "Critique of Violence." In *Walter Benjamin: Selected Writings*, edited by Marcus Bullock and Michael W. Jennings, translated by Edmund Jephcott, 1:236–52. Cambridge, MA: Belknap Press, 1996.

Berger, John. *And Our Faces, My Heart, Brief as Photos*. New York, NY: Vintage International, 1984.

Berlant, Lauren. *Cruel Optimism*. Durham, NC: Duke University Press, 2011.

Bermúdez Liévano, Andrés. "El asesinato con el que acusan a las Farc de romper la tregua." *La Silla Vacía*, August 6, 2015. https://www.lasillavacia .com/silla-nacional/pacifico/el-asesinato-con-el-que-acusan-a-las-farc-de -romper-la-tregua/.

Bernes, Jasper. "Revolutionary Motives." *Endnotes*, no. 5 (2019): 192–246.

Bernstein, Henry, and Terence J. Byres. "From Peasant Studies to Agrarian Change." *Journal of Agrarian Change* 1, no. 1 (2002): 1–56.

Berry, Maya J., Claudia Chávez Argüelles, Shanya Cordis, Sarah Ihmoud, and Elizabeth Velásquez Estrada. "Toward a Fugitive Anthropology: Gender, Race, and Violence in the Field." *Cultural Anthropology* 32, no. 4 (2017): 537–65.

Bhandar, Brenna. *Colonial Lives of Property: Law, Land, and Racial Regimes of Ownership*. Durham, NC: Duke University Press, 2018.

Birenbaum Quintero, Michael. *Rites, Rights, and Rhythms: A Genealogy of Musical Meaning in Colombia's Black Pacific*. Oxford, UK: Oxford University Press, 2018.

Bonefeld, Werner. "Social Constitution and the Form of the Capitalist State." In *Open Marxism*, edited by Werner Bonefeld, Richard Gunn, and Kosmas Psychopedis, vol. 1, Dialectics and History, 93–132. London, UK: Pluto Press, 1992.

Bonilla-Silva, Eduardo. "The Invisible Weight of Whiteness: The Racial Grammar of Everyday Life in Contemporary America." *Ethnic and Racial Studies* 35, no. 2 (February 1, 2012): 173–94. https://doi.org/10.1080/01419870.2011.613997.

Brittain, James J. *Revolutionary Social Change in Colombia: The Origin and Direction of the FARC-EP*. New York, NY: Pluto Books, 2010.

Brown, Wendy. "Wounded Attachments." *Political Theory* 21, no. 3 (1993): 390–410.

Burnyeat, Gwen. "'We Were Not Emotional Enough': Cultural Liberalism and Social Contract Imaginaries in the Colombian Peace Process." *Critique of Anthropology* 42, no. 3 (2022): 286–303.

Burnyeat, Gwen, and Miranda Sheild Johansson. "An Anthropology of the Social Contract: The Political Power of an Idea." *Critique of Anthropology* 42, no. 3 (2022): 221–37.

Butler, Judith. *The Psychic Life of Power: Theories in Subjection*. Stanford, CA: Stanford University Press, 1997.

Butler, Judith, Ernesto Laclau, and Slavoj Žižek. *Contingency, Hegemony, Universality: Contemporary Dialogues on the Left*. New York, NY: Verso, 2000.

Caicedo Fernández, Alhena. "Vida campesina y modelo de desarrollo: Configuraciones de despojo/privilegio en el norte del Cauca." *Revista Colombiana de Antropología* 53, no. 1 (2017): 59–89.

CAJAR. "Defensores de derechos humanos: Bajo el estigma del Presidente Álvaro Uribe," November 2, 2009. https://www.colectivodeabogados.org/defensores-de-derechos-humanos-bajo-el-estigma-del-presidente-alvaro-uribe/.

Campo Palacios, Daniel Felipe. "Los desafíos del gobierno propio: Poder e identidad étnica nasa en el norte del Cauca, Colombia." Master's thesis, Benemérita Universidad Autónoma de Puebla, 2020.

——. "Los cambios conceptuales de los principios organizativos del CRIC: Unidad, tierra, cultura, autonomía y resistencia" (unpublished).

Campo Palacios, Daniel, and Anthony Dest. "Empty Seats and Full Streets in the Colombian Minga." *NACLA*, October 23, 2020. https://nacla.org/news/2020/10/23/empty-seats-and-full-streets-colombian-minga.

Canetti, Elias. *Crowds and Power*. New York, NY: Continuum, 1978.

Cano, Alfonso. "A las comunidades indígenas del Cauca," March 2009. https://www.weready.cedema.org/digital_items/3201.

——. *Colección crónicas de tiempos duros VI: Nuevo gobierno y continuación de fuego*, n.d. https://partidocomunes.com.co/nuevo-gobierno-y-continuacion-del-fuego/.

Cárdenas, Roosbelinda. *Raising Two Fists: Struggles for Black Citizenship in Multicultural Colombia*. Stanford, CA: Stanford University Press, 2024.

———. "'Thanks to My Forced Displacement': Blackness and the Politics of Colombia's War Victims." *Latin American and Caribbean Ethnic Studies* 13, no. 1 (2018): 72–93.

Casa de Pensamiento de la Çxhab Wala Kiwe ACIN. "Módulo I: Paz, conflicto armado y resistencia." Bogotá, DC: Ediciones Antropos, 2012.

Castellanos, M. Bianet. *Indigenous Dispossession: Housing and Maya Indebtedness in Mexico.* Stanford, CA: Stanford University Press, 2020.

Castilla Salazar, Alberto. "Reconocimiento político del campesinado." *Revista Semillas*, December 10, 2015. https://semillas.org.co/es/revista/reconocimiento-pol-2.

Celis Ospina, Juan Carlos, ed. *Estallido social 2021: Expresiones de vida y resistencias.* Bogotá, Colombia: Siglo Editorial, Universidad del Rosario, 2023.

Chaves Chamorro, Margarita, and Marta Zambrano Escobar. "From *Blanqueamiento* to *Reindigenización*: Paradoxes of Mestizaje and Multiculturalism in Contemporary Colombia." *Revista Europea de Estudios Latinoamericanos y Del Caribe*, no. 80 (2006): 5–23. https://doi.org/10.18352/erlacs.9652.

Cienfuegos, Camila. "El último abrazo del camarada Alfonso." *Gaskua* (blog), November 4, 2017. https://gaskua.blogspot.com/2017/11/el-ultimo-abrazo-del-camarada-alfonso.html.

Ciro Rodríguez, Estefanía. *Levantados de la selva: Vidas y legitimidades en los territorios cocaleros del Caquetá.* Bogotá, Colombia: Ediciones Uniandes, 2020.

Clastres, Pierre. *Society against the State: Essays in Political Anthropology.* New York, NY: Zone Books, 1987.

Clover, Joshua. *Riot. Strike. Riot: The New Era of Uprisings.* New York, NY: Verso, 2016.

Colectivo Contrainformativo Sub*Versión. *For War, Nothing.* Translated by Flora & Fauna Collective. Brooklyn, NY: Fugitive Materials, 2023.

Colectivo Darién. "Trafficking as Settler Colonialism in Eastern Panama: Linking the Americas via Illicit Commerce, Clientelism, and Land Cover Change." *World Development* 145 (2021).

Colectivo Otras Negras y . . . ¡Feministas!, Elba Palacios, María Mercedes Campo, Martha Rivas, Natalia Ocoró, and Betty Ruth Lozano, eds. *Feminicide and Global Accumulation: Frontline Struggles Resist the Violence of Patriarchy.* Translated by Veronica Carchedi, Liz Mason-Deese, and Susana Draper. Brooklyn, NY: Common Notions, 2021.

Colectivo Situaciones. *19 & 20: Notes for a New Social Protagonism.* Translated by Nate Holdren and Sebastián Touza. Brooklyn, NY: Autonomedia & Common Notions, 2002.

Colectivo Situaciones and MTD de Solano. *Hipótesis 891: Más allá de los piquetes.* Buenos Aires, Argentina: Ediciones de Mano en Mano, 2002.

Collazos Cayapu, Diana, Daniela Soto Pito, and Daniel Campo Palacios. "Mirar desde adentro para encontrar el camino." *Unidad Alvaro Ulcué*, no. 7 (2022): 20–29.

Comisión de la Verdad. *Resistir no es aguantar: Violencias y daños contra los pueblos étnicos de Colombia*. Vol. 9. 24 vols. Bogotá, Colombia: Comisión de la Verdad, 2022.

Comisión de Seguimiento a la Política Pública sobre Desplazamiento Forzado. "III encuesta nacional de verificación de los derechos de la población desplazada: Resumen de resultados preliminares en materia de bienes rurales." Bogotá, Colombia, 2010.

Congreso de Colombia. "Acto legislativo 01 de 2023: Por medio del cual se reconoce al campesinado como sujeto de especial protección constitucional." 2023. https://www.funcionpublica.gov.co/eva/gestornormativo/norma.php?i=213790.

CONPA (Consejo Nacional de Paz Afrocolombiano). "Asesinado Genaro García, líder de un consejo comunitario afrocolombiano," August 5, 2015. https://afrocolombian.wordpress.com/2015/08/06/asesinado-genaro-garcia-lider-de-un-consejo-comunitario-afrocolombiano/.

Contravía Capítulo 186. *Entrevista a H.H. (6/6)*, 2008. https://www.youtube.com/watch?v=peL-uYJdFds.

Corporación Ensayos. "¿Es posible superar las economías ilegales? Aproximación a las variables económicas e institucionales del cannabis en Toribío, Cauca." *Patacrítica*, November 2020.

Costa Vargas, João H. "Hyperconsciousness of Race and Its Negation: The Dialectic of White Supremacy in Brazil." *Identities* 11, no. 4 (October 1, 2004): 443–70. https://doi.org/10.1080/10702890490883803.

Coulthard, Glean Sean. *Red Skin, White Masks: Rejecting the Colonial Politics of Recognition*. Minneapolis: University of Minnesota Press, 2014.

Courtheyn, Christopher. *Community of Peace: Performing Geographies of Ecological Dignity in Colombia*. Pittsburgh, PA: University of Pittsburgh Press, 2022.

CRIC (Consejo Regional Indígena del Cauca). *CRIC: Diez años de lucha; historia y documentos*. Bogotá, Colombia: Centro de Investigación y Educación Popular, 1981.

———.*"Entonces ¡hablamos!" Informe sobre las afectaciones del conflicto político armado a los pueblos indígenas que conforman el Consejo Regional Indígena del Cauca—CRIC, 1971–2021*. Popayán, Cauca: Editorial Universidad del Cauca, 2022.

———. "Terminar la guerra, Defender la autonomía, reconstruir los bienes civiles y construir la paz." Toribío, 2011.

CrimethInc Ex-Workers' Collective. *From Democracy to Freedom: The Difference between Government and Self-Determination*. Salem, OR: CrimethInc, 2017.

Cuero Campaz, Harrinson, Anthony Dest, and Esther Yemisi Ojulari. "Buenaventura Strikes against Racial Capitalism." *NACLA Report on the Americas*, 2021.

Cuero Campaz, Harrinson, and Esther Yemisi Ojulari. "Colombia: 500 años luchando en la primera línea por la defensa de la dignidad humana." *desInformémonos*, May 22, 2021. https://desinformemonos.org/colombia-500-anos-luchando-en-la-primera-linea-por-la-defensa-de-la-dignidad-humana/.

Çxhab Wala Kiwe ACIN, Tejido de Defensa de la Vida y los Derechos Humanos. *Informe de desarmonías territoriales 2024 resumen*, 2025.

DANE (Departamento Administrativo Nacional de Estadística). "Medición de empleo informal y seguridad social: Trimestre abril–junio 2021." Boletín Técnico Gran Encuesta Integrada de Hogares, August 11, 2021a.

——. "Principales indicadores del mercado laboral: Junio de 2021." Boletín Técnico Gran Encuesta Integrada de Hogares, July 30, 2021b.

Das, Veena, and Deborah Poole. "State and Its Margins: Comparative Ethnographies." In *Anthropology in the Margins of the State*. Santa Fe, NM: School of American Research Press, 2004.

Dauvé, Gilles. *From Crisis to Communisation*. Revolutionary Pocketbooks, no. 3. Oakland, CA: PM Press, 2019.

de la Cadena, Marisol. *Indigenous Mestizos: The Politics of Race and Culture in Cuzco, Peru, 1919–1991*. Durham, NC: Duke University Press, 2000.

Delgado Montenegro, Raúl Alejandro. "Vida y territorio: Las luchas de las comunidades negras del Consejo Comunitario Alto Mira y Frontera en Tumaco, Nariño—Colombia." Universidade Federal do Rio de Janeiro, 2023.

Dest, Anthony. "'Disenchanted with the State': Confronting the Limits of Neoliberal Multiculturalism in Colombia." *Latin American and Caribbean Ethnic Studies* 15, no. 4 (2020): 368–90.

——. "La tierra no es solo para trabajarla . . . : Luchar por la vida y la paz en el norte del Cauca." *Pueblos En Camino* (blog), August 27, 2022. https://pueblosencamino.org/?p=9679.

de Zubiría Samper, Sergio. "Aproximaciones conceptuales a la noción de 'Paz Total.'" In *Paz total: Insumos para la formulación de una política pública integral de paz*, edited by Carlos Medina Gallego, 21–27. Bogotá, Colombia: Universidad Nacional de Colombia, 2022.

Dinerstein, Ana Cecilia. *The Politics of Autonomy in Latin America: The Art of Organising Hope*. London, UK: Palgrave Macmillan, 2015.

Dixon, Paul. "'Hearts and Minds'? British Counter-Insurgency from Malaya to Iraq." *Journal of Strategic Studies* 32, no. 3 (2009): 353–81. https://doi.org/10.1080/01402390902928172.

Duarte, Carlos. *Desencuentros territoriales: La emergencia de los conflictos interétnicos e interculturales en el departamento del Cauca.* Vol. 1. 2 vols. Bogotá, Colombia: Instituto Colombiano de Antropología e Historia, 2015.

DuBois, W. E. Burghardt. *Black Reconstruction: An Essay toward a History of the Part Which Black Folk Played in the Attempt to Reconstruct Democracy in America, 1860–1880.* New York, NY: Harcourt, Brace, 1935.

Echeverri, Marcela. *Indian and Slave Royalists in the Age of Revolution: Reform, Revolution, and Royalism in the Northern Andes, 1780–1825.* Cambridge, UK: Cambridge University Press, 2016.

Edelman, Marc. "Landlords and the Devil: Class, Ethnic, and Gender Dimensions of Central American Peasant Narratives." *Cultural Anthropology* 9, no. 1 (1994): 58–93.

——. "What Is a Peasant? What Are Peasantries? A Briefing Paper on Issues of Definition." Paper presented at the First Session of the Intergovernmental Working Group on a United Nations Declaration on the Rights of Peasants and Other People Working in Rural Areas. Geneva, Switzerland, 2013.

El Espectador. "¿El palo en la rueda?" February 12, 2013. Editorial. https://www.elespectador.com/opinion/editorial/el-palo-rueda-articulo-404470/.

El Tandil, una masacre que aún continúa en la impunidad, 2018. https://www.youtube.com/watch?v=gDJOMtIXJFw.

El Tiempo. "Asociaciones de cultivadores ilícitos deben desaparecer: Eduardo Díaz." January 19, 2017. https://www.eltiempo.com/archivo/documento/CMS-16796510.

Escobar, Arturo. *Pluriversal Politics: The Real and the Possible.* Durham, NC: Duke University Press, 2020.

——. *Territories of Difference: Place, Movements, Life, Redes.* Durham, NC: Duke University Press, 2008.

Espitia Cueca, Carlos Eduardo, and Salomón Majbub Avendaño. "La economía de la marihuana en el enclave productivo del norte del Cauca." INDEPAZ. *Puntos de Encuentro,* no. 81 (2024).

EZLN (Ejército Zapatista de Liberación Nacional). *Critical Thought in the Face of the Capitalist Hydra: Contributions by the Sixth Commission of the EZLN.* Vol. 1. Durham, NC: PaperBoat Press, 2016.

Fajardo, Darío. *Las guerras de la agricultura Colombiana, 1980–2010.* Bogotá, Colombia: Instituto Latinoamericano para una Sociedad y un Derecho Alternativos, 2014.

Fanon, Frantz. *The Wretched of the Earth.* Translated by Constance Farrington. New York, NY: Grove Press, 1963.

FARC. "Programa agrario de los guerrilleros." Centro de Documentación de los Movimientos Armados, July 20, 1964. https://www.weready.cedema.org/digital_items/4018.

FARC-EP. "Conclusión de la investigación sobre muerte del líder afro Genaro García." Centro de Documentación de los Movimientos Armados, August 24, 2015. https://www.weready.cedema.org/digital_items/6840.

———. "Desarrollo rural y agrario para la democratización y la paz con justicia social de Colombia: 100 propuestas mínimas," n.d.a.

———. "Participación política para la democratización real, la paz con justicia social y la reconciliación nacional: 100 propuestas mínimas," n.d.b.

———. "Pleno ampliado, febrero 17-20 de 1987," 1987.

———. "Política anti-droga para la soberanía y el buen vivir de los pobres del campo: 50 propuestas mínimas," n.d.c.

———. "Programa agrario de las FARC-EP." Centro de Documentación de los Movimientos Armados, April 2, 1993. https://www.weready.cedema.org/digital_items/8568.

———. "Tesis de abril: Por un partido para construir la paz y la perspectiva democrático-popular," March 2017. https://cedema.org/digital_items/7596.

FARC-EP CCO (Comando Conjunto de Occidente). "Mensaje a las comunidades indígenas del norte del Cauca," March 2012. https://www.weready.cedema.org/digital_items/4843.

Fassin, Didier. "On Resentment and Ressentiment: The Politics and Ethics of Moral Emotions." *Current Anthropology* 54, no. 3 (2013): 249–267.

Fernández Tovar, Carolina Rocío. "Ustedes y nosotros: Finca San Rafael un conflicto ¿'interétnico'?" Master's thesis, Universidad del Cauca, 2014.

Forero Álvarez, Jaime, ed. *El campesino colombiano: Entre el protagonismo económico y el desconocimiento de la sociedad.* Bogotá, Colombia: Pontificia Universidad Javeriana, 2010.

Freire, Paulo. *Pedagogy of the Oppressed.* Translated by Myra Bergman Ramos. 30th anniversary ed. New York, NY: Continuum, 2000.

Friede, Juan. "De la encomienda indiana a la propiedad territorial y su influencia sobre el mestizaje." *Anuario Colombiano de Historia Social y de La Cultura* 4 (1969): 35–61.

———. *El indio en lucha por la tierra: Historia de los resguardos del macizo central.* Popayán, Cauca: Editorial Universidad del Cauca, 2010.

Gago, Verónica. *Feminist International: How to Change Everything.* Brooklyn, NY: Verso, 2020.

———. *Neoliberalism from Below: Popular Pragmatics and Baroque Economies.* Translated by Liz Mason-Deese. Durham, NC: Duke University Press, 2017.

Galtung, Johan. "Violence, Peace, and Peace Research." *Journal of Peace Research* 6, no. 3 (1969): 167–91.

García, Martha Cecilia, and Santiago Garcés. "Notas sobre un 'estallido social' en Colombia. El Paro Nacional 28 A." *Cien Días*, 2021.

Gaviria Díaz, Víctor Manuel. "El Paro Nacional desde el Comité del Paro." In *Estallido social 2021: Expresiones de vida y resistencias*, edited by Juan Carlos Celis Ospina, 243–88. Bogotá, Colombia: Siglo Editorial, Universidad del Rosario, 2023.

Gilmore, Ruth Wilson. *Golden Gulag: Prisons, Surplus, Crisis, and Opposition in Globalizing California*. Berkeley: University of California Press, 2007.

Gilmore, Ruth Wilson, and Craig Gilmore. "Beyond Bratton." In *Policing the Planet: Why the Policing Crisis Led to Black Lives Matter*, edited by Jordan T. Camp and Christina Heatherton. Brooklyn, NY: Verso, 2016.

Goett, Jennifer. *Black Autonomy: Race, Gender, and Afro-Nicaraguan Activism*. Stanford, CA: Stanford University Press, 2017.

Gómez Correal, Diana. "Mujeres, género y el acuerdo de la Habana." *LASA Forum* 48, no. 1 (2017): 13–16.

González, Fernán E. "'En Colombia, nadie representa a nadie'. Una aproximación preliminar al análisis del significado político del paro." *Cien Días*, 2021.

González Casanova, Pablo. "Colonialismo interno (una redefinición)." In *La teoría marxista hoy: Problemas y perspectivas*, 409–34. Buenos Aires, Argentina: Consejo Latinoamericano de Ciencias Sociales, 2006.

Gordon, Gretchen, and Noah Smith. "Truth behind Bars: Colombian Paramilitary Leaders in U.S. Custody." Berkeley: University of California, International Human Rights Law Clinic, School of Law, 2010.

Gott, Richard. "Latin America as a White Settler Society" 26, no. 2 (2007): 269–89.

Gramsci, Antonio. *Selections from the Prison Notebooks*. Edited and translated by Quintin Hoare and Geoffrey Nowell Smith. New York, NY: International Publishers, 1971.

Gros, Christian. *Colombia indígena: Identidad cultural y cambio social*. Bogotá, Colombia: CEREC, 1991.

———. "Ser diferente por (para) ser moderno, o las paradojas de la identidad: Algunas reflexiones sobre la construcción de una nueva frontera étnica en América Latina." *Análisis Político*, no. 36 (1999): 3–20.

Grupo de Memoria Histórica. "Bojayá: La guerra sin límites." Bogotá, Colombia: Comisión Nacional de Reparación y Reconciliación, 2010. https://centrodememoriahistorica.gov.co/wp-content/uploads/2020/01/Bojay%C3%A1-La-guera-sin-l%C3%ADmites.pdf.

Guevara, Ernesto (Che). *Guerrilla Warfare: The Authorised Edition*. London, UK: Ocean Press, 2006. First published 1961 by MR Press.

Gutiérrez Aguilar, Raquel. "América Latina: De la revuelta a la estabilización." In *Conversaciones en el impasse: Dilemas políticos del presente*, edited by Colectivo Situaciones, 167–86. Buenos Aires, Argentina: Tinta Limón, 2009.

———. *Horizontes comunitario-populares: Producción de lo común más allá de las políticas estado-céntricas*. Madrid, Spain: Traficantes de Sueños, 2017.

Gutiérrez Aguilar, Raquel, and Huáscar Salazar Lohman. "Reproducción comunitaria de la vida: Pensando la trans-formación social en el presente." *El Apantle* 1 (2015): 15–50.

Gutiérrez-Sanín, Francisco. "Mangling Life Trajectories: Institutionalised Calamity and Illegal Peasants in Colombia." *Third World Quarterly* 43, no. 11 (2022): 2577–96.

Hale, Charles R. "Neoliberal Multiculturalism: The Remaking of Cultural Rights and Racial Dominance in Central America." *Political and Legal Anthropology Review* 28, no. 1 (2005): 10–28.

Hall, Stuart. "Race, Articulation, and Societies Structured in Dominance." In *Sociological Theories: Race and Colonialism*, 305–46. Paris: UNESCO, 1980.

Hall, Stuart, Chas Critcher, Tony Jefferson, John Clarke, and Brian Roberts. *Policing the Crisis: Mugging, the State, and Law and Order*. London, UK: Macmillan, 1978.

Harris, Cheryl I. "Whiteness as Property." *Harvard Law Review* 106, no. 8 (1993): 1707–91.

Hartman, Saidiya. *Scenes of Subjection: Terror, Slavery, and Self-Making in Nineteenth-Century America*. New York, NY: Oxford University Press, 1997.

———. *Wayward Lives, Beautiful Experiments: Intimate Histories of Riotous Black Girls, Troublesome Women, and Queer Radicals*. New York, NY: W. W. Norton, 2019.

Harvey, David. "The "New" Imperialism: Accumulation by Dispossession." *Socialist Register* 40 (2004): 63–87.

Hekatombe. "La cartografía de la resistencia caleña." *Revista Hekatombe*, June 4, 2021. https://www.revistahekatombe.com.co/la-cartografia-de-la-resistencia-calena/.

Holloway, John. *Change the World without Taking Power: The Meaning of Revolution Today*. New York, NY: Pluto Press, 2010a.

———. *Crack Capitalism*. New York, NY: Pluto Press, 2010b.

———. "Global Capital and the National State." *Capital and Class* 18, no. 1 (1994): 23–49.

———. *Hope in Hopeless Times*. London, UK: Pluto Press, 2022.

Hooker, Juliet, ed. *Black and Indigenous Resistance in the Americas: From Multiculturalism to Racist Backlash*. Lanham, MD: Lexington Books, 2020.

———. *Race and the Politics of Solidarity*. Oxford, UK: Oxford University Press, 2009.

IEI (Instituto de Estudios Interculturales). "Estructura de la propiedad rural y necesidad de tierras en el norte del Cauca," 2017.

James, C. L. R., Grace C. Lee, and Pierre Chaulieu. *Facing Reality*. Detroit, MI: Bewick Editions, 1974. First published 1958. Citations refer to the 1974 edition.

Jaramillo, Alejandro. "Peace for Sale: The Mutual Lives of History and Commodity in Transitional Colombia." PhD diss., New York University, forthcoming.

Jimeno, Myriam. "La descomposición de la colonización campesina en Colombia." *Estudios Rurales Latinoamericanos* 6, no. 1 (1983): 65–76.

Johnson, Lyndon B. "Remarks at a Dinner Meeting of the Texas Electric Cooperatives, Inc." May 4, 1965. https://www.presidency.ucsb.edu/documents/remarks-dinner-meeting-the-texas-electric-cooperatives-inc.

Johnson, Nikola Garcia. "Emergent Citizenships: Mapuche and Chilean Politics and Belonging in the Peri-Urban (Santiago, Chile)." PhD diss., Emory University, 2023.

Juris, Jeffrey S. *Networking Futures: The Movements against Corporate Globalization*. Durham, NC: Duke University Press, 2008.

Juventud y protesta social: Las voces de los puntos de resistencia 2do encuentro, Ciclo de conferencias / Filosofía y cognición. 2021. https://www.youtube.com/watch?v=0DdKrfgqQvw.

Kadalie, Modibo. "Pan-African Social Ecology: A Conversation with Dr Modibo Kadalie." Occupied Tsalagi Land in Southern Appalachia (Asheville, NC), June 21, 2020. https://thefinalstrawradio.noblogs.org/post/2020/06/21/pan-african-social-ecology-a-conversation-with-dr-modibo-kadalie/.

King, Martin Luther, Jr. "Letter from the Birmingham Jail." In *Why We Can't Wait*, 77–100. San Francsico, CA: Harper & Row, 1963.

La ley del monte. Colombia: Citurna Producciones, 1989.

LA MINA (Video Clip), 2014. https://www.youtube.com/watch?v=mq6TTc3ThVk.

Lasso, Marixa. *Myths of Harmony: Race and Republicanism during the Age of Revolution, Colombia, 1795–1831*. Pittsburgh, PA: University of Pittsburgh Press, 2007.

Le Bon, Gustav. *The Crowd: A Study of the Popular Mind*. Translated by T. Fisher Unwin. Mineola, NY: Dover Publications, 2002.

Lederach, Angela Jill. *Feel the Grass Grow: Ecologies of Slow Peace in Colombia*. Stanford, CA: Stanford University Press, 2023.

Lefebvre, Henri. *The Explosion: Marxism and the French Upheaval*. Translated by Alfred Ehrenfeld. New York, NY: Monthly Review Press, 1969.

LeGrand, Catherine. "Colonization and Violence in Colombia: Perspectives and Debates." *Canadian Journal of Latin American and Caribbean Studies* 14, no. 28 (1989): 5–29.

——. *Frontier Expansion and Peasant Protest in Colombia, 1850–1936*. Albuquerque: University of New Mexico Press, 1986.

Lemaitre Ripoll, Julieta, ed. *Derechos enterrados: Comunidades étnicas y campesinas en colombia, nueve casos*. Bogotá, Colombia: Universidad de los Andes, Facultad de Derecho, Centro de Investigaciones Sociojurídicas, Ediciones Uniandes, 2011.

Lenin, V.I. "The Collapse of the Second International." In *Collected Works*, translated by Julius Katzer, vol. 21 (August 1914–December 1915). Moscow: Progress Publishers, 1964. https://www.marxists.org/archive/lenin/works/1915/csi/ii.htm.

——. "What Is to Be Done? Burning Questions of Our Movement." In *Collected Works*, translated by Joe Fineberg and George Hanna, vol. 5 (May 1901–February 1902): 347–530. Moscow: Progress Publishers, 1902.

Liebman, Alexander. "Cannabis, Cane, and Campesinos: Identity, Resistance, and Negotiation at the Plantation Interface in Northern Cauca, Colombia." PhD diss., Rutgers University, forthcoming.

Londoño, Julio César. "La 'primera línea' y las otras cuatro." In *Voces en primera línea*, edited by Freya Liv Quintana and Juan Sebastián Rojas, 59–61. Colombia: Librería Expresión Viva, Fundación Crear Ciudad, Sic Semper Editorial, Oromo Café Librería y Editorial, Ediciones El Silencio, 2021.

Loperena, Christopher A. *The Ends of Paradise: Race, Extraction, and the Struggle for Black Life in Honduras*. Stanford, CA: Stanford University Press, 2022.

——. "Settler Violence? Race and Emergent Frontiers of Progress in Honduras." *American Quarterly* 69, no. 4 (2017): 801–7.

López Hernández, Claudia, ed. *Y refundaron la patria*. Bogotá, Colombia: Debate, 2010.

Lorde, Audre. *Sister Outsider: Essays and Speeches*. Berkeley, CA: Crossing Press, 1984.

Lozano Lerma, Betty Ruth. "Social Uprising, Racism, and Resistance in Cali's National Strike." *South Atlantic Quarterly* 121, no. 2 (2022): 425–34.

Lugones, María. "The Coloniality of Gender." *Worlds and Knowledges Otherwise* 2, no. 2 (2008): 73–101.

Maldonado Tovar, Juan Camilo. "Digna putería: La historia de la Unión de Resistencias Cali." *Mutante*, October 4, 2021. https://www.mutante.org/contenidos/digna-puteria-union-resistencias-cali.

Mallon, Florencia E. *Peasant and Nation: The Making of Postcolonial Mexico and Peru*. Berkeley: University of California Press, 1995.

Mao Zedong. "On Guerrilla Warfare." In *Selected Works of Mao Tse-Tung*, vol. 9, 1937. https://www.marxists.org/reference/archive/mao/works/1937/guerrilla-warfare/index.htm.

Marcos, Subcomandante Insurgente. "Durito IV: Neoliberalism and the Party-State System." In *Conversations with Durito: Stories of the Zapatistas and Neoliberalism*, 87–94. Brooklyn, NY: Autonomedia, 2005.

———. "La historia de las preguntas," December 13, 1994. https://enlacezapatista.ezln.org.mx/1994/12/13/la-historia-de-las-preguntas/.

———. "Respuesta a la organización político-militar vasca Euskadi Ta Askatasuna (ETA)," January 9, 2003. https://enlacezapatista.ezln.org.mx/2003/01/09/respuesta-a-la-organizacion-politico-militar-vasca-euskadi-ta-askatasuna-eta/.

Mariátegui, José Carlos. *José Carlos Mariátegui: An Anthology*. Edited by Harry E. Vanden and Marc Becker. New York, NY: Monthly Review Press, 2011.

Marrugo Gómez, Ana. "Afectos y ollas comunitarias después del Paro Nacional del 2021 en Colombia." Paper presented at the Latin American Studies Association Annual Conference, Bogotá, Colombia, June 2024.

Martínez, Felipe. *Desborde popular: La rebelión caleña en el paro de abril de 2021 en Colombia*. Bogotá, Colombia: Desde Abajo, 2023.

Marx, Karl. *Capital: A Critique of Political Economy*. Vol. 1. London, UK: Penguin Classics, 1990.

———. *The Eighteenth Brumaire of Louis Bonaparte*. Paris: Foreign Languages Press, 2021.

Marx, Karl, and Frederick Engels. *The Manifesto of the Communist Party*. In *Karl Marx and Frederick Engels: Selected Works*, 1:98–137. Moscow, USSR: Progress Publishers, 1969.

Mattick, Paul. "The Scum of Humanity." *International Council Correspondence* 1, no. 6 (1935): 9–18.

Mbembé, J.-A. "Necropolitics." Translated by Libby Meintjes. *Public Culture* 15, no. 1 (2003): 11–40.

McAllister, Carlota, and Diane M. Nelson, eds. *War by Other Means: Aftermath in Post-Genocide Guatemala*. Durham, NC: Duke University Press, 2013.

McSweeney, Kendra, Nazih Richani, Zoe Pearson, Jennifer Devine, and David. J. Wrathall. "Why Do Narcos Invest in Rural Land?" *Journal of Latin American Geography* 16, no. 2 (2017): 3–29.

Medina Pineda, Medófilo. "Inscripción histórica, personalidad sociocultural del estallido social 2021." In *Estallido social 2021: Expresiones de vida y resistencias*, edited by Juan Carlos Celis Ospina, 25–66. Bogotá, Colombia: Siglo Editorial, Universidad del Rosario, 2023.

Medios Libres Cali. "'Instead, We Became Millions': Inside Colombia's On-going General Strike." CrimethInc, May 20, 2021. https://crimethinc .com/2021/05/20/instead-we-became-millions-inside-colombias-ongoing -general-strike.

Mejía, Daniel. "Plan Colombia: An Analysis of Effectiveness and Costs." Washington, DC: Brookings Institution, 2016.

Mezzadra, Sandro, and Verónica Gago. "In the Wake of the Plebeian Revolt: Social Movements, 'Progressive' Governments, and the Politics of Autonomy in Latin America." *Anthropological Theory* 17, no. 4 (2017): 474–96.

Midnight Notes Collective. *The New Enclosures*. Vol. 10. Jamaica Plain, MA: Midnight Notes, 1990.

Mills, Charles W. "The Racial Contract." In *The Racial Contract*. Ithaca, NY: Cornell University Press, 1997.

Mina, Mateo. *Esclavitud y libertad en el valle del río Cauca*. Bogotá, Colombia: Universidad de los Andes, 2011.

Ministerio de Defensa (Colombia). "Balance general—paro nacional 2021: 28 de abril al 27 de junio de 2021—corte a las 23.59 HR." 2021. https://www .mindefensa.gov.co/irj/go/km/docs/Mindefensa/Documentos/descargas/ estudios_sectoriales/info_estadistica/InformeCorrido_Balance_Paro _2021.pdf.

Ministerio del Interior (Colombia). "Presidente Gustavo Petro, sancionó la Ley de la Paz Total," November 4, 2022. https://www.mininterior.gov .co/presidente-gustavo-petro-sanciono-la-ley-de-la-paz-total/#:~:text=La %20Ley%20418%20de%20Paz,despeje%20de%20la%20Fuerza%20P%C3 %BAblica.

Mintz, Sidney W. "A Note on the Definition of Peasantries." *Journal of Peasant Studies* 1, no. 1 (1973): 91–106.

Molano, Alfredo. *Selva adentro: Una historia oral de la colonización del Guaviare*. Bogotá, Colombia: El Áncora Editores, 2006.

Montenegro Lancheros, Hernán Camilo. "Ampliaciones y quiebres del reconocimiento político del campesinado colombiano: Un análisis a la luz de la Cumbre agraria, campesina, étnica y popular (Cacep)." *Revista Colombiana de Antropología* 52, no. 1 (2016): 169–95.

Moodie, Ellen. *El Salvador in the Aftermath of Peace: Crime, Uncertainty, and the Transition to Democracy*. Philadelphia: University of Pennsylvania Press, 2010.

Moreton-Robinson, Aileen. *The White Possessive: Property, Power, and Indigenous Sovereignty*. Minneapolis: University of Minnesota Press, 2015.

Morris, Courtney Desiree. *To Defend This Sunrise: Black Women's Activism and the Authoritarian Turn in Nicaragua*. New Brunswick, NJ: Rutgers University Press, 2023.

Movilización de Mujeres Afrodescendientes por el Cuidado de la Vida y los Territorios Ancestrales. "Comunicado a las comunidades organizadas y no organizadas, al gobierno nacional y sus instituciones y actores en el marco del acuerdo para la salida negociada al fin del conflicto, a la opinión pública," April 21, 2018.

———. "Comunicado N° 1," November 15, 2014. https://mujeresnegrascaminan .com/comunicado-1/.

Nahuelpan, Héctor. "Formación colonial del Estado y desposesión en Ngulumapu." In *Ta iñ fijke xipa rakizuameluwün: Historia, colonialismo y resistencia desde el país mapuche*, 19–152. Temuco: Ediciones Comunidad de Historia Mapuche, 2012.

Nash, June C. *We Eat the Mines and the Mines Eat Us: Dependency and Exploitation in Bolivian Tin Mines*. New York, NY: Columbia University Press, 1979.

Nasioka, Katerina. "The Proletariat versus the Working Class: Shifts in Class Struggle in the Twenty-First Century." In *Open Marxism 4: Against a Closing World*, edited by Ana Cecilia Dinerstein, Alfonso García Vela, Edith González, and John Holloway, 125–41. London, UK: Pluto, 2020.

National Center for Historical Memory. *Basta Ya! Colombia: Memories of War and Dignity*. Translated by Jimmy Weiskopf. Colombia, 2016.

Negotiation Table. "Final Agreement to End the Armed Conflict & Build a Stable and Lasting Peace," 2017. https://peaceaccords.nd.edu/wp-content/ uploads/2023/02/Colombia-Final-Accord-Text-in-English.pdf.

Neocleous, Mark. *War Power, Police Power*. Edinburgh, Scotland: Edinburgh University Press, 2014.

Newton, Huey P. "Intercommunalism (1974)." *Viewpoint Magazine*, 2018. https://viewpointmag.com/2018/06/11/intercommunalism-1974/.

Ng'weno, Bettina. *Turf Wars Territory and Citizenship in the Contemporary State*. Stanford, CA: Stanford University Press, 2007.

Nkrumah, Kwame. *Neo-Colonialism: The Last Stage of Imperialism*. New York, NY: International Publishers, 1966.

Nunes, Rodrigo. *Neither Vertical nor Horizontal: A Theory of Political Organization*. London, UK: Verso, 2021.

Observatorio de Drogas de Colombia. "Cultivos ilícitos," 2024. https://www .minjusticia.gov.co/programas-co/ODC/Paginas/SIDCO-departamento -municipio.aspx.

Ojulari, Esther Yemisi, and Harrinson Cuero Campaz. "Ethno-Racial Analysis of Excessive Use of Force by State Agents in Cali." Translated by Sarah Soanirina Ohmer, Anthony Dest, Wilson Orlando Salazar, and Katherine Díaz Tamayo. Cali Regional Office: CODHES, May 21, 2021. https://codhes.files .wordpress.com/2021/05/codhes-entho-racial-analisis-ecc81tnicoracial-of -the-strikes-in-cali-eng-d.pdf.

ONIC (Organización Nacional Indígena de Colombia). *Los indígenas y la paz: Pronunciamientos, resoluciones, declaraciones y otros documentos de los pueblos y organizaciones indígenas sobre la violencia armada en sus territorios, la búsqueda de la paz, la autonomía y la resistencia.* Bogotá, Colombia: Ediciones TURDAKKE, 2002.

Oslender, Ulrich. *The Geographies of Social Movements: Afro-Colombian Mobilization and the Aquatic Space.* Durham, NC: Duke University Press, 2016.

Paley, Dawn. "Cold War, Neoliberal War, and Disappearance: Observations from Mexico." *Latin American Perspectives* 48, no. 1 (2021): 145–62.

——. *Drug War Capitalism.* Oakland, CA: AK Press, 2014.

Pardo, Daniel. "Por qué en Colombia casi no hay sindicatos (y qué tiene que ver eso con los asesinatos de líderes sociales)." *BBC News Mundo,* November 25, 2020. https://www.bbc.com/mundo/noticias-america-latina-55060513.

Paschel, Tianna. "'The Beautiful Faces of My Black People': Race, Ethnicity and the Politics of Colombia's 2005 Census." *Ethnic and Racial Studies* 36, no. 10 (2013).

——. *Becoming Black Political Subjects: Movements and Ethno-Racial Rights in Colombia and Brazil.* Princeton, NJ: Princeton University Press, 2016.

Pateman, Carole. *The Sexual Contract.* Stanford, CA: Stanford University Press, 1988.

PCN (Proceso de Comunidades Negras). "Alerta sobre incriminación de las defensoras de derechos humanos y activistas del Proceso de Comunidades Negras en Colombia," April 20, 2018. https://renacientes.net/blog/2018/04/20/alerta-sobre-incriminacion-de-las-defensoras-de-derechos-humanos-y-activistas-del-proceso-de-comunidades-negras-en-colombia-pcn/.

——. "El narcotrafico no es lo nuestro: Somos comunidades negras no cocaleras," May 2017.

Peñaranda Supelano, Daniel Ricardo. *Guerra propia, guerra ajena: Conflictos armados y reconstrucción identitaria en los andes colombianos, el Movimiento Armado Quintín Lame.* Bogotá, Colombia: Centro Nacional de Memoria Histórica-Instituto de Estudios Políticos y Relaciones Internacionales, 2015.

Permaneceremos—We Shall Remain. 2015. https://www.youtube.com/watch?v=WeZoPACOOVU.

Perry, Keisha-Khan Y. *Black Women against the Land Grab: The Fight for Racial Justice in Brazil.* Minneapolis: University of Minnesota Press, 2013.

Petro, Gustavo. *Discurso Gustavo Petro—29 mayo de 2022.* 2022. https://www.youtube.com/watch?v=3_bjsCrAF5Y.

——. "Intervención del Presidente Gustavo Petro durante el foro de reactivación económica 'confianza para crecer.'" August 9, 2024. https://www.presidencia.gov.co/prensa/Paginas/Intervencion-del-presidente-Gustavo

-Petro-durante-el-Foro-de-Reactivacion-Econ-mica-Confianza-para-crecer
-240809.aspx.

———. *Una vida, muchas vidas.* Bogotá, Colombia: Editorial Planeta, 2021.

Petro, Gustavo, and Francia Márquez. "Colombia potencia mundial de la vida: Programa de gobierno, 2022–2026," 2022. https://www.cancilleria.gov.co/sites/default/files/FOTOS2020/Programa%20de%20Gobierno%20Gustavo%20Petro.pdf.

Plazas Díaz, Leydi Carolina. "Tierra y colonos en la legislación agraria colombiana." *Revista Andina De Estudios Políticos* 9, no. 1 (2019): 16–45.

PLMT (Proceso de Liberación de la Madre Tierra). "Freedom and Joy with Uma Kiwe." Northern Cauca, Colombia, 2024.

———. "Libertad y alegría con Uma Kiwe." Northern Cauca, Colombia, 2016.

Proclama del Cauca. "Norte del Cauca: Nuevo departamento autónomo, proponen comunidades negras." March 22, 2015a, sec. Actualidad. https://www.proclamadelcauca.com/norte-del-cauca-nuevo-departamento-autonomo-proponen-comunidades-negras/.

———. "Paloma Valencia propone dividir el departamento del Cauca en dos: Uno para indígenas y otro para los demás," March 15, 2015b, sec. Actualidad. https://www.proclamadelcauca.com/paloma-valencia-propone-dividir-el-departamento-del-cauca-en-dos-uno-para-indigenas-y-otro-para-los-demas/.

Pueblos en Camino. "Y ahora nos mataron a Fredy," July 27, 2023. https://pueblosencamino.org/?p=9860.

Quijano, Anibal. "Coloniality of Power, Eurocentrism, and Latin America." Translated by Michael Ennis. *Nepantla: Views from South* 1, no. 3 (2000): 533–80.

Quintana, Laura. *Rabia: Afectos, violencia, inmunidad.* Barcelona, Spain: Herder, 2021.

Ramírez, María Clemencia. *Between the Guerrillas and the State: The Cocalero Movement, Citizenship, and Identity in the Colombian Amazon.* Durham, NC: Duke University Press, 2011.

———. "Genealogía de la categoría de colono: Imágenes y representaciones en las zonas de frontera y su devenir en campesino colono y campesino cocalero." *Revista Colombiana de Antropología* 58, no. 1 (2022): 29–60.

Ramírez, William. "La guerrilla rural en Colombia: ¿Una vía hacia la colonización armada?" *Estudios Rurales Latinoamericanos* 4, no. 2 (1981): 144–205.

Rappaport, Joanne. *Cumbe Reborn: An Andean Ethnography of History.* Chicago, IL: University of Chicago Press, 1994.

———. *The Disappearing Mestizo: Configuring Difference in the Colonial New Kingdom of Granada.* Durham, NC: Duke University Press, 2014.

———. *Intercultural Utopias: Public Intellectuals, Cultural Experimentation, and Ethnic Pluralism in Colombia.* Durham, NC: Duke University Press, 2005.

———. *The Politics of Memory: Native Historical Interpretation in the Colombian Andes.* Durham, NC: Duke University Press, 1998.

Rebollo, Esther. "Santos: 'El modelo económico y político no está en discusión con las FARC.'" *Revista Semana,* November 15, 2012. https://www.semana.com/nacion/articulo/santos-el-modelo-economico-politico-no-esta-discusion-farc/267919-3/.

Restrepo, Eduardo. *Etnización de la negridad: La invención de las "comunidades negras" como grupo étnico en Colombia.* Popayán, Cauca: Editorial Universidad del Cauca, 2013.

Richmond, Oliver P. "The Problem of Peace: Understanding the 'Liberal Peace.'" *Conflict, Security and Development* 6, no. 3 (2006): 291–314.

Rivera Cusicanqui, Silvia. "Ch'ixinakax Utxiwa: A Reflection on the Practices and Discourses of Decolonization." Translated by Brenda Baletti. *South Atlantic Quarterly* 111, no. 1 (2012): 95–109.

———. "The Politics and Ideology of the Colombian Peasant Movement: The Case of ANUC (National Association of Peasant Smallholders)." Geneva: United Nations Research Institute for Social Development; Centro de Investigación y Educación Popular, 1987.

———. *Violencias (re)encubiertas en Bolivia.* La Paz, Bolivia: Piedra Rota, 2010.

Rocio Valdivia, Fatima del, and Juan Okowí. "Drug Trafficking in the Tarahumara Region, Northern Mexico: An Analysis of Racism and Dispossession." *World Development* 142 (2021).

Rojas, Cristina. *Civilization And Violence: Regimes of Representation in Nineteenth-Century Colombia.* Minneapolis: University of Minnesota Press, 2001.

Romero, Mauricio, ed. *Parapolítica: La ruta de la expansión paramilitar y los acuerdos políticos.* Bogotá, Colombia: Intermedio, 2007.

Ross, Kristin. *Communal Luxury: The Political Imaginary of the Paris Commune.* London, UK: Verso, 2015.

———. *The Commune Form: The Transformation of Everyday Life.* London, UK: Verso, 2024.

Rousseau, Jean-Jacques. "The Social Contract." In The Social Contract *and* The First and Second Discourses, 149–254. Rethinking the Western Tradition. New Haven, CT: Yale University Press, 2002.

Rozental, Emmanuel, and Vilma Almendra. "La paz de los pueblos sin dueños." *desInformémonos,* May 5, 2013. https://desinformemonos.org/la-paz-de-los-pueblos-sin-duenos/.

Rozental, Manuel. "¿Qué palabra camina la minga?" *Deslinde,* August 21, 2009.

Saade, Marta, ed. *Elementos para la conceptualización de lo "campesino" en Colombia*. Bogotá, Colombia: Instituto Colombiano de Antropología e Historia, 2018.

Sabogal, John Edison. "Entre el Cauca y la Habana: La participación de las organizaciones étnicas en el proceso de paz en Colombia." Master's thesis, École des Hautes Études en Sciences Sociales, 2019.

Sakai, J. *The "Dangerous Class" and Revolutionary Theory: Thoughts on the Making of the Lumpen/Proletariat*. Montreal, Quebec: Kersplebedeb, 2017.

Scahill, Jeremy. *Dirty Wars: The World Is a Battlefield*. New York, NY: Nation Books, 2013.

Scott, James C. *The Art of Not Being Governed: An Anarchist History of Upland Southeast Asia*. New Haven, CT: Yale University Press, 2009.

———. *The Moral Economy of the Peasant: Rebellion and Subsistence in Southeast Asia*. New Haven, CT: Yale University Press, 1976.

———. *Seeing Like a State: How Certain Schemes to Improve the Human Condition Have Failed*. New Haven, CT: Yale University Press, 1998.

Semana. "El dilema de la consulta previa." February 26, 2012. https://www.semana.com/nacion/articulo/el-dilema-consulta-previa/254088-3/.

Serje, Margarita. *El revés de la nación: Territorios salvajes, fronteras y tierras de nadie*. Bogotá, Colombia: Ediciones Uniandes, 2011.

Shanin, Teodor, ed. *Peasants and Peasant Societies: Selected Readings*. 2nd ed. Oxford, UK: Basil Blackwell, 1987.

Simpson, Leanne Betasamosake. *As We Have Always Done: Indigenous Freedom through Radical Resistance*. Minneapolis: University of Minnesota Press, 2017.

Skinner, Quintin. "The State." In *Political Innovation and Conceptual Change*, 90–131. Cambridge, UK: Cambridge University Press, 1989.

Smith, Christen A. *Afro-Paradise: Blackness, Violence, and Performance in Brazil*. Champaign: University of Illinois Press, 2016a.

———. "Facing the Dragon: Black Mothering, Sequelae, and Gendered Necropolitics in the Americas." *Transforming Anthropology* 24, no. 1 (2016b): 31–48.

Speed, Shannon. "Structures of Settler Capitalism in Abya Yala." *South Atlantic Quarterly* 69, no. 4 (2017).

Stutzman, Ronald. "El Mestizaje: An All-Inclusive Ideology of Exclusion." In *Cultural Transformations and Ethnicity in Modern Ecuador*, edited by Norman E. Whitten, 45–94. Champaign: University of Illinois Press, 1981.

Tate, Winifred. "The Aspirational State: State Effects in Putumayo." In *State Theory and Andean Politics: New Approaches to the Study of Rule*, 234–53. Philadelphia: University of Pennsylvania Press, 2015b.

———. *Drugs, Thugs, and Diplomats: U.S. Policymaking in Colombia*. Stanford, CA: Stanford University Press, 2015a.

Taussig, Michael. *The Devil and Commodity Fetishism in South America*. Chapel Hill: University of North Carolina Press, 1980.

———. *Palma Africana*. Chicago, IL: University of Chicago Press, 2018.

Temblores, PAIIS (Programa de Acción por la Igualdad y la Inclusión Social), and INDEPAZ. "Resumen ejecutivo informe de Temblores ONG, Indepaz y PAIIS a la CIDH sobre la violación sistemática de la Convención Americana y los alcances jurisprudenciales de la Corte IDH con respecto al uso de la fuerza pública contra la sociedad civil en Colombia, en el marco de las protestas acontecidas entre el 28 de abril y el 26 de junio de 2021," June 8, 2021. https://en.temblores.org/_files/ugd/7bbd97 _00f4e54bbb3742d9ac4a3e21dfddeac4.pdf.

Tickner, Arlene B. "Intervention by Invitation: Keys to Colombian Foreign Policy and Its Main Shortcomings." *Colombia Internacional* 65 (2007): 90–111.

Todorov, Tzvetan. *The Conquest of America: The Question of the Other*. Translated by Richard Howard. Norman: University of Oklahoma Press, 1982.

Trujillo, Ciro. *Páginas de su vida*, 1965. https://www.yumpu.com/es/document/ read/25111618/ciro-trujillo-paginas-de-su-vida.

Twinam, Ann. *Purchasing Whiteness: Pardos, Mulattos, and the Quest for Social Mobility in the Spanish Indies*. Stanford, CA: Stanford University Press, 2015.

UNHCR (United Nations High Commissioner for Refugees). "Forced Displacement Growing in Colombia despite Peace Agreement," 2017. https:// www.unhcr.org/us/news/briefing-notes/forced-displacement-growing -colombia-despite-peace-agreement.

UNODC (United Nations Office on Drug Control). "2008 World Drug Report," 2008.

———. "2024 World Drug Report," 2024.

———. "Coca Cultivation in the Andean Region: A Survey of Bolivia, Colombia and Peru," 2008.

———. "Colombia: Censo de cultivos de coca en diciembre de 2003," 2004.

———. "Colombia: Survey of Territories Affected by Illicit Crops—2016," 2017.

———. "Cultivos de coca: Estadísticas municipales censo 31 de diciembre de 2013," 2014.

UNODC (United Nations Office on Drug Control) and BIESIMCI. "Estadísticas municipales año 2020," 2021. https://www.biesimci.org/index.php?id=134.

Uprimny Yepes, Rodrigo. "Para que el campesinado cuente tiene que ser contado." *Dejusticia*, November 23, 2017. https://www.dejusticia.org/wp -content/uploads/2018/02/Tutela-censo-campesino-final-.pdf.

Valencia, Paloma, @PalomaValenciaL. "Propongo un referendo o una consulta para que el departamento del Cauca se divida en dos. Un departamento indígena y otro para los ,estizos." *Twitter* (blog), March 16, 2015. https://twitter.com/PalomaValenciaL/status/577574125947994112.

Van Cott, Donna Lee. *The Friendly Liquidation of the Past: The Politics of Diversity in Latin America*. Pittsburgh, PA: University of Pittsburgh Press, 2000.

Vargas Meza, Ricardo. "Economías de guerra en escenarios de posacuerdos: Drogas en Colombia y los desafíos de la paz liberal." In *Violencias Que Persisten: El Escenario Tras Los Acuerdos de Paz*, edited by Mario Aguilera Peña and Carlos Mario Perea Restrepo, 1–76. Bogotá, Colombia: Universidad del Rosario, 2020.

Vega Cantor, Renán. "El motín del CAI: La masacre policial del 9 y 10 de septiembre de 2020 en Bogotá." *Rebelión*, September 9, 2021. https://rebelion.org/wp-content/uploads/2021/09/colombia_cai-2.pdf.

Velasco Olarte, Mónica Eliana. "Quiénes son hoy los/as campesino/as: Un acercamiento al proceso de construcción de identidad campesina en el marco del conflicto armado en Colombia. Caso de estudio: Las zonas de reserva campesina." Master's thesis, Facultad Latinoamericana de Ciencias Sociales (FLACSO), 2014.

Vergara-Figueroa, Aurora. *Afrodescendant Resistance to Deracination in Colombia: Massacre at Bellavista-Bojayá-Chocó*. Cham, Switzerland: Palgrave Macmillan, 2018.

Víctimas de la masacre de el Tandil llegaron a Bogotá exigiendo justicia, 2020. https://www.youtube.com/watch?v=4VSAvmgCY9k.

Villarraga, Álvaro. "Bloque Calima de las AUC: Depredación, paramilitarismo y narcotráfico en el suroccidente colombiano." Informes Sobre el Origen y Actuación de Las Agrupaciones Paramilitares en Las Regiones. Bogotá, Colombia: Centro Nacional de Memoria Histórica (CNMH), 2018.

Wade, Peter. *Blackness and Race Mixture: The Dynamics of Racial Identity in Colombia*. Baltimore, MD: Johns Hopkins University Press, 1993.

———. "Race in Latin America." In *Companion to Latin American Anthropology*, edited by Deborah Poole, 177–92. Oxford, UK: Blackwell, 2008.

Wallerstein, Immanuel. *The Modern World-System I: Capitalist Agriculture and the Origins of the European World-Economy in the Sixteenth Century*. Berkeley: University of California Press, 2011.

Warren, Kay B., and Jean E. Jackson, eds. *Indigenous Movements, Self-Representation, and the State in Latin America*. Austin: University of Texas Press, 2003.

Weeks, Kathi. "The Lumpenproletariat and the Politics of Class." *Crisis and Critique* 10, no. 1 (May 18, 2023): 325–47.

Williams, Raymond. *The Long Revolution*. Middlesex, UK: Penguin Books, 1961.

Wolfe, Patrick. "Settler Colonialism and the Elimination of the Native." *Journal of Genocide Research* 8, no. 4 (2006): 387–409.

Wolford, Wendy. *This Land Is Ours Now: Social Mobilization and the Meanings of Land in Brazil.* Durham, NC: Duke University Press, 2010.

Worsley, Peter. "Frantz Fanon and the 'Lumpenproletariat.'" *Socialist Register* 9:193–230 (1972).

Wynter, Sylvia. "Unsettling the Coloniality of Being/Power/Truth/Freedom: Towards the Human, after Man, Its Overrepresentation—An Argument." *CR: The New Centennial Review* 3, no. 3 (2003): 257–337. https://doi.org/10.1353/ncr.2004.0015.

Yashar, Deborah J. *Contesting Citizenship in Latin America: The Rise of Indigenous Movements and the Postliberal Challenge.* Cambridge, UK: Cambridge University Press, 2005.

Ybarra, Megan. *Green Wars: Conservation and Decolonization in the Maya Forest.* Berkeley: University of California Press, 2018.

Yie Garzón, Soraya Maite. "Vea, los campesinos aquí estamos! Etnografía de la (re)aparición del campesinado como sujeto político en los andes nariñenses colombianos." PhD diss., Universidad Estadual de Campenias, 2018.

Zambrano, Angelica. "Los discursos de la instalación de la Mesa de Diálogos." *Razón Publica,* October 22, 2012. https://razonpublica.com/los-discursos-de-la-instalacion-de-la-mesa-de-dialogos/.

Zamosc, Leon. *The Agrarian Question and the Peasant Movement in Colombia: Struggles of the National Peasant Association, 1967–1981.* Cambridge, UK: Cambridge University Press, 1986.

Zibechi, Raúl. "El antimonumento, puño-corazón." *La Jornada,* June 18, 2021. https://www.jornada.com.mx/2021/06/18/opinion/015a2pol.

INDEX

Note: Page numbers in italics indicate figures and tables.

ACIN (Çxhab Wala Kiwe Association of Indigenous Cabildos of Northern Cauca/Asociación de Cabildos Indígenas del Norte del Cauca): autonomy and, 52–53, 54, 55–56, 58, 158; in Chaux, 101, 111; Coca Growers' Associations and, 107; "Ending the War, Defending Our Autonomy, Reconstructing the Public Good, and Building Peace," 52–53; FARC-EP and, 42, 48, 49, 50, 52–54, 55–56; Life Plans (Planes de Vida), 58, 103. *See also* Indigenous Guard

ACONC (Association of Afro-Colombian Community Councils of Northern Cauca/Asociación de Consejos Comunitarios del Norte del Cauca), 95, 107, 111

activism: activists characterized as guerillas, 18; activists in government, 31, 33; Afro-Colombian, 126, 140, 141, 156, 174n29 (see also *individual activists and organizations*); delegation from Guatemala and, 15; development opposition and, 26, 85; indigenous, 15, 47, 126, 156 (see also *individual activists and organizations*); mestizo, 97 (*see also* campesinos: post–Peace Accord organizing and; identity politics); professionalized, 15, 17

Afro-Colombian Community Council of Alto Mira and Frontera, *xvi*; autonomy and, 6–9, 15–18; coca cultivation in territory of, 8, 75–76; collective land title of, 8; leadership displacement and return, 9–10, 75–76; leadership imprisonment, 17, 18

Afro-Colombian Community Council of Alto Mira and Frontera, violence and: the El Tandil Massacre and, 5–6; FARC-EP and, 8–9, 15–17, 54; increase in, 18–19; murders of leaders/members, 7, 8, 9, 15–17

Afro-Colombian Community Council of La Toma, viii, ix, 25, 27, 28. *See also* Afro-Descendant Women's Mobilization for the Care of Life and Ancestral Territories

Afro-Colombian Community Council of Nuevo Amanecer (pseudonym): autonomy and, 62–63, 71, 88–89; coca and, 61–64, 79, 81, 87, 88, 108 (*see also* enclosure); Coca Growers' Association of, 82, 87; coca in, 61–64, 77–80, 79, 81–82, 84–87, 86, 88, 108; COCCAM and, 111; collective land title and, 64, 88; *colono/foráneo* and mestizo participation in, 63, 77, 84, 182n34; demographic change and, 63–64, 108–9, 123; displaced people migrating to, 84; enclosure in, 66, 74, 84, 88–89; FARC-EP and, 77, 78, 85; *foráneos* in, 84, 85, 88; formation of, 62–63; foundation of, 77; Julio (pseudonym) and, 81, 88, 109, 182n36; mestizos and, 63, 77, 84, 85, 88, 182n34; Peace Accords workshops and, 43–46, 61–62, 70; PNIS and, 61–62, 109; resistance to coca eradication and, 62–63, 70; settler mentality in, 88; threat of violence and, xii, 85, 182n34; violence in, xii, 76–77, 78, 81, 84, 85

Afro-Colombian Community Council of Nuevo Amanecer, individual interlocutors: Alfredo (pseudonym), 82, 87; Carmen (pseudonym), 36, 84, 87; Jorge (pseudonym), 35–36, 47–48, 84, 87; Juan (pseudonym), 76–77; Julio (pseudonym), 81, 88, 109, 182n36; Roberto (pseudonym), 77, 78–79, 80, 81, 82

Afro-Colombian Community Council of the Iscuandé River, 24

Afro-Colombians: collective land titles and, 6, 8–9, 64, 75, 88, 100, 101; collective rights of, 6–7, 27, 97, 100, 101, 110, 174n22; congressional seats for, 6; difference and, 97, 110 (*see also* race; racialization); exclusion from campesino discourse, 120; exclusion from peace negotiations, 21, 56; free, prior, and informed consultation and, 63, 100; Law 70 and, 6–7; lawsuit use, 100; mining and, 24–25, 26, 27, 104; as obstacles to state formation, 2; place in government, 30 (*see also* Márquez Mina, Francia). *See also* autonomy, black; resistance, black; slavery; *individual people and organizations*

Afro-Colombians, violence and: Armenio Cortés, 9; death threats and, ix–x, xii, 25, 27, 76, 88, 182n34; FARC-EP and, 8–9, 15–17, 43–44, 54; Genaro García, 15–17; Pablo Gutiérrez, 9; Francisco Hurtado Cabezas, 7; Jose Jair Cortes, 17

Afro-Descendant Women's Mobilization for the Care of Life and Ancestral Territories, 18, 25–28, 30. *See also* Garzón Valencia, Sofía; Márquez Mina, Francia

agriculture: agrarian reform and, 6; FARC-EP Agrarian Program, 39, 49, 51, 57–58; FARC-EP Rural and Agrarian Development for Democratization and Peace with Social Justice in Colombia, 105,

119; National Agrarian Summit, 119; oil palms, 6–7, 8, 74; sugarcane, 15, 23, 74, 105. *See also* campesinos; coca; COCCAM; coffee; ORGANICHAUX

Alfredo (pseudonym), 82, 87

alienation, 32, 42–43, 55, 148, 149, 158, 161

Allen, Jafari, 140

Almendra Quiguanás, Vilma, 29, 31, 161, 176n69

Álvaro (pseudonym), 109–11

Alves, Jaime Amparo, 192n49, 193n55

Andrés (pseudonym), 112–18, 120–22

ANP (National Popular Assembly/ Asamblea Nacional Popular), 131–32, 144

Anti-disturbance Mobile Squad (ESMAD), 92–93, 144–48, *145*

ANUC (National Association of Peasant Users/Asociación Nacional de Usuarios Campesinos), 50–51, 102, 119, 186n40

ANZORC (National Association of Peasant Reserve Zones/Asociación Nacional de Zonas de Reserva Campesina), 98, 105, 107, 111, 118, 119, 186n40

Archila Neira, Mauricio, 189n18

arrests and warrants, 17–18, 23–24, 77, 132, 150

ASOMINUMA (Peasant Association of the Mira, Nulpe, and Mataje Rivers/Asociación de Juntas de Acción Comunal de los Ríos Mira, Nulpe y Mataje), 8, 15, 18, 174n27, 175n40

Association of Afro-Colombian Community Councils of Northern Cauca. *See* ACONC

AUC (United Self-Defense Forces of Colombia/Autodefensas Unidas de Colombia): Colombian military support of, 73; drug trafficking and, 83; expansion of state power and, 19; the Naya Massacre and, 83; private property and, 19–20; private-sector ties, 73, 83; school propaganda and, 20; state ties, 20, 73; Uribe administration's negotiations with, 19, 20. *See also* paramilitary groups

authoritarianism, 13, 22, 43, 60

authority: black and indigenous, 75, 108–9, 178n14 (see also *cabildos*; *individual organizations*); European forms of, 4; gendered, 46; loss of, 128; the social contract and, 3; state, 2, 100, 195n67; struggle for, 8, 54, 58, 75, 108–9

autonomy: authorized, 55, 158; Cali uprising murals and, 149, *149*; contradictory process of, 31; critical consciousness and, 32–33; as doing of dissidence, 157; inclusion and, 176n70; the law and, 158; left-wing critiques of, 29, 157–58; as "minority trap," 54–55, 157–58; Pueblos en Camino and, 29; refusal and, 128–29, 156; shared moments of revolt and, 148; state-centric, 54, 100, 123, 158, 160; state retreat and, 161. *See also* resistance

autonomy, black: asserted through the state, 54, 123, 158; contradictions of, 71; enclosure and, 88–89; everyday practices of, 160–61; FARC-EP and, 7–9, 11, 16–18, 54; *mestizaje* and, 96; mutual recognition with indigenous autonomy,

autonomy, black: (*cont.*)
109–10; PCN and, ix, 32, 100–101; political consciousness and, 30; revenge of the system and, 89; *sentipensar* (feeling-thinking) and, 161–62; undermining/limiting, 9–10, 101, 108. *See also* resistance, black; struggle, black; *individual organizations*

autonomy, indigenous: Abiayala/Abya Yala and, 156, 196n10; asserted through the state, 54, 123, 158; *cabildos* and, 49, 51, 54, 55–56, 110, 123, 178n14; CAMPOCAUCA and, 112; contradictions of, 71; FARC-EP and, 48–50, 53–55, 59–60; *mestizaje* and, 96–97; *mingas hacia adentro* and, 153–55; mutual recognition with black autonomy, 109–10; the Nasa people and, 31; *resguardos* and, 51, 75, 110, 120, 153–56, 178n14; respect for, 112; as self-determination, 55; undermining/limiting, 108 (*see also* ORGANICHAUX). *See also* resistance, indigenous; struggle, indigenous; *individual organizations*

Bakunin, Mikhail, 135
Balibar, Etienne, 185n31
Bautista Taquinás, Cristina, 156
Berger, John, xiii
Berlant, Lauren, 82
Bhandar, Brenna, 186n45
black Colombians. *See* Afro-Colombians
Black Communities' Process (Proceso de Comunidades Negras). *See* PCN
Bogotá: Afro-Descendant Women's Mobilization for the Care of Life and Ancestral Territories march to, 25–27, 28; Pablo Catatumbo in, 10, 11; CNP in, 137; the Ethnic Commission in, 10; Peace Accords signing in, 14–15; professionalized human rights activism in, 15, 17; riots in, 127, 188n11
Bojayá Massacre, 43–44, 46, 48, 57
Bolivia, 31, 39–40, 72–73, 186n43
Bonefeld, Werner, 191n37
Brown, Wendy, 99
Buenos Aires, Cauca, vii, *xi, xiii*, 39, 40
Burnyeat, Gwen, 172n11
Butler, Judith, 123

cabildos: ACIN's move away from, 178n14; association with the state, 178n14; autonomy and, 49, 51, 54, 55–56, 110, 123, 178n14; campesino organizing and, 109–11, 116–17 (*see also* CAMPOCAUCA; COCCAM); Chaux indigenous *cabildo*, 109–11, 117; corruption and, 58, 117; ex-FARC-EP indigenous and, 57–58; school curricula and, 117; threats of violence and, 152; undermining of, 54, 107, 122 (*see also* ORGANICHAUX); ZRCs and, 98–99. *See also* ACIN; CRIC
Caicedo Fernández, Alhena, 182n34
Cali, *xvi*, 12, 69, 83
Cali, 2021 uprising in: the ANP and, 131–32; arrests and, 132, 150; beginnings of, 126, 187n4, 188n11; black contributions sidelined in, 139–41, 143, 192n49; Camilo, paso aguante CALI and, 125, 128, 130; the *chirrete/ñeros* and, 133–34, 138; end of, 148, 150, 187n4; ESMAD attack on Dignity Hill, 144–48,

145, 147; exploitation of, 143–44, 150; improvised weaponry and, 129, 146–47; Iván Duque and, 126, 127–28; legacy of, 150, 194n65; "lumpenproletariat" discourse and, 134–35, 136–37, 138, 150–51; mainstream view on source of, 137, 148; Medios Libres updates and, 148, 149; the Minga and, 137–38, 155; motivations for joining, 132–34, 138; mutual aid and, 129, 144, 149, *149*, 150; Olla Rodante collective and, 144, 194n60; *ollas comunitarias* (communitarian kitchens) and, 129, 144, 149, 150, 187n6, 194n60; Gustavo Petro and, 134; rejection and self-determination in, 128–29, 188n14; the *Resiste* statue and, 141–43, *142*, 193n57; toppling the Belalcázar statue and, 127–28; Universidad del Valle occupation, 131, 132; the URC and, 141, 145–46, 193n51; Álvaro Uribe and, 128; William (pseudonym) and, 131, 132–34, 135, 138

Cali, 2021 uprising in (front line of): Fredy Campo Bomba and, 155; class struggle and, 133; construction of, 129 (*see also* Cali, 2021 uprising in (resistance points of)); ESMAD attack on Dignity Hill and, 144, 146–48, *147*; the Minga and, 137–38; the *Resiste* statue and, *142*; "Tod@s Somos Primera Línea" and, 130–31, 138, *139*, 140, 143, 148, 150. *See also* ANP

Cali, 2021 uprising in (resistance points of): the end of the uprising and, 150; Loma de la Dignidad (Dignity Hill), 129, 131, 132, 144,

146, 147, *159*; modeling self-determination, 129–30, 161; popular libraries and, 129, *130*, 149, *149*; Puerto Resistencia (Resistance Port), 129, *130*, *133*, 140–42, *142*, 143, 145, *149*, 156; racism in leadership and, 141, 150–51; reception of the Minga in, 138

Cali Resistance Union (Unión de Resistencia Cali, URC), 141, 145–46, 193n51

Camilo, paso aguante CALI, 125, 128, 130

campesinos: Afro-Colombian, 9, 99, 185n39; Afro-Colombians excluded from discourse of, 120; conflict with indigenous peoples and, 103–4, 109–11, 116–17; definition of, 93; as disadvantaged/oppressed, 93–94, 97–98, 103, 108, 110, 117, 119–20, 121 (*see also* identity politics); displacement of, 48, 74–75, 84, 93; drug trafficking and, 91–92, 93, 107; identity and difference, 98–99, 101, 110, 117–18, 120, 122, 123–24 (*see also* identity politics; ZRCs); indigenous people excluded from discourse, 120; *La ley del monte* (Trujillo and Castaño) and, 67–68; legal rights/recognition and, 93–94, 103, 117–19, 121; *mestizaje* and, 93, 99, 123, 183n4; as mestizos, 62, 63, 93, 97–99, 103–4, 123; national censuses and, 119–21; as needing to be represented, 194n65; peasant nationalism and, 93, 183n4; post–Peace Accords organizing and, 44–46, 94, 101–2, 110 (*see also* ASOMINUMA; CAMPOCAUCA; COCCAM; ORGANICHAUX);

campesinos: (*cont.*)
settler colonialism and, 98, 124;
as targets of Plan Colombia, 73.
See also ANUC; ANZORC
campesinos FARC-EP and: campesino platform, 105, 107–8, 119; as
FARC-EP base, 69, 102, 105–6, 116,
123–24; organizing and, 38–39,
44–45, 47–48, 50, 69
Campo Bomba, Fredy, 152, 155–56
CAMPOCAUCA (pseudonym), 109,
110–12, 116–18, 120–21. *See also*
Andrés
Campo Palacios, Daniel, 196n7
Canetti, Elias, 192n46
Cano, Alfonso, *40*; correspondence
with the ACIN and CRIC, 48, 49;
death/Operation Odysseus and,
35–36, 42, 53, 59, 126; diaries of,
39; as FARC-EP model, 36; in
hiding, 35, *37*, 51–52; KOMSOMOL
and, 59
Cano, Manuel, 67–68, 70
capitalism: agriculture and, 70;
alienation and, 148, 149; compulsion to work and, 157; dispossies-
sion and, 74, 182n34; expansion
of, 158; extraction and, 7; the
lumpenproletariat and, 135,
136, 138; modernity and, 2, 3, 71,
96–97, 148, 149; Petro administration and, 3, 172nn9–10; refusal of,
129, 150, 157, 161–62; rejection of,
158, 160; Santos administration
and, 13–14, 23; sphere of dominance of, 3, 19, 69–70, 158; state
formation and, 3, 172n19; violence
producing, 3, 19, 88; the war on
drugs and, 74
capitalism, colonial: enclosure
within, 18–19, 156, 158 (*see also*

enclosure); genocide and, 4; the
law and, 4; modernity and, 2,
96–97; multiculturalism and, 7;
political economy of, 158; preserved in the Peace Accords, 15,
21; promises of, 129; refusal of,
24, 28–29, 157; the social contract
and, 2, 3, 129; as state character,
5, 21, 23, 60. *See also* colonialism,
settler
Caquetá department, 67, 72, 74, *75*,
83, 84. See also *La ley del monte*
Carmen (pseudonym), 36, 84, 87
Casa Cultural Chontaduro (Chontaduro Cultural House), 139–40,
152
Castaño, Carlos, 19–20
Castaño, Patricia: *La ley del monte*
(The law of the jungle, with Adelaida Trujillo), 67–68, 70, 73
Catatumbo, Pablo: Camila Cienfuegos and, 34; the Colombian
oligarchy and, 41, 47; early life,
10–13; on FARC-EP's appeal to the
poor, 58; on FARC-EP's failure in
armed struggle, 40–42; friendship with Alfonso Cano, 59;
KOMSOMOL and, 59; the murder
of Genaro García and, 16–17; role
in strengthening FARC-EP, 42; as
senator, 10, 42
Cauca, northern, *xvi*, 28; black
demographics in, 94–95, 108–9,
183n10; Corinto, 51–52, 69, 104,
104; FARC-EP coordinated attacks
in, 51–52, 53; indigenous demographics in, 183n10; mestizo demographics in, 183n10; PLMT in,
23; San Antonio, 24–25. *See also*
ACIN; Afro-Colombian Community Council of Nuevo Amanecer;

Chaux; coca; CRIC; *foráneos*; *individual people and organizations*

CCO (FARC-EP Joint Western Command), 42, 53, 55, 56

Chaux (pseudonym): ACIN and CRIC in, 101, 111; Coca Growers' Associations in, 107–8, 109; coca in, 107–8, 109, 116; cocaine processing in, 116; FARC-EP and, 105–6, 116; indigenous *cabildo* of, 109–11, 117; ORGANICHAUX and, 101–7, 109, 111; paramilitary violence in, 112–13, 116; postconflict development and, 101; recognized *resguardo* in, 120; reputation for violence and, 101, 115, 116. *See also* COCCAM

Chaves, Margarita, 122

Cienfuegos, Camila, 34, 39, 43

civil society participation: the ANP and, 131; campesino identity and, 117–18, 120; in development projects, 100; FARC-EP demands for, 20–21; government funding for, 14; inclusivity and, 14, 21; ORGANICHAUX and, 106

class: class struggle and, 133, 191n37, 192n49, 193n59; COCCAM's messaging and, 93; definitions of, 191n37, 192n49; FARC-EP's conception of allies and, 13, 38, 42, 55; indigenous difference and, 38, 50–51, 55; political consciousness and, 47, 158. *See also* Cali, 2021 uprising in; lumpenproletariat, the; politics, left-wing

CNP (National Strike Committee/ Comité Nacional del Paro), 127, 128, 131, 137–38, 194n64

coca: Afro-Colombian Community Council of Alto Mira and Frontera and, 8, 75–76; Afro-Colombian Community Council of Nuevo Amanecer and, 61–64, 77–80, 79, 81–82, 84–87, 86, 87, 88, 108 (*see also* enclosure); anti-culture of, 66, 71, 81, 83, 88, 114; booms in, 62, 65, 67, 74, 81–83, 89, 114; cash flow and, 77–78; Chaux and, 107–8, 109, 116; coca paste, 72–73, 76, 77, 80, 85, 86; community resistance to intervention and, 62–63, 64; cultivation shift to Colombia, 39–40; disease losses, 84–85; expansion of, 68–69, 71–72, 75, 75–76, 89–91, 123 (*see also* enclosure); *foráneos* and, 70–71, 88 (see also *colonos cocaleros*; enclosure); fumigation of (glyphosate), 8, 62, 66, 73–74; growers' protests in the 1990s, 91, 94; growth on less-arable land, 68; growth rate of, 79, 80; increased income and, 67, 81–82, 85, 87, 88, 89, 112; indigenous traditional use of, 81, 87; La Isla eradication effort, 154; *La ley del monte* (Trujillo and Castaño) and, 67–68; Law 30 and, 68; minimizing risks of cultivating, 62; Naya and, 82–83, 113, 114; pickers (*raspachínes*), 57, 77, 79, 79–80, 81, 82, 113; Plan Colombia and, 65, 71–72, 73, 74–75, 76, 92, 181n19; processing laboratories (*chongos* and *cristalizaderos*), 76, 77–78, 80, 85, 86, 116; productivity compared to coffee, 79, 82, 82, 87; subsidizing coffee, 87. *See also* COCCAM

coca, crop substitution and: Agency for the Substitution of Illicit Crops, 91; COCCAM and, 106–7;

coca, crop substitution and: (*cont.*)
coffee and, 78–79, 82–83, 87; community council membership and,
63, 64; failure to implement, 1, 63;
PISDA and, 107, 109; PNIS and,
14, 61–62, 89, 107, 109; Solution
to the Problem of Illicit Drugs
(Peace Accords), 13, 61, 70, 81, 85,
91, 105–6; violence and, 17, 85, 88,
115–16. *See also* CAMPOCAUCA
Coca Growers' Associations (Asociaciones de Cocaleros), 82, 87,
106–8. *See also* COCCAM
cocaine: coca anti-culture and, 81,
87; cocaleros as base of supply
chain, 73, 182n34; Colombia as
transshipment point, 72–73; El
Tandil coca cultivation and, 1;
FARC-EP and, 116; global market
for, 1, 67; U.S. market for, 67, 73
COCCAM (National Coordinating
Committee of Cultivators of Coca,
Poppy, and Marijuana/Coordina-
dora Nacional de Cultivadores y
Cultivadoras de Coca, Amapola y
Marihuana): campesino agency
and, 105; FARC-EP and, 107; *foráneo* advocacy for, 89–90; founding Coca Growers' Associations
(Asociaciones de Cocaleros),
106–7; government mistrust of,
91; launch march of, 91–93, *92*
coffee: coca subsidizing, 87; comparative productivity of, 82, *82*,
87; land suitable for, 68; northern
Cauca economy and, 62; pickers,
45, 78, 118, 182n37; switch from
coca to, 87; switch to coca from,
78–79, 82–83, 87
Colectivo Situaciones, 128, 189n24
Collazos Cayapu, Diana, 196n7

collectivity: collective land titles
and, 6, 64, 75, 88, 100, 101;
freedom and, 28; labor and, 137,
153–54; mutual aid and, 129, 144,
149, *149*, 150. *See also* *individual
collectives*
Colombia: census-taking in, 88,
95–96, 97, 119–21, 184n14; coca
eradication plans, 91 (*see also* Plan
Colombia); Congress of, 20, 30;
Free Trade Agreement with U.S.,
viii, 74; mestizo identity of, 95,
96–97, 104, 121–22, 124, 184n13
(see also *mestizaje*); Ministry of
Defense, 126; Ministry of Interior,
23, 25–26, 121; U.S. military aid
to, 35, 40 (*see also* Plan Colombia).
See also nation-state, the; state,
the
Colombia, 1991 constitution of:
collective land titles and, 6, 101;
community council formation
and, 6, 63, 110; indigenous rights
and, 6, 97, 100, 101, 110, 117–18;
mestizaje and, 97, 99; multiculturalism and, 6, 7, 63, 97, 99, 174n22;
recognition and, 6, 7, 62–63, 97,
103, 174n22; violence following,
40
Colombia, presidents of: Iván
Duque, 21–22, 126, 127–28; Carlos
Lleras Restrepo, 11; Juan Manuel
Santos, 10, 13–15, 20–21, 22–23,
36, 172n11; Álvaro Uribe Vélez,
18, 19, 20, 73, 94–95, 128. *See also*
Petro, Gustavo
Colombian military: ASOMINUMA
and, 175n40; the Cali uprising and,
128, 138; coca eradication and,
62, 63, 64 (*see also* Plan Colombia);
growth of, 41–42; in indigenous

land, 52–53; informants and, 115; mobilization against protest, 128; Operation Odysseus and, 35–36; support of AUC and, 83; suspected in coca robberies, 78; targeting Chaux community leaders, 115; torture and, 57; US aid to, 35, 40 (*see also* Plan Colombia)

colonialism, 4, 70–71, 73, 127, 136, 143, 181n16. *See also* capitalism, colonial

colonialism, settler: drug trafficking and, 71, 88, 180n7; enclosure and, 66, 76, 180n7; Latin American context and, 173n18; logic of elimination and, 23; mentality of, 88; mestizo campesinos and, 98, 124; recognition and, 123; reproduction of inequality of, 64; as war, 24, 143. See also *colonización*; *colonos cocaleros*; enclosure; peace: state-centric

coloniality of power, 140, 158, 173nn18–19, 181n16

colonización (colonization): capitalist expansion and, 69–70, 158; contemporary definition, 64–65; contradictions of, 68; enclosure and, 69–70, 71–72, 88, 89, 158, 181n16; justification for, 4; logic of, 28; resistance to, 50; scholarship of, 69; of struggle, 32, 71; waves of, 68, 69, 71–72, 75, 88–89. See also *colonos cocaleros*; *foráneos*

colonos cocaleros: Afro-Colombian community council membership and, 63–64; ASOMINUMA and, 8, 15; enclosure and, 70, 71–72, 76, 83–84, 88; *La ley del monte* (Trujillo and Castaño) and, 67–68;

Plan Colombia and, 65–66, 73, 74–75; state formation and, 64–65; state support and, 69; uprising of, 62; violence and, 153. *See also* campesinos; *colonización*; *foráneos*

communism: the Cold War and, 72; Communist Party of Colombia, 67; guerillas and, 7 (*see also* FARC-EP); the lumpenproletariat and, 135, 190n36; paramilitary violence against, 7, 58; reforms against, 14; Soviet, 39, 59

Community Action Committees (Juntas de Acción Comunal), 101–2, 110. *See also* campesinos

community councils: authority of, 75; death threats and, xii, 76, 88, 182n34; formation in Pacific Colombia, 174n21; land usage and, 103; murder of members, 7, 8, 9, 15–17; poisoned water and, 76. See also *individual Afro-Colombian councils*

Comprehensive Community and Municipal Crop Substitution and Alternative Development Plans (PISDA), 107, 109

Comprehensive Program for the Substitution of Illicit Crops (PNIS), 14, 61–62, 89, 107, 109

Comprehensive Rural Reform (RRI), 13, 14, 21, 102–3

consciousness, critical, 32–33, 172n1

consciousness, political, ix, 42, 46–47, 193n59

conservatives, 14, 70, 78, 95, 148, 150, 178n16

corporations, multinational, 21, 74, 81, 83, 106

Costa Vargas, João, 96, 122

counterinsurgency, 4, 40, 54, 65, 74, 126
creoles, 2, 96–97, 98, 184n21
creole whiteness, 2, 96–97, 98
CRIC (Çxhab Wala Kiwe Regional Indigenous Council of Cauca/ Consejo Regional Indígena del Cauca): autonomy and, 51, 54, 158, 179n31; in Chaux, 111; defining political community and, 50; FARC-EP and, 42, 48, 49, 50, 51, 53–54, 55; murder of Sandra Liliana Peña Chocué and, 154–55; split from ANUC, 50–51; the Vitoncó Resolution and, 51
CrimethInc Ex-Workers' Collective, 148, 189n24
Cuba, 9, 10, 21, 36, 41, 50, 140
Cuero Campaz, Harrinson, 141, 143
Çxhab Wala Kiwe, xvi, 32. See also ACIN; Cauca, northern; CRIC; Nasa people

Das, Veena, 68
death threats: Afro-Colombian community councils and, xii, 76, 88, 182n34; Afro-Descendant Women's Mobilization for the Care of Life and Ancestral Territories and, 25, 27; the AUC and, 20; Fredy Campo Bomba and, 155; coca substitution meetings and, 85; community council fracture and, 27; FARC-EP and, 48, 57, 175n40, 178n13; foráneos and, 70, 85, 182n34; gold mining and, viii, 25, 27, 85; "no tocar" raft as, 9; Sandra Liliana Peña Chocué and, 153, 154; PNC members and, ix–x; Pueblos en Camino and, 29; ZRC members and, 98

de la Cruz, José Hernán, 1–2, 3–4
democracy, 3–4, 47, 59, 69
development: activist opposition and, 26, 85; agrarian, 105, 119; areas of, 115; Chaux and, 101; displacement and, 26; free, prior, and informed consultation and, 63, 100; as genocidal, 4; the Peace Accords preserving, 14; resistance and, 90; total peace preserving, 3. See also capitalism; PISDA
Development Program with a Territorial Focus. See PDET
de Zubiría Samper, Sergio, 23, 175n53
difference: Afro-Colombian, 97, 110; campesino identity and, 98–99, 101, 110, 117, 122, 123–24 (see also identity politics); ideology and, 136–37; indigenous, 50–51, 97, 110, 122; the lumpenproletariat and, 136; protest and, 138, 146, 192n46; state definitions of, 6–7, 123 (see also Colombia: census-taking in). See also race; racialization
Dinerstein, Ana Cecilia, 31
disarmament camps, vii, xi, xiii, 40, 80–81
displacement: of campesinos, 48, 74–75, 84, 93; development and, 26; dispossession and, 26, 39, 93; FARC-EP violence and, 7, 48, 175n40; foráneos purchasing land and, 83, 84; the Naya Massacre and, 83; Plan Colombia and, 65, 74–76; poisoned water and, 76; violence in general and, 36, 39, 83–84, 134. See also enclosure
dispossession: capitalism and, 74, 182n34; displacement by, 26, 39, 93; drug war capitalism and, 74,

182n34; following coca fumigation, 73–74; resistance to, 7–8, 25, 52–53; state policy and, 13, 24, 181n16 (*see also* colonialism, settler). See also *colonización*; enclosure; land

drug trafficking: Afro-Colombian community councils and, 8, 27; the AUC and, 83; balloon effect and, 72; blamed for Cali uprising, 137; campesinos and, 91–92, 93, 107, 108, 116–17; community dependence on, 64, 89; FARC-EP and, 37–38, 39, 42, 72, 73, 107–8, 116; *foráneos* and, 70–71, 81, 85, 116, 153 (see also *colonos cocaleros*); indigenous banning of, 155–56 (*see also* Campo Bomba, Fredy); new organizations post–Peace Accords, 58, 85; the oligarchy and, 41; routes of, 65–66, 85; settler colonialism and, 71, 76, 88, 180n7 (*see also* enclosure); Solution to the Problem of Illicit Drugs (Peace Accords) and, 13, 61, 70, 81, 85, 91, 105–6 (*see also* coca, crop substitution and; PNIS); Total Peace negotiations and, 22; violence and, 68, 71, 72, 89, 115, 116, 153 (*see also* mafias; murder). *See also* coca; cocaine; Plan Colombia

Duarte, Carlos, 97–98

DuBois, W. E. B., 24

Duque, Iván, 21–22, 126, 127–28

economies: boom, 25, 65, 68, 82; illicit, 64 (*see also* drug trafficking); informal, 134; legal, 1; models of, 13, 14, 23, 29; political, 66, 158; subsistence, 71. *See also* capitalism; capitalism, colonial

Ecuador, 1, 6, 31

elites: the 2021 Cali uprising and, 138, 144, 150, 193n57; as controlling the government, 10–11, 13, 195n67; control/repression of campesino organizing, 94, 99 (*see also* ORGANICHAUX); influence on the Peace Accords, 21; "lumpenproletariat" terminology and, 136–37; oligarchy and, 41, 47; paramilitary force and, 7; Plan Colombia and, 76; racism and, 94–95, 137; traditional, 30. *See also* conservatives; *mestizaje*; racism

ELN (National Liberation Army/ Ejército de Liberación Nacional), 17–18, 44, 67

El Tandil Massacre, the, 1–2, 3–4, 5, 9

enclosure: in the Afro-Colombian Community Council of Nuevo Amanecer, 66, 74, 84, 88–89; black autonomy and, 88–89; colonial capitalism and, 18–19, 156, 158; *colonización/colonos cocaleros and*, 69–70, 71–72, 76, 83–84, 88, 89, 158, 181n16; definition, 66; as lens, 180n5; marijuana and, 181n7; resources and, 66; settler colonialism and, 66, 76, 180n7; violence and, 69–70, 75, 83, 84, 86, 88; the war on drugs provoking, *75*, 181n16 (*see also* displacement: campesino)

Engels, Frederick, 135

ESMAD (Anti-disturbance Mobile Squad), 92–93, 144–48, *145*

Ethnic Commission for Peace and the Defense of Territorial Rights (Comisión Étnica para la Paz y la Defensa de los Derechos Territoriales): community workshops and, x, xii, *22*, 32, 80–81, 89–90; consul-

Ethnic Commission (*cont.*)
tation with Guatemalan activists,
15; division of Cauca and, 95;
exclusion from peace negotiations
and, 10, 56; negotiations with
FARC-EP and, x, 10–11, 15, 50, 56
evangelical Christianity, 14, 87, 113,
114, 117, 187n54
extraction: capital and, 7; impoverishment and, 26; politics of,
52–53; relationship to the land
and, 66, 84, 186n43; of resources,
7, 8, 53, 54, 103 (*see also* gold)

Fanon, Frantz, 97, 135–36, 190n36
FARC-EP (Revolutionary Armed
Forces of Colombia–People's
Army/Fuerzas Armadas Revolucionarias de Colombia–Ejército
del Pueblo): action against paramilitary groups, 114; the Afro-Colombian Community Council
of Nuevo Amanecer and, 77, 78,
85; Agrarian Program, 39, 49,
51, 57–58; alienation from base,
42–43, 55; anniversary celebration, vii, *xi*, xii, 144; ANZORC and,
107; approach to revolution, 42,
47, 48, 60; AUC's presence in Naya
and, 83; authoritarianism and,
13, 60; blamed for the El Tandil
Massacre, 1; CCO (Joint Western
Command/Comando Conjunto de
Occidente), 42, 53, 55, 56; Chaux
and, 105–6, 116; civil society
participation and, 20–21; claims
of victory, 11; class conception
of allies and, 13, 38, 42, 55; Coca
Growers' Associations and, 107–8;
COCCAM and, 107; Daniel Aldana
Mobile Column, 15–17, 175n40;
decimation of cohorts and, 57,
59; disarmament and, vii, *xi*,
xiii, 13, 18–19, 20, *40*, 58, 80–81,
85; discourse of liberation, 48;
drug trafficking and, 37–38, 39,
42, 72, 73, 107–8, 116; elimination
of Peace Accords participants,
2; expectations of recruits, 45;
failure of armed struggle and,
40–42; FARC-phobia and, 13,
21–22, 175n52; foreign nationals
in, vii; genocide accusations,
11; ideology of, 116; impoverishment and support for, 37–38, 49,
57–58; internal conflict in, 47, 59;
kidnapping and, 37–38, 39; land
dispossession and, 8–9; mafia
ties and, 116; military force of, 34,
39, 43, 44, 48, 56, 57, 59 (*see also*
violence, FARC-EP); as narco-ter-
rorists, 39–40, 42; origins of, 38;
the Patriotic March and, 107; the
Patriotic Union and, 41, 178n13;
post–Peace Accords reimagining/
splintering, 59–60, 172n1, 175n37;
post–Peace Accords support for,
46; power vacuum left by, xii,
58; pre–Peace Accords negotiations, x, 10, 67, 73; prosecution
of, 14; providing a revolutionary
framework, 47, 59; recruitment
in Naya, 113; refusal of as enmity,
47; reintegration to civilian life,
57, 58, 144, 180n46; as representing the people, 39, 42–43, 47, 55,
60, 116; as target of Plan Colombia, 73; vanguardism of, 11, 37, 43,
47, 59–60, 158; war of the masses
and, 37; ZRCs associated with, 98.
See also Cano, Alfonso; Sandino,
Victoria; violence, FARC-EP

FARC-EP, Afro-Colombians and: black autonomy and, 7–9, 11, 16–18, 54; the Bojayá Massacre and, 43–44, 46, 48, 57; Ethnic Commission and, x, 10–11, 15, 50, 56; the murder of Genaro García and, 15–17; racism and, 10–11, 42–43, 54

FARC-EP, campesinos and: campesino platform, 105, 107–8, 119; as FARC-EP base, 69, 102, 105–6, 116, 123–24; organizing and, 38–39, 44–45, 47–48, 50, 69

FARC-EP, indigenous people and: ACIN and, 42, 48, 49, 50, 52–56; autonomy and, 48–50, 53–55, 59–60; CRIC and, 42, 48, 49, 50, 51, 53–55; expectations of allyship, 49–50, 51, 53–54, 56, 179n24; Jhon (pseudonym), 56–58, 59; racism and, 10–11, 42–43, 49–50, 54, 60; as representing indigenous, 10–11, 42, 49–50, 55, 56, 60; struggle approaches differing, 42, 47, 49–50, 56; violence and, 11, 55–56, 60

FARC-EP, individual interlocutors: Camila Cienfuegos, 34, 39, 43; Jhon (pseudonym), 56–58, 59; René Nariño, 144; Tomás (pseudonym), 43–44, 45–46, 48. See also Catatumbo, Pablo

feminism, 39, 160, 187n6

foráneos (outsiders): Afro-Colombian Community Council of Nuevo Amanecer and, 63, 77, 84, 85, 182n34; the anti-culture of coca and, 81; attempts at undermining community spaces, 89–90; coca production and, 71, 75, 88, 89–90, 116 (see also colonos cocaleros); as coca workers, 84; COCCAM and, 89–90; colonos as, 65, 70, 71; death

threats and, 70, 85, 182n34; drug traffickers and, 70, 85, 116, 153; mestizo, 70, 83–85, 88, 89–90, 108–9; privatized infrastructure and, 89. See also enclosure

free trade, viii, 74, 92

Freire, Paulo, 46, 177n74, 178n19

frontiers, 3, 65, 66, 69, 74, 97, 180n1

Gago, Verónica, 187n6, 195n66

Gaitanista Self-Defense Forces of Colombia (Autodefensas Gaitanistas de Colombia), 85

gangs, 76–77, 132, 133, 137, 143

Garcés, Santiago, 194n64

García, Genaro, 15–16, 17

García Velandia, Martha Cecilia, 189n18, 194n64

Garzón Valencia, Sofía, 26–29

genocide: creole whiteness and, 96; failure to stop, 18; FARC-EP accused of, 11; police violence and, 141; the Spanish Empire and, 4; state formation and, 5, 156; state heroes and, 142, 143

Gilmore, Ruth Wilson, 192n49

gold: chemicals used in mining, 78; control of Cauca and, 24–25, 27, 100; illicit mining of, 24–25, 27, 83, 85; "La Mina" and, 24; as nonrenewable, 68; opposition to mining, viii, 26, 104, 106

Gómez Correal, Diana, 14

Gramsci, Antonio, 46, 47, 195n67

Gros, Christian, 178n16, 184n20

guerillas: activists characterized as, 18; AUC rhetoric and, 19–20; connections with the people and, 38, 41, 46–47; ELN, 17–18, 44, 67; growth of groups, 38–39; indigenous clashes with, 51, 178n16

guerillas: (*cont.*)
  (*see also* FARC-EP: indigenous people and); *La ley del monte* (Trujillo and Castaño) and, 67; M-19, 3, 11, 19, 131; mafia association and, 25, 116; MAQL, 19, 51; power and, xii, 69, 178n16; state violence provoking membership, 13; suspected collaborators, 115; urban strength and, 41, 42; as vanguard of the people, 34. *See also* FARC-EP
Guevara, Ernesto (Che), 12, 34, 37, 59
Gutiérrez Aguilar, Raquel, 31, 177n75
Gutiérrez-Sanín, Francisco, 65

Hall, Stuart, 192n49, 193n59
Hartman, Saidiya, 29, 176n68
Holloway, John, 54–55, 156, 157, 176n71
Hooker, Juliet, 174n22
human rights, viii–ix, 15, 18, 74, 97, 119, 139, 175n40
hunger, 26, 73–74, 87, 129. *See also* impoverishment
Hurtado Cabezas, Francisco, 7, 8

identity politics: *mestizaje* and, 95, 99, 121–22, 123–24; multiculturalism and, 55, 63, 96, 99–100, 123; race relations theory and, 185n31; Paloma Valencia and, 94–95. *See also* ORGANICHAUX; race
ideology: of assimilation, 187n61; commitment to, 171n5; of creole whiteness, 96; difference and, 136–37; domination and, 29; of the FARC-EP, 116; of gender, 14; justifying colonization, 4; rural land use/ownership and, 103; subject elision and, xi–xii, 171n5;

supporting counter-narcotics militarization, 72
impoverishment: capitalism and, 160; coca and, 67, 68, 89; dispossession and, 7; extraction and, 26; FARC-EP support and, 37–38, 49, 57–58; increased income from coca and, 67, 81–82, 85, 87, 88, 89, 112; state promises and, 68, 138; urban resistance and, 129, 133–34
inclusion: autonomy and, 176n70; census categories and, 120; civil society participation and, 14, 21; conditional, 4, 173n15 (*see also* multiculturalism); illusion of, 21; limitations of, 143; metabolizing resistance, 7; negotiating, 13. *See also* multiculturalism; recognition
Indigenous Guard (Guardia Indígena), 52, *52*, 53, 138, 154, 155, 156
indigenous people: census categories and, 120–21; collective land titles and, 6, 75, 100, 101; constitutional and legal rights of, 6, 68, 71, 97, 100, 101, 110, 117–18; exclusion from campesino discourse, 120; exclusion from peace negotiations, 21, 50, 56; FARC-EP expectations of allyship, 49–50, 51, 53–54, 56, 179n24; free, prior, and informed consultation and, 63, 100; Guatemalan, 15; increase in coca cultivation and, 76; the "indigenous question" and, 37, 49; individuals severed from community, 50; land occupation and, 51; *mestizaje* suppressing expression and, 96, 104; Mingas (Mingas of Social and Communitarian Resistance) and, 137–38, 155, 191n42; *mingas hacia adentro* and, 23, 154–55; Misak,

127; Nasa, xiv, 31, *32*, 49, 103–4, 117, 155–56, 178n14; as obstacles to state formation, 2; ORGAN-ICHAUX positioning against, 102; protest and, 94; "reindianization" and, 122; resistance to FARC-EP, 42, 48, 49, 50, 51, 52–54, 55–56, 60 (*see also* FARC-EP, indigenous people and; resistance, indigenous); spirituality of, 81, 117, 118; traditional coca use and, 81. *See also* ACIN; CRIC; PLMT

indigenous people, *resguardos* (reservations) and: authority and, 75; "conditional inclusion" and, 4; Laguna Siberia Indigenous Reservation, 153 (*see also* Peña Chocué, Sandra Liliana); legal standing and, 120, 178n14; representation at PNIS workshops, 61, 70; right to autonomy in, 51, 104, *104*, 110, 178n14; school curricula and, 117

indigenous people, violence and, *32*; Cristina Bautista Taquinás, 156; Fredy Campo Bomba, 152, 155–56; clashes with guerillas, 51, 178n16 (*see also* FARC-EP, indigenous and); Javier Oteca, 15, *16*, 19, 153; Sandra Liliana Peña Chocué, 153, 154, 155, 156; Alvaro Ulcué, xiv

infrastructures, 7, 14, 83, 89, 90, 100, 116

JACs (Community Action Committees/Juntas de Acción Comunal), 101–2, 110. *See also* campesinos
Jaime (pseudonym), 110, 111, 117
Jhon (pseudonym), 56–58, 59
Jimeno, Myriam, 69–70
Johansson, Miranda Sheild, 172n11
Johnson, Lyndon, 38

Jorge (pseudonym), 35–36, 47–48, 84, 87
Juan (pseudonym), 76–77
Julio (pseudonym), 81, 88, 109, 182n36

Kadalie, Modibo, 158
kidnapping, 10, 37–38, 39

labor: *cambio de mano* and, 81, 182n37; coca pickers (*raspachínes*), 57, 77, *79*, 79–80, 81, 82, 113; COCCAM messaging and, *92*, *93*; coffee pickers, 45, 78, 118, 182n37; collective, 137, 153–54; land ownership and, 103–4
La ley del monte (The law of the jungle, Trujillo and Castaño), 67–68, 70, 73
land: ASOMINUMA and, 8–9; campesino rights and, 69, 88, 93–94, 98, 99, 103–4, 117–18 (*see also* ZRCs); collective title to, 6, 8–9, 64, 75, 88, 100, 101 (*see also* indigenous people, *resguardos* (reservations) and); development and, 26; FARC-EP and Afro-Colombian land, 8–9; FARC-EP and indigenous land, 49, 51, 53; individual title to, 8–9, 69, 84, 186n45; lack of formal title and, 77, 88; land grabs, 6–7, 8–9, 74, 83, 182n34 (see also *colonos cocaleros*; enclosure; *foráneos*); large landowners, 7, 49, 74, 105; oil palm cultivation and, 6–7, 8, 74; overlapping claims to, 99; paramilitary violence and dispossession, 7, 83; PLMT and, 23–24, 60; reclaimed, 10, 23, 51, 53; return of, 39; subaltern perspective on, 103; sugarcane monoculture and, 15, 23, 74, 105;

land: (cont.)
    total peace and, 24; use concepts
    and, 103–4. See also agriculture;
    extraction
land reform, 6, 13, 14, 21, 65, 102–3,
    186n43
law: Afro-Colombians and, 6–7, 27,
    71, 97, 100, 101, 110, 174n22; the
    AUC and, 19–20; autonomy and,
    158; colonial capitalism and, 4;
    colonization of, 68; environmen-
    tal, 67; inclusion and, 4; indige-
    nous people and, 6, 68, 71, 97, 100,
    101, 110, 117–18; international,
    20–21; the judicial system and,
    6, 18; Law 21 (1991), 97; Law 30
    (1986), 68; Law 70 (1993), 6–7, 15,
    97; Law 89 (1890), 173n15; Law
    160 (1994), 98, 110, 123; Law 2272
    (Total Peace Law, 2022), 22–23
    (see also Peace Accords); lawsuits,
    100, 119–20, 121; private property
    and, 4, 186n45; the social contract
    and, 3, 4; state formation and, 4.
    See also Plan Colombia
law, rule of: assimilation and, 4,
    187n61 (see also recognition); the
    AUC and, 20; capitalist expan-
    sion and, 14; myth of, 69; private
    property and, 4, 186n45; revolt
    against, 126, 128, 150; settler so-
    ciety and, 187n61; state formation
    and, 2. See also property, private
Lefebvre, Henri, 188n14, 193n58
LeGrand, Catherine, 69
Lenin, Vladimir I., 41, 47
liberalism, 38, 97, 128, 172n11,
    176n54
liberation: beyond the state, 157;
    black exclusion from, 44, 143,
    179n25; critical consciousness

and, 32; FARC-EP's approach to,
    11, 44, 48; impediments to, 138;
    the PLMT and, 23; racism and,
    126–27, 150–51, 179n25; state-cen-
    tric peace and, 24, 33; terrain of
    rebellion and, 149–50. See also
    Cali, 2021 uprising in
Lleras Restrepo, Carlos, 11
Londoño, Rodrigo (Timochenko),
    14–15, 50, 55
Lozano Lerma, Betty Ruth, 192n49
lumpenproletariat, the: elitist
    terminology and, 136–37, 190n32;
    left-wing discourse and, 134–35,
    136–37, 150–51, 190n36; as racist
    term, 136–37, 150–51, 191n39;
    rejecting term, 138

M-19, 3, 11, 19, 131
mafias, 25, 114–15, 116
Mallon, Florencia E., 183n4
Mao Zedong, 38
MAQL (Quintín Lame Armed Move-
    ment), 51
Mariátegui, José Carlos, 49, 53
marijuana, 69, 89–90, 91, 106–7, 180n7
Márquez, Iván, 13, 175n37
Márquez Mina, Francia, viii, ix, xiii–
    xiv, 3, 26–27, 30–31, 126
massacres: Bojayá Massacre, 43–44,
    46, 48, 57; El Tandil Massacre,
    1–2, 3–4, 5, 9; Naya Massacre,
    83–84, 112; paramilitary groups
    and, 43–44, 45, 83, 112, 113
Mattick, Paul, 190n36
Medina Pineda, Medófilo, 188n11
Medios Libres, 148–50
mestizaje: campesinos and, 93, 99,
    123, 183n4; exclusion and,
    96, 184nn19–20; ideology of,
    96; indigenous and black auton-

omy and, 96–97; multiculturalism and, 96, 97, 122; national identity and, 95, 96–97, 104, 121–22, 124, 184n13; the 1991 constitution and, 97, 99; reversed, 122; suppressing black/indigenous expression and, 96, 104. *See also* identity politics

mestizos: activism and, 97, 123, 139, 141 (*see also* campesinos: post-Peace Accord organizing and; identity politics); the Afro-Colombian Community Council of Nuevo Amanecer and, 63, 77, 84, 85, 88, 182n34; the Cali uprising and, 131, 132–34, 135, 138, 139, 141; campesinos as, 62, 63, 93, 97–99, 103–4, 123 (*see also* identity politics); *colonos/foráneos* as, 70, 83–85, 88, 89–90, 108–9; FARC-EP members, 54–55 (*see also* Tomás); *La ley del monte* (Trujillo and Castaño) and, 67–68; Law 160 (ZRCs) and, 123; racial identity and, 95–96, 184n20, 185n24 (*see also* identity politics); as spokespeople for resistance, 141

Mezzadra, Sandro, 195n66

Mingas (Mingas of Social and Communitarian Resistance/Mingas de Resistencia Social y Comunitaria), 137–38, 155, 191n42

mingas hacia adentro, 23, 153–54, 155

modernity: agricultural, 49; capitalist, 2, 3, 71, 96–97, 148, 149; rural projects of, 65, 97 (see also *colonización*)

Molano, Alfredo, 70

Moreno, Vicenta, 139–40, 192n48

Moreno Mina, Victor Hugo, 95

Mother Earth Liberation Process. *See* PLMT

multiculturalism: "conditional inclusion" and, 4; constitutional recognition of, 6, 7, 63, 97, 174n22; identity politics and, 55, 63, 96, 99–100, 123; as interethnic competition, 97–98, 99, 118, 123; *mestizaje* and, 93, 96, 97, 122; neoliberal, 7, 54, 93, 99, 123, 158; state recognition and, 6–7, 63, 71, 94, 97–98, 118–19, 123, 158; as a trap, 7, 54–55. *See also* inclusion; race; recognition

murder: Afro-Colombian community councils and, 7, 8, 9, 15–17; the AUC and, 83; the Cali uprising and, 128, 140–41, 150; FARC-EP's arbitrary use of, 39, 48; leading up to the Bojayá Massacre, 43–44; military, 57, 128; the "no tocar" raft and, 9; paramilitary in general, 45, 85, 112, 113; of PCN members, ix–x; of PLMT liberators, 23; of snitches, 16, 113, 115; of trade unionists, 190n29; of ZRC members, 98. *See also* violence

murder, individual victims: Cristina Bautista Taquinás, 156; Fredy Campo Bomba, 152, 155–56; Armenio Cortés, 9; Genaro García, 15–17; Pablo Gutiérrez, 9; Francisco Hurtado Cabezas, 7; Jose Jair Cortes, 17; Javier Ordóñez, 127; Javier Oteca, 15, *16*, 19, 153; Sandra Liliana Peña Chocué, 153, 154, 155, 156; Alvaro Ulcué, xiv

Nariño, René, 144, 193n59

Nasa people, xiv, 31, *32*, 49, 103–4, 117, 155–56, 178n14

National Association of Peasant Reserve Zones (Asociación Nacional

National Association (*cont.*)
de Zonas de Reserva Campesina,
ANZORC), 98, 105, 107, 111, 118,
119, 186n40
National Association of Peasant
Users (Asociación Nacional de
Usuarios Campesinos, ANUC),
50–51, 102, 119, 186n40
National Coordinating Committee
of Cultivators of Coca, Poppy, and
Marijuana. *See* COCCAM
National Liberation Army (Ejército
de Liberación Nacional, ELN),
17–18, 44, 67
National Popular Assembly (Asamblea Nacional Popular, ANP),
131–32, 144
National Strike Committee (Comité
Nacional del Paro, CNP), 127, 128,
131, 137–38, 194n64
National Strikes: 2019, 187n5, 188n11;
2021, 128, 154, 187n5, 188n11 (*see
also* Cali, 2021 uprising in)
nation-state, the: formation of, 70–71,
95, 96–97, 104, 121–22, 124, 183n4;
legal subjects in, 38; *mestizaje*
and, 95, 96–97, 104, 121–22, 124;
multicultural recognition by, 6–7,
63, 71, 94, 97–98, 118, 119, 158; as
patriarchal, 14. *See also* state, the
Naya, 82–83, 90–91, 113, 114
Naya Massacre, the, 83–84, 112
Neocleous, Mark, 5
neoliberalism: demonstration
against, 126, 195n66; the Duque
administration and, 22, 127;
economic markets and, 64;
economic precarity and, 134,
190n36; FARC-EP criticism of, 53;
multiculturalism and, 7, 54, 93,
99, 123, 158; private property and,

8; reforms of, 6, 74, 81, 127, 128;
rejection of, 137
Ng'weno, Bettina, 100
Nkrumah, Kwame, 73

oil palms, 6–7, 8, 74
Ojulari, Esther, 141, 143
Operation Odysseus, 35–36, 53
ORGANICHAUX (pseudonym), 101–7,
109, 111
Oteca, Javier, 15, *16*, 19, 153
Other, the, 28, 32, 71, 137

pacification, 4–5, 150, 173n18. *See
also* violence, state
Palacios Córdoba, Elba Mercedes,
160–61
Palechor, Gregorio, 50–51
Paley, Dawn, 74, 177n75, 181n19
paramilitary groups: Chaux and,
112–13, 116; confiscation of livestock and, 112; FARC-EP action
against, 114; Gaitanista Self-Defense Forces of Colombia, 85;
gold mining and, 25, 27; government negotiations with, 19;
land dispossession and, 7; mafia
association and, 25; response
to the 2021 Cali uprising, 138;
state collaboration and, 20; ZRC
threats and, 98. *See also* AUC;
FARC-EP; violence, paramilitary
Paschel, Tianna, 6
patriarchy: monuments and, 142;
persistence of, 140, 150, 192n46;
the social contract and, 173n19;
the state and, 2, 14, 30–31
Patriotic March (Marcha Patriótica),
the, 107
PCN (Black Communities' Process/
Proceso de Comunidades Negras):

advocacy workshops, 17, 32; arrest of activists of, 17–18; autonomy and, ix, 32, 100–101; the Bojayá Massacre and, 44; documenting land dispossession and, 9; land use and, 103; legacies of enslavement and, 29; the "revenge of the system" in black life and, 89; systemic violence and, ix–x; as threatening political dominance, 100–101; the war on drugs and, 76; Zapatista parallels, ix

PDET (Development Program with a Territorial Focus), 101

peace: dissident forms of, 5, 28, 29, 32, 33, 157, 177n75; as framework, 5, 23, 33; illusion of, 2, 21; persistence of violence and, 15–17, *16*, 19; potential of, 33; promise of, 10, 15, 19, 26–27, 40, 126 (*see also* Ethnic Commission for Peace and the Defense of Territorial Rights); state-centric, 5, 23–24, 29, 31, 33, 102–3, 176n54; struggles for, 24; total, 3, 19, 22–24, 176n64. *See also* pacification

Peace Accords: Afro-Colombian Community Council of Nuevo Amanecer workshops, 43–46, 61–62, 70; Afro-Colombian exclusion from negotiations, 21, 56; alleged gender ideology of, 14; campesinos and, 93, 102, 103, 104, 105–6, 110, 115; Pablo Catatumbo's senate seat and, 10, 42; colonial capitalism preserved in, 15, 21; elite influence on, 21; Ethnic Commission workshops and, x, xii, *22*, 32, 80–81, 89–90; FARC-EP demands and, 20, 102, 105; indigenous exclusion from

negotiations, 21, 50, 56; lack of implementation, 1, 58; national plebiscite on, 14, 21, 62; as not ending the war, vii, 2, 10, 18–19; Operation Odysseus and, 36; PDET and, 101; preserving the political and economic model and, 13, 14; private property and, 15, 21; right-wing opposition to, 21–22; signing of, vii, xii; Subcommission on Gender, 14, 15, 21; unfulfilled promises of, 22; victim testimony and, 21; violence during negotiations, 15–17, *16*, 19. *See also* COCCAM; Ethnic Commission for Peace and the Defense of Territorial Rights

Peace Accords, chapters of: End of the Conflict and Disarmament, 13 (*see also* FARC-EP: disarmament and); ethnic chapter as appendix, 15; Political Participation, 13 (*see also* civil society participation); Solution to the Problem of Illicit Drugs, 13, 61, 70, 81, 85, 91, 105–6 (*see also* coca, crop substitution and; PNIS); Toward a New Colombian Countryside, 13, 102 (*see also* RRI)

Peasant Association of the Mira, Nulpe, and Mataje Rivers (Asociación de Juntas de Acción Comunal de los Ríos Mira, Nulpe y Mataje, ASOMINUMA), 8, 15, 18, 174n27, 175n40

peasants. *See* campesinos

Peña Chocué, Sandra Liliana, 153, 154, 155, 156

Peru, 39–40, 49, 72–73, 185n22

Petro, Gustavo: the Cali uprising and, 134–35; capitalism and,

Petro, Gustavo: (*cont.*)
3, 172nn9–10; co-optation in
Petro-Marquéz administration,
31; M-19 and, 3, 11; support for,
195n66; total peace and, 3, 19,
22–23, 24; ZRC recognition and, 98
PISDA (Comprehensive Community
and Municipal Crop Substitution
and Alternative Development
Plans), 107, 109
Plan Colombia, 65, 71–72, 73, 74–75,
76, 92, 181n19
plebiscite, Peace Accords, 14, 21, 62
PLMT (Mother Earth Liberation
Process/Proceso de Liberación de
la Madre Tierra), 23–24, 60
PNIS (Comprehensive Program for
the Substitution of Illicit Crops),
14, 61–62, 89, 107, 109
politics: convictions during war,
38; of death, 30; establishment,
14; extractive, 52–53; philosophy
and, 23; political action limits,
31; political consciousness, 42,
46–47, 193n59; political power, 73,
93, 100–101, 118 (*see also* elites);
prefigurative, 149; of representation, 50, 128, 136–37, 150, 189n24.
See also identity politics
politics, left-wing: critiques of autonomy and, 29, 157–58; guerilla
groups and, 83, 100 (*see also*
FARC-EP); lumpenproletariat
discourse and, 134–35, 136–37,
150–51, 190n36; the Patriotic
Union and, 41, 178n13; a *primera
línea* party and, 143; uprising
skeptics in, 132. *See also* communism; Márquez Mina, Francia;
Petro, Gustavo; racism, left-wing
politics and; Zapatistas

politics, right-wing: Democratic
Center Party, 14; Iván Duque and,
21–22, 126, 127–28; opposition to
the Peace Accords and, 21–22;
paramilitary groups and, 39, 73,
100 (*see also* AUC); "Peace with
Guarantees" and, 19
Poole, Deborah, 68
Popayán, *xvi*, 91, 92, 95, 106, 107, 111,
127
poppies, 69, 89–90, 91, 106–7
power: change without taking,
54–55; coloniality of, 140,
173nn18–19, 181n16; community,
62, 110, 137–38 (*see also* autonomy; Cali, 2021 uprising in); drug
trafficking and, 58, 64, 153; elite,
30; guerilla, xii, 69, 178n16 (*see
also* FARC-EP); international, 3;
legitimacy of, 40–41, 128, 188n14,
195n67; micropower, 132, 134;
outsiders and, 109; personal,
130; political, 73, 93, 100–101, 118;
promises of, 60; relations of, 13, 47
power, state: as corrupt and oppressive, x, 176n71; expansion of, 19;
as locus of transformation, 30–31;
myth of totality, 69, 98; revolution taking, 47, 55, 59, 60. *See also*
violence, state
"progressive" institutions, ix, 3, 31,
134, 135, 150, 195n66
property, collective, 119. *See also*
land: collective title to
property, private: the AUC and,
19–20; FARC-EP aggression in
Alto Mira and Frontera and, 8–9;
the law and, 4, 186n45; the Peace
Accords and, 15, 21; racial tension
and, 104, *104*; territorial claims
and, 103

protest: "bad protesters" and, 137, 139–40, 191n39 (*see also* lumpen-proletariat, the); coca growers', 1, 62, 63, 64, 91; destruction of police stations and, 127, 129, 189n18; difference and, 138, 146, 192n46; indigenous, 94 (*see also* Mingas); National Strikes and, 128, 154, 188n11. *See also* Cali, 2021 uprising in

Pueblos en Camino, 29, 161, 176n69. *See also* Almendra Quiguanás, Vilma; Rozental, Emmanuel

Putumayo, 74, 75, 83, 84

Quijano, Aníbal, 140, 173n19

Quiñones, Juan David, 136–37, 191n39

Quiñonez, Sara, 17–18

Quintín Lame Armed Movement (MAQL), 19, 51

race: census identity and, 95–96, 120–21; creole whiteness and, 2, 96–97, 98 (see also *mestizaje*; whiteness); hierarchies of, 64, 96, 98, 143, 160, 181n16, 185n26 (see also *mestizaje*); Latin American terms and, 95–96, 184n14; Law 70 and, 6–7; peasant identity/organizing and, 94, 101, 110, 111–12, 120–21 (*see also* identity politics; *mestizaje*; ORGANICHAUX); racial justice and, 26; resentment politics and, 94, 99, 116–17, 123, 185n32 (*see also* campesinos; identity politics; mestizos); state definitions of difference and, 6–7, 123; whitening and, 4, 96, 122, 185n23. *See also* identity politics; *mestizaje*; multiculturalism; whiteness

racialization, 2, 96, 122, 137, 160, 179n25

racism: campesino rights obscuring, 98; colorblindness and, 141–42; dispossession and, 9–10, 53; elites and, 94–95, 137; foundations of Colombia and, 2; ideal revolutionaries and, 136–37, 140–41; liberation and, 126–27, 150–51, 179n25; Mingas and, 137; state violence and, 139–40, 192n49, 193n52; stoking, 102, *104*, 104–5. *See also* coloniality of power

racism, left-wing politics and: the Cali uprising and, 140, 141, 150–51; FARC-EP and, 10–11, 42–43, 49–50, 54, 60; liberation discourse and, 126–27, 150–51, 179n25; lumpenproletariat discourse and, 136–37, 150–51, 191n39; the *Resiste* statue and, 143

Ramírez, María Clemencia, 94, 180n3

Rappaport, Joanne, 178n14, 184n13, 185n24

reactionaries, 14, 21–22, 29, 135, 150. *See also* AUC

recognition: agrarian reform and, 6; *cabildos* operating without, 178n14; campesino, 93–94, 97–98, 103, 117–19, 120–22, 123–24; constitutional, 6, 7, 62–63, 97, 103, 174n22; metabolizing resistance, 7, 27, 54–55, 71; politics based on, 94, 118, 119; protection/belonging and, 62–63, 100, 123–24; racial definitions and, 6–7, 62–63, 110, 120–21, 122; of resistance, 161; state support and, 120, 178n14. *See also* inclusion; multiculturalism

reform: land and, 6, 13, 14, 21, 65,
102–3, 186n43; neoliberal, 6, 74,
81, 127, 128; the peace negotiation
process and, 21. *See also* Colombia, 1991 constitution of; RRI
religion and spirituality: Cathol-
icism, 44, 187n54; evangelical
Christianity, 14, 87, 113, 114, 117,
187n54; indigenous, 81, 117, 118
resistance: coca catalyzing, 62–63,
64; to collectivity, 64; to *colonización*, 50, 89–90; to colonization
of struggle, 32; to development,
90; ecologies of, 161–62; as
everyday issue, 160–61, 196n18;
mestizos as spokespeople for,
141; metabolized, 7, 31, 193n59;
organization of, 193n59 (see also
individual organizations); pacification and, 4–5, 150, 194n64; persistence of, 193n58; racism and,
140; reproducing life and, 196n18;
the *Resiste* statue and, 141–43, *142*,
193n57; solidarity and, 129, 150,
156, 158; urban impoverishment
and, 129, 133–34; URC and, 141,
145–46, 193n51. *See also* Cali, 2021
uprising in (resistance pints of);
FARC-EP; struggle
resistance, black: to coca eradication, 62–63, 70; cultural history
of, 89–90; to dispossession, 7–8,
25; as everyday issue, 160–61;
importance in Colombian history, 143, 161; sidelined in Cali
uprising, 139–41, 143, 192n49. *See
also* autonomy, black; FARC-EP,
Afro-Colombians and; *individual
organizations*
resistance, indigenous: counterinsurgency and, 4; cultural history

of, 50, 89–90, 155; the Indigenous Guard and, 52, *52*, 53, 138,
154, 155, 156; Mingas (Mingas of
Social and Communitarian Resistance) and, 137–38, 155, 191n42.
See also autonomy, indigenous;
FARC-EP: indigenous and; *individual organizations*
resources: community control of,
6, 117; competition for, 100, 102;
enclosure and, 66; extraction of,
7, 8, 53, 54, 68, 103; government
spending of, 116; nonrenewable,
68 (*see also* gold); obtained from
the state, 62, 100, 101, 102, 107. *See
also* property, private
revolution: assembly models and,
131–32, 189n24, 190n25; blocking,
41, 42; counterrevolution and, 41,
189n24; FARC-EP's approach to,
42, 47, 48, 60; ideal revolutionaries and, 136–37, 140–41; the
lumpenproletariat and, 135–36;
making possible, 128; potential
for, 46; prevention of, 38; professional revolutionaries and, 37, 59
(*see also* vanguardism); strength
needed for, 13; support of the
people necessary for, 38, 39, 41;
taking state power, 47, 55, 59, 60.
See also Cali, 2021 uprising in;
resistance; struggle
Rivera Cusicanqui, Silvia, 4, 172n6,
184n19, 186n43
Roberto (pseudonym), 77, 78–79, 80,
81, 82
Rosero, Carlos, 32
Ross, Kristin, 196n15, 196n17
Rousseau, Jean-Jacques, 3
Rozental, Emmanuel, 29, 153–54,
176n69

RRI (Comprehensive Rural Reform/ Reforma Rural Integral), 14, 102–3

Sáenz Vargas, Guillermo León. *See* Cano, Alfonso
Salazar Lohman, Huáscar, 196n18
Sánchez, Gonzalo, 177n11
Sandino, Victoria, 10–11, 180n46
Santos, Juan Manuel, 10, 13–15, 20–21, 22–23, 36, 172n11
Sa'th Tama Kiwe, *xvi*, 155–56
schools, 20, 102–3, 114–15, 117
Scott, James, 66, 182n36
Serje, Margarita, 180n1, 181n16
Simpson, Leanne Betasamosake, 28
Situationist International, 148, 194n63
slavery, 4, 24, 25, 29, 96, 161, 185n26
Smith, Christen, 9
snitches, 16, 113, 114, 115
social contract, the: authority and, 3; character of, 3–4; colonial capitalism and, 2, 3, 129; as hollow, 28; the law and, 3, 4; liberal, 172n11; patriarchy and, 173n19; the Petro-Marquéz administration and, 3; private property and, 15; state violence imposing, 2, 3; total peace as, 23
social movements: coca anti-culture and, 81; colonization/manipulation of, 105, 111, 178n16; consciousness-raising and, 101; FARC-EP conflict with, 47–48, 56; judicial system as weapon against, 18; lumpenproletariat discourse and, 135; Mingas and, 137; perseverance and, 100; rejection of, 128; subject elision and, xi–xii, 171n5; violence and,

88, 156 (*see also* murder). *See also* activism; ANP; National Strikes; vanguardism; *individual organizations*
solidarity: coca and, 62, 64; ethnic, 186n43; FARC-EP/Ethnic Commission, 10–11; growth of, 196n17; resistance and, 129, 150, 156, 158
Solution to the Problem of Illicit Drugs (Peace Accords), 13, 61, 70, 81, 85, 91, 105–6. *See also* coca, crop substitution and; PNIS
Soto Pito, Daniela, 196n7
state, the: abandonment by, 94; alienation and, 32; authority and, 2, 100, 195n67; blocking revolution, 41, 42; *cabildos* associated with, 178n14; capitalism and, 5, 21, 23, 54, 60; collusion with paramilitary violence, 20; crisis of, 150, 195n67; defining difference, 6–7, 123; disenchantment with, 27, 30–31; disidentification with, 28; expectations of, 27–28; impoverishment and promises of, 68, 138; liberation beyond, 157; as locus of transformation, 3, 29, 30–31, 157–58; logic of, 32–33; margins of, 68, 69, 71; policy of dispossession and, 13, 24, 181n16 (*see also* colonialism, settler); recognition and multiculturalism, 6–7, 63, 71, 94, 97–98, 118, 119, 123, 158; recognition and support, 120, 178n14; replication of, 100; resources obtained from, 62, 100, 101, 102, 107, 120, 178n14; retreat of, 161; revolution taking the power of, 47, 59, 60; state-centric autonomy and, 54, 100, 123, 158, 160; state-centric peace and, 5, 23–24, 29, 31,

state, the: (*cont.*)
33, 102–3, 176n54; state-centric struggle, 174, 194n65; state heroes and genocide, 142, 143; support of *colonos cocaleros*, 69. *See also* colonialism, settler; nation-state, the; power, state; violence, state

state formation: authorized autonomy and, 158; capitalism as necessary to, 3, 172n19; colonial approach to, 173n15; *colonos cocaleros and*, 64–65; failed states and, 40, 177n12; genocide and, 5, 156; the law as crucial to, 4; obstacles to, 2; subaltern participation in, 183n4

strikes, general, 24, 127, 187n6. *See also* National Strikes

struggle: campesino, 102, 115–16 (*see also* campesinos: post–Peace Accords organizing and); class, 133, 191n37, 192n49, 193n59 (*see also* FARC-EP: class conception of allies and); colonization of, 32, 66, 71, 88, 123, 158, 196n7 (*see also* enclosure); co-optation and, 31; critical consciousness and, 32–33; diversity of, 13; FARC-EP analysis of, 10–11, 40–42, 45–46, 47–48, 53–55, 60; freeing the means of, 149; limits in government participation, 31; normalization of, 32–33; for peace, 24–25; reduced space and, 158; reproducing life and, 160–61, 196n18; state-centric, 174, 194n65; terrain of, 28–29, 194n65; transformation of, 32–33; urban, 41, 42 (*see also* Cali, 2021 uprising in)

struggle, black: for autonomy, vii–viii, ix, 8–10, 71 (*see also* autonomy, black); for constitutional reform, 6; differing from FARC-EP approach, 47; the legacy of enslavement and, 25, 29; sidelined in Cali uprising, 139–41, 143, 192n49; threat of violence and, ix–x, 18. *See also* resistance, black; *individual organizations*

struggle, indigenous: Abiayala/Abya Yala and, 156, 196n10; for constitutional reform, 6; differing from FARC-EP approach, 42, 47, 49–50, 56; institutionalization of, 196n7; Laguna Siberia Indigenous Reservation and, 153–55; Pioya and, 155–56; recognition of, 110; threat of violence and, 31, *32*. *See also* autonomy, indigenous; resistance, indigenous; *individual organizations*

Stutzman, Ronald, 96

sugarcane, 15, 23, 74, 105

Tate, Winifred, 72

Taussig, Michael, 7

Tickner, Arlene, 73

Timochenko (Londoño, Rodrigo), 14–15, 50, 55

Todorov, Tzvetan, 4

"Tod@s Somos Primera Línea" (We Are All Front Liners), 130–31, 138, *139*, 140, 143, 148, 150. *See also* Cali, 2021 uprising in

Tomás (pseudonym), 43–44, 45–46, 48

total peace, 3, 19, 22–23, 24

transformation: desire for, 24, 128, 149, 193n59; drug trafficking producing, 65, 66, 68, 75–76, 88, 89 (*see also* coca: anti-culture of); movement participation and,

171n5; mutual, 194n61; negotiation of peace and, 29; political base for, 54, 55, 144, 193n59; the state as locus of, 3, 29, 30–31, 157–58; of struggle, 32–33. *See also* Cali, 2021 uprising in; struggle
Trujillo, Adelaida: *La ley del monte* (The law of the jungle, with Patricia Castaño), 67–68, 70, 73
Tumaco, *xvi*, 9, 75–76

unions, 50–51, 127, 135, 188n14, 190n29, 190n36. *See also* CNP
United Nations: Declaration on the Rights of Indigenous Peoples, 55; Declaration on the Rights of Peasants, 94; Human Rights Council, 97; internally displaced Colombians and, 7; Office on Drug Control, 69, 76; peace negotiation forums, 21
United Self-Defense Forces of Colombia/Autodefensas Unidas de Colombia. *See* AUC
United States, the: extradition to, 83; imperialism of, 76, 181n19 (*see also* Plan Colombia); military aid to Colombia, 35, 128, 179n24 (*see also* Plan Colombia); U.S.-Colombia Free Trade Agreement, viii, 74
Uprimny, Rodrigo, 119, 120
URC (Cali Resistance Union/Unión de Resistencia Cali), 141, 145–46, 193n51
Uribe Vélez, Álvaro, 18, 19, 20, 73, 94–95, 128

Valencia, Paloma, 94–95, 96–97
vanguardism: criticism of, 178n15; defining, 37; FARC-EP and, 11, 13, 37, 43, 47, 59–60, 158; Che

Guevara on, 34; knowing subject of, 177n3; the lumpenproletariat and, 136; Marxist-Leninist, 47; Zapatistas and, 178n15
Veloza, Herbert (H.H.), 83
violence: in the Afro-Colombian Community Council of Nuevo Amanecer, xii, 76–77, 78, 81, 84, 85; Afro-Colombians and, ix–x, xii, 18–19, 54, 85, 86, 156, 182n34 (*see also* autonomy, black; struggle, black; violence, FARC-EP: Afro-Colombians and); in Chaux, 111, 112–13, 115, 116; coca substitution and, 17, 85, 88, 115–16; *colonos cocaleros* and, 153; against communism, 7, 58; corporate, 7; decimation of FARC-EP cohorts and, 57, 59; desperation and, 30; displacement and, 36, 39, 83–84, 134; drug trafficking and, 68, 71, 72, 89, 115, 116, 153 (*see also* mafias; murder); fleeing, 9, 36; following the Constitutional Assembly (1991), 40; *foráneos* as threat of, 70, 85, 182n34; illicit gold mining and, viii, 25, 83, 85; mafias and, 25, 114–15, 116; the Naya Massacre and, 83–84, 112; overlapping land claims and, 99; Peace Accords negotiations and, 15–17, *16*, 19; PMLT liberators and, 23; the politics of death and, 30; producing capital, 3, 19, 88; sexual, x, 192n49; structures of, 47, 192n49; torture, 9, 57. *See also* death threats; murder
violence, FARC-EP: Afro-Colombians and, 8–9, 11, 15–17, 43–44, 54, 55–56, 60; arbitrary use of murder, 39, 48; attacks related

violence, FARC-EP: (*cont.*)
  to Alfonso Cano, 51–52, 53; the
  Bojayá Massacre and, 43–44, 46,
  48, 57; contract killing and, 113,
  114; death threats and, 48, 57,
  175n40, 178n13; displacement
  and, 7, 48, 175n40; indigenous
  people and, 11, 55–56, 60; post–
  Peace Accords factions and,
  172n1; suspected collaborators
  and, 114; vanguardism justifying, 43
violence, indigenous people and,
  32; Cristina Bautista Taquinás,
  156; Fredy Campo Bomba, 152,
  155–56; clashes with guerillas,
  51, 178n16 (*see also* FARC-EP,
  indigenous people and); Javier
  Oteca, 15, *16*, 19, 153; Sandra Liliana Peña Chocué, 153, 154, 155,
  156; Alvaro Ulcué, xiv
violence, paramilitary: anti-communist, 7, 58; against community organization, 85, 98, 113;
  invasion of northern Cauca and,
  112–13, 116; land grabs and, 7, 83;
  murder/massacres, 43–44, 45,
  112, 113; resource extraction and,
  7, 25, 27, 85; state collusion with,
  20. *See also* AUC
violence, state: challenge of, 126;
  counterinsurgency and, 126;
  effects of, 9; imposition of the
  social contract and, 2, 3; imprisonment and, 13, 17, 18, 144;
  Operation Odysseus and, 35–36;
  protest and, 11–13, 127–28, 129,
  130, 132–33, 138, 144, 150
  (*see also* Cali, 2021 uprising in:
  ESMAD attack on Dignity Hill;

El Tandil Massacre, the); provoking further protest, 128,
  138; provoking guerilla membership, 13; racism and, 139–41,
  192n49, 193n52; suppressing
  social change, 2. *See also* power,
  state

war: the Cold War, 72, 137; conditions of survival and, 30, 38;
  conditions underlying, xi, 38;
  continuing after Peace Accords,
  vii, 2, 10, 18–19; counterinsurgency and, 4, 40, 54, 65, 74, 126;
  crimes of, 14, 43–44, 46, 48,
  57; "degradation" and, 40, 59,
  177n11; dirty, 42; excesses of, 11,
  43; exclusion from power in, 53;
  forces of persisting, vii; funding, 38, 39 (*see also* Colombia:
  U.S. military aid to); intention
  of, 26; logic of, 48; producing
  precarity, 134; psychological, 42;
  reality of conducting, 48; settler
  colonialism as, 24, 143; state
  military strength and, 41–42;
  theft of land and, 7; U.S. Civil
  War, 24; wastelands of, 87–88.
  See also Colombian military;
  FARC-EP; guerillas; paramilitary groups
war on drugs, the: isolation and, 84;
  Plan Colombia and, 65, 71–72, 73,
  74–75, 76, 92, 181n19; provoking
  enclosure, *75*, 181n16 (*see also* displacement: campesino). *See also*
  coca; marijuana
Washington Office on Latin America
  (WOLA), viii–ix
Weeks, Kathi, 190n36

whiteness: census-taking and, 95–96; creole, 2, 96–97, 98 (see also *mestizaje*); mestizos and, 96, 139, 141 (see also *mestizaje*); national belonging and, 2, 142; whitening processes and, 4, 96, 122, 185n23. *See also* race; racism

William (pseudonym), 131, 132–34, 135, 138

Wolfe, Patrick, 187n61

Wolford, Wendy, xi, 171n5

Worsley, Peter, 190n36

Zambrano, Marta, 122

Zapatistas (Zapatista Army of National Liberation/Ejército Zapatista de Liberación Nacional), ix, xiv, 87–88, 128, 158, 178n15, 193n58

Zibechi, Raúl, 142

ZRCs (peasant reserve zones/zonas de reserva campesinas): ANZORC and, 98, 105, 107, 111, 118, 119, 186n40; demographic change and, 108–9; FARC-EP and, 98, 119; legal standing of, 98–99

The authorized representative in the EU for product safety and compliance is:
Mare Nostrum Group
B.V Doelen 72
4831 GR Breda
The Netherlands

www.ingramcontent.com/pod-product-compliance
Lightning Source LLC
Chambersburg PA
CBHW020848270326
41928CB00006B/597